'The book's power stems from its devastating details; Cossins establishes a tone so vivid it's reminiscent of Dickens.'
US Publisher's Weekly

'a story of convict heritage, family betrayal, and forensic science still in its infancy... fascinating.'
Richard Weinstein, *Bar News*

'shines a spotlight on the complex social factors that made infanticide commonplace.'
Sydney Morning Herald

'a welcome addition to the field of Australian true crime writing... a compelling... read.'
Australian Book Review
'

A passionate interest in the wretched choices facing women in the 19th century, before contraception, has produced interesting testaments... Criminologist Cossins raises the bar with this thoroughly researched story of the most infamous trial in Australian legal history.'
Australian Women's Weekly

'This scrupulously researched and referenced history of the baby farmers Sarah and John Makin introduces the reader to every available detail not only of their sordid lives, but also of the parents they betrayed, the policeman who pursued them, and the lawyers and judges who defended and condemned them... The *Baby Farmers* is part thriller, part biography, part social history, and part legal studies textbook... a gripping read.'
Marian Quartly, *Australian Journal of Politics and History*

'a fascinating slice of social history... with its portraits of the relinquishing mothers and the unstinting efforts of Sergeant James Joyce to uncover the Makins' crimes... a compelling read.'
Linda Funnell, *The Newtown Review of Books*

Annie Cossins is an author, actor and criminologist. She is an Associate Professor in the Law School at the University of NSW and a leading legal expert on evidence law and sexual assault law reform. In 2009 she played the role of Sarah Makin in an episode of a TV series, *Deadly Women*.

ANNIE COSSINS

The BABY FARMERS

A CHILLING TALE OF MISSING BABIES, SHAMEFUL SECRETS AND MURDER IN 19TH CENTURY AUSTRALIA

ALLEN&UNWIN
SYDNEY · MELBOURNE · AUCKLAND · LONDON

First published in 2013

Allen & Unwin
83 Alexander Street
Crows Nest NSW 2065
Australia
Phone: (61 2) 8425 0100
Email: info@allenandunwin.com
Web: www.allenandunwin.com

Cataloguing-in-Publication details are available
from the National Library of Australia
www.trove.nla.gov.au

ISBN 978 1 74331 401 2

Set in 12/16 pt Granjon by Midland Typesetters, Australia
Printed and bound in Australia by Griffin Press

10 9 8 7 6 5 4 3

Contents

Author's note	vii
Prologue	1
Part I: Who were the Makins?	**7**
1 The hanging	9
2 Sarah Makin: convict daughter	13
3 John Makin: son of the middle class with a past	29
4 The deadly secret in Sarah Makin's body	48
Part II: Digging up the baby farmers' secrets	**59**
5 The baby trade	61
6 The Macdonaldtown discoveries	68
7 To catch a baby farmer	75
8 The first inquest: two babies called A and B	79
9 Constable James Joyce: Joycean fictions and the art of deceit	88
10 More digging and the strange behaviour of the Makins	95
11 The next five inquests: the Makins' lives stripped bare	106
12 The longest, saddest inquest: clothing and other complications	116
13 The mysterious Mr and Mrs Wilson give evidence	131
14 The obsessions of James Joyce: digging, redigging and more digging	147
15 Mothers, mothers everywhere: the George Street inquests begin	157
16 The day Miss Amber Murray visited the Makins	173

Part III: Trials, appeals and various petitions   189

17 The trial of the century: a judge out of his depth   191

18 The first appeal: the Makins' struggle against the hand of fate   209

19 The law passes sentence   221

20 Last stop, London   225

21 Makin's last chance: an 'innocent' man under the thumb
    of a 'fiendish' woman   230

Part IV: Sarah Makin, reformed woman   239

22 From convict daughter to convict   241

23 Was Sarah Makin really an evil, deadly woman?   257

24 The lives that were left   260

Notes   267

Acknowledgements   288

Index   289

Author's note

A many years ago
When I was young and charming
As some of you may know
I practised baby-farming[1]

In 2009, I played the role of a murderer by the name of Sarah Makin in a television docu-drama called *Deadly Women*. Despite evidence to the contrary, Sarah was portrayed as the 'deadly woman' who murdered all the babies found buried in the backyards of various houses in which she had lived with her husband John. By doing so, the program sacrificed many of the facts as carelessly as Sarah was supposed to have sacrificed 13 babies 120 years ago.

But one must be careful with facts. To kill them off unnecessarily not only robs us of the opportunity of ferreting down many a 'dunny' lane, it stops us from slipping back into the world of the 1890s—into the narrow, smelly streets of the inner city where the rustling of long skirts and petticoats can be heard along with hurried ruttings in back lanes or secretive seductions on night walks. We would miss a girl's furtive cover-ups as her skirts and petticoats stretched to accommodate her growing belly and then the shocked gasp of her first labour pains—perhaps as she served her master's breakfast or stood on the street, trying to earn a living. Sometimes she was assisted by a kindly midwife in a dim-lit room where she gave birth to a red-faced, mewling infant she neither wanted nor knew what to do with. Perhaps, instinctively, she cuddled him close to her leaking breasts, knowing that she could not keep him.

In an age without telephones, a discreet advertisement in the local newspaper brought the baby farmer out of the shadows, caught briefly by the halo of a gas lamp as he visited his next client. And if we look closely, we will glimpse the luxuriant handlebar moustache of John Makin, his hands in his pockets as he strides past the gas light on his way to the home of one of his last customers just a few days before another man with a handlebar moustache, a constable by the name of James Joyce, brought him undone in the best murder mystery tradition.

As I follow in the footsteps of Constable Joyce, I will take you on a tour through the lives of the most notorious baby farmers in Australia—Sarah and John Makin, not young and from all accounts not always charming but with sufficient gravitas to come across as a most dependable, caring couple. By examining their lives in the economic times of the late 1800s, I reveal some things about Australian society towards the end of the 'virtuous' Victorian age that will surprise.

In this biography of murder, I describe the most unexplained, unexamined and unbelievable murders ever committed in the Australian colonies, which came to light in the 55th year of the reign of Queen Victoria. At the time of their conviction John and Sarah Makin were said to have committed 'the worst crime ... which has ever disfigured the criminal records of Australia'.[2] But based on the evidence presented in this book, it appears the Makins were convicted of the death of the wrong baby.

The crude beginnings of the colony of New South Wales in 1788 meant that it bred vice, crime and corruption which, 104 years later in 1892, still moulded the lives and deaths of the poor, the weak and the dispossessed. This was the Sydney of Sarah Makin, John Makin and a cast of other characters who took part in surreptitious pacts to deal with the unwanted babies from seduction and prostitution, imitating what had been happening in Mother England for generations. It was also the Sydney of the obsessive but secretive Constable James Joyce, who changed the lives of the Makins and the course of legal history.

Although television cast Sarah Makin as Australia's first female serial killer, the whole of her secrets was not guessed at in the television program or in any of the documentation from the 1890s. There was much more to her troubled and criminal life than the shame of being a convicted murderer, although you might think that was enough. There were other dead babies, her own, and the deadly secret harboured in her body.

This book aims to be careful with the facts, although at times the facts find themselves in competition with the opinions of the day. Sometimes I have given my own opinions if they are supported by the facts. Yet the lives of those involved in the events surrounding the gruesome discovery of the Makins' activities have been, largely, lost to history. Many of them were working-class folk who either did not record what happened or, if they did, their letters and diaries have not survived. Without that information it is difficult to imagine the immediacy and drama of the extraordinary events of this time.

In chronicling the careers of the Makins, there are large gaps in the decades of their lives when they are invisible. They only appear from the silent under-class when they have an encounter with the law that is recorded in newspapers, trial transcripts or prison records. When the voices of the Makins are heard, it is difficult to know how accurately they are reported and whether they include embellishments made by report-ers who might have emphasised certain words and conduct in pursuit of a good story. People have had a long fascination with the 'bad' and the 'mad', especially of the murdering kind. It was no less so in 1892 when the Makins were arrested and crowds of people clambered to snatch seats in the courtroom when they were finally put on trial.

The main sources relied on in this book are contemporary newspaper reports, including those of the Makins' trial,[3] law reports of the Makins' two appeals, family histories and family trees of Sarah and John Makin, *Sands Directories of Sydney*, original sources such as birth, death and marriage certificates, and the findings from the inquests into the deaths of the 13 babies. Other sources include articles from medical journals as well as histories of the social conditions of Sydney, all of which cover the mid to late 1800s.

Prologue
11 August 1892

On the afternoon of Thursday 11 August 1892, an unmarried couple who called themselves Mr and Mrs Wilson bought a bunch of flowers on a lonely train platform for the last journey they would make to 25 Burren Street, Macdonaldtown. Their destination was a small workers' suburb squeezed in between Newtown and Erskineville along the train line. Along with a telegram in his pocket, Horace had money to pay for a funeral. He and his girlfriend, Minnie, were the teenage parents of a baby girl called Mignonette. While they had hidden her birth, the flowers and a funeral were the final things they were able to do for their daughter, who became known as the baby who cried too much.

Minnie Davies was a domestic servant living at 31 Greens Road, Paddington. Horace, whose real name was Bothamley, was a proofreader for *The Daily Telegraph* and lived in Oatley Road, Paddington. Perhaps this is where they met since the two streets are on opposite sides of what was once a reserve. Or perhaps they met at a dance at the nearby Paddington Town Hall which opened in 1891, the year their baby was conceived.

Mignonette Lavinia was born on 10 June 1892 at the home of Mrs Taylor, a midwife who lived at 31 Church Street, Newtown, a good distance from Paddington and Minnie's inquisitive employer. Named after her mother, Baby Mignonette was a strong child with no deformities who took well to the Nestlé's milk she was fed. To make sure no-one knew of the birth, Minnie gave Mrs Taylor a false name while Horace registered his daughter's birth in the name of Wilson.

On 21 June, Horace sought a solution to the birth of his illegitimate child by placing an advertisement in *The Sydney Morning Herald* in the name of Mr Franklin:

> Wanted, kind person to take charge of Baby. Apply, stating terms, to 333 Herald Office, King-st.

This advertisement appeared alongside another ad seeking a kind, motherly person to care for a baby and various ads for clothing, lead and old tools. Although unstated, Horace was seeking a baby farmer, someone who purchased unwanted children.

Horace received a letter the next day from Mr John Burt of 109 George Street, Redfern. That evening he and Minnie walked to George Street from Newtown with their baby, whom they had nicknamed Vinnie. When they arrived at the 'pleasant-looking' worker's cottage in George Street, Horace waited outside while Minnie and her daughter were invited into the house. In the sparsely furnished front room, Mr John Burt introduced his eldest daughter, Blanche, explaining that his wife was ill in bed.

After a discussion of terms, John agreed to adopt Mignonette for a payment of ten shillings a week and to allow Minnie to visit whenever she wished. When they talked about what to feed her child, Minnie insisted on Nestlé's milk. This was a commerically available substitute for breast milk, produced from cow's milk, wheat flour and sugar. By cooking the wheat flour with malt, Henri Nestlé had managed to convert the indigestible starch of wheat flour into dextrin, which infants were able to absorb.[1] Considered to be the world's first baby formula, it was cheap, although the concentration of the formula was easy to manipulate by those short of money, such as a Sydney baby farmer, to make a tin of Nestlé's milk last as long as possible.

After saying a painful goodbye to their precious daughter, Minnie and Horace returned to 109 George Street two days later with a pile of baby clothing. This time, they met Mrs Sarah Burt and introduced themselves as Mr and Mrs Wilson. Neither couple realised the other was using a false name. Mr Burt announced the family was intending to move 'up the line' to a house they had purchased. He gave Minnie and Horace their new address as 25 Burren Street, Macdonaldtown. During their visit, neither Horace nor Minnie saw or heard the sound of any other babies.

Devoted to their daughter, Minnie and Horace visited her every Saturday when they paid the weekly nursing fee of ten shillings to the Burts. Since they both lived in Paddington, perhaps they arranged to meet up secretly on Minnie's day off on a street corner, transforming into Mr and Mrs Wilson as, arm in arm, they strolled down Oxford Street on their way to Central train station to catch the next train to Macdonaldtown.

When they visited their baby on 9 July, Minnie and Horace learnt that Mignonette had been seen by a doctor for an apparently 'turned' foot, for which they reimbursed the Burts two shillings and sixpence. One week later, their baby had a slight cold but was otherwise in good health. John reassured them that Mignonette was taking her food well and had even been started on solids. Despite spending an hour and a half in the house Minnie and Horace still did not see or hear the sound of any other babies.

During one of their visits, Sarah confessed to Minnie and Horace that she and John had deceived them, revealing that their name was not Burt but Makin. While Mr and Mrs Wilson did not return the confidence by confessing their real names, they may have wondered what the Makins were hiding. Sadly, Sarah's confession was not enough for them to make further inquiries or reclaim their daughter. If they had, their story would have had a different ending.

As Minnie would later tell a Coroner's Court, from the middle of July onwards Mignonette's cold worsened so that by Saturday, 30 July, her daughter was 'very sick'. So sick that she and Horace returned to Burren Street the next day. On Tuesday 9 August, Makin sent a telegram asking Horace to 'come at your earliest convenience'. On his own, Horace hurried to Burren Street to hear the worst news. John informed him that his daughter 'might not live till tomorrow' as she was suffering from a 'wasting disease'. Two days later Horace received another telegram:

> To 333, HERALD Office, King-st. Letter waiting at address, King-st. Come at once.
> (Sgd) JOHN BURT, 'Eilleen House,' 25 Burren-st, Macdonaldtown.

The letter waiting for Horace contained the news that Mignonette had died the day before, on 10 August.

When the Wilsons arrived at Burren Street with their bunch of flowers between three and four o'clock that fine day, John carried the body of Mignonette into the sitting room. She was laid out on a board and dressed in a long white gown. For the couple who could not bear to reveal their daughter's existence, theirs was a very private grief.

Minnie and Horace asked whether their child had been taken to a doctor. John reassured them that a Dr Agassiz had diagnosed the baby as suffering from marasmus, a wasting disease, 'to which all children are liable'. When later asked in court if there were any marks on the child's head, arms or legs, Minnie said no, that her baby appeared well cared for, clean and comfortably clothed. She and Horace had not noticed that their child was wasting away.

While Minnie and Horace viewed their daughter's body, John asked Horace whether he had made any funeral arrangements. In turn, Horace asked if John could see to the burial as well as organise a death certificate. John agreed to do so for £2. Apparently grateful that someone else would deal with these difficult matters, Horace agreed to pay the money in instalments. When John asked whether he or Minnie would like to attend the funeral, Horace replied they were unable to because of work commitments.

But John did not arrange an undertaker to collect Mignonette's body as promised. Instead, that night he dug a small grave in the backyard close to the house. As she was laid in the damp clay soil by John or Sarah, Baby Mignonette was dressed in a white flannel gown with scarlet edging, a blue and white striped petticoat and pink and white woollen bootees. Perhaps the Makins' two teenage daughters looked on in the chilly night. This was the last burial the family would hold before John, Sarah and their four children left Burren Street in a hurry, leaving no forwarding address for their landlord, who was seeking unpaid rent.

John later sent a letter to Horace informing him of his new address at 55 Botany Street, Redfern, where he accepted Horace's final instalment for the funeral even though he knew where Mignonette's body lay.

It was several months before Minnie and Horace found out what had happened to the body of their daughter. But first they would have to reveal their shameful secret in a Coroner's Court packed with journalists and curiosity seekers, and the Makins looking on. When they did, their secret was published in every newspaper in Australia.

PART I

❖

WHO WERE THE MAKINS?

❧

CHAPTER ONE

The hanging
14–15 August 1893

After Mr and Mrs Wilson exposed their secret lives in a Coroner's Court in November 1892, Sarah and John Makin were committed to stand trial for the manslaughter of Baby Mignonette. But the police were not satisfied with a manslaughter charge. A constable called James Joyce was convinced the Makins were murderers and set out to gather enough evidence to prove it.

Despite the intense publicity about the Wilsons' shameful secret, it was one of the painful ironies of the Makin case that Sarah and John were never tried for the death of Mignonette. Horace and Minnie had to console themselves with the thought that their evidence had given Constable Joyce enough information to recommence his investigation into the suspicious activities of the Makins. Eventually, he gathered enough evidence to send the Makins to trial for the murder of another child. The Great Baby Farming Case became the trial of the century, with Joyce's investigations being the most dogged, persistent and obsessive Sydney had ever seen.

On Tuesday 15 August 1893, Constable Joyce and the Wilsons were able to privately celebrate the demise of Australia's most notorious baby farmer. On that day John Sidney Makin was executed at Darlinghurst Gaol for the murder of Horace Amber Murray, a four-week-old baby who had been given the name of an adult but the future of a back-street child. At the time no-one realised or cared that John and Sarah had been wrongly convicted.

Before his death John wrote letters and spent 'the greater part of the night' in prayer.[1] To the end he denied murdering Baby Horace, leaving an intriguing letter in which he 'solemnly declared' that the body of the infant for which he was convicted was not Horace but failing to leave any clues as to who the child was, how it came to be buried in his backyard and what happened to Horace.

He left an affectionate letter to his daughters, asking them to be good and to urge their mother to beg God's forgiveness so that she might join him in heaven. Like his bravado in life, when faced with death he seemed to have every confidence that his crimes would not prevent his entry into heaven. Yet John also declared that his wife 'did not murder the child supposed to be Amber Murray's', leaving an intriguing question mark over Sarah's need to ask for God's forgiveness and who, out of John and Sarah, was guilty of what.

At his end, John Makin was fortunate since his execution was a professional job. As he had meted out death so he received his. His death was instantaneous as he swung from the gallows with a broken neck.

When John learnt of his fate the day before his execution, he said he was ready to die: 'I thought as much. Well, I am quite prepared for the end'. On that Monday afternoon, he was visited by his brothers, Daniel and Joseph, who had done so much to try to save his neck, as well as his step-daughter and step-son-in-law, Mr and Mrs Helbi, and his devoted daughters, Blanche and Florence. He had already said a passionate goodbye to his wife, Sarah, the previous Thursday before she was transferred to Bathurst Gaol to begin her term of life imprisonment.

During the family's one hour visit, perhaps John's brothers lamented the unfairness of his death sentence, since they believed that Sarah had drawn an innocent man into her murderous world. No doubt John's daughters did their best to patch up past accusations as they contemplated the loss of the stern but sturdy presence in their lives.

When their time was up, what followed was 'a most pitiful leave taking'. As John kissed them through the bars of his cell, he 'fervently embraced his two daughters ... saying, "Good-bye my children, I'll be better off. This is the last time you will see me alive"'. Although it was reported that Makin, a man always in control of his emotions, 'did not appear to be much affected', as his daughters left the gaol 'the bitter cries of the two girls sent a painful thrill through every warder as they passed'.

Like many who are condemned to death, John made a late conversion, spending most of his final day in prayer with Canon Rich, the Darlinghurst Gaol chaplain, who believed he had saved another soul. John then wrote his various letters until midnight.

On Tuesday morning, just before nine o'clock, Mr Howard, the executioner, entered the cell and pinioned John's arms behind his back. Makin said nothing but his eyes must have shown that his final moment had arrived. Followed by Canon Rich, John walked with a firm step to the scaffold, where one more prayer was said for him.

The first hanging in Australia took place on the shores of Port Jackson on 28 February 1788, just one month after the arrival of the First Fleet, when Thomas Barrett was hanged for stealing food.[2] While capital punishment was common for minor crimes such as theft in Britain and the Australian colonies in the 1700s and early 1800s, by the late 1800s it was only used to punish serious offences such as rape and murder. Between 1841 and 1852, hangings had been public affairs at Darlinghurst Gaol with people jostling to grab the best spot at the front gates in Forbes Street. The expectant audience must have been a horrifying sight for a condemned prisoner as he was led onto the wooden platform of the gallows, built above the gaol gate, exposed to the jeering and clapping crowd. The hangman lived in a cottage just outside the gaol wall. At the appointed time he would climb the steps to the gallows as the crowd jeered or cheered. The gaol's first hangman, Alexander Green, 'was frequently drunk and botched many hangings' by misjudging the length of the rope needed—something that added to the entertainment value of this gruesome public spectacle.[3]

Unlike the public executions of former times, there were no crowds to witness Makin's demise since he was executed on the permanent gallows located inside the main walls of the gaol in the corner of the Y-shaped E-Wing which faced the rising morning sun.[4]

The only witnesses were the executioner, his assistant and the sheriff. The hangman, Robert Rice Howard, was known as 'Nosey Bob' since he had no visible nose after being kicked in the face by a horse. Unlike previous hangmen, he took a professional approach to his job and was known as the 'gentleman hangman' because he wore a black frockcoat and white necktie to all his executions.[5]

As Nosey Bob fastened the rope around John's neck and dropped the cap over his pale face, John's lips 'moved in prayer', as if he still believed he needed help on his ascent to heaven. In order to get him there, the assistant gave the signal, Nosey Bob pulled a lever and the trapdoor underneath John gave way. Abruptly his 12 stone body fell through and 'hung almost without a quiver'. Without a struggle, John died instantaneously, the ten foot drop and the strong rope snapping his neck at 9.08 a.m. His body hung for another ten minutes before being cut down to ensure that death had indeed paid its visit.

After his death, the Deputy Coroner carried out an inquest to determine John's cause of death: 'dislocation of the cervical vertebrae'.[6] Unlike many executed prisoners who were buried in unconsecrated ground within the gaol walls, John was buried in the Anglican Section of Rookwood Cemetery with only his brother Daniel and a brother-in-law present[7] to witness the burial of the family's shame.

While the New South Wales Government had been determined to carry out John's execution, refusing all petitions for his reprieve, Sarah Makin's death sentence had been commuted to life imprisonment. Although she was convicted along with her husband for the murder of Baby Horace, the law threw a paternalistic cloak around her in its belief that, as John's wife, she had acted under his direction.

The daughter of a convict, Sarah was now a convicted murderer whose crimes overshadowed the misdemeanours of her convict father. She spent the next eighteen years being moved between Darlinghurst and Bathurst Gaols as her health worsened and her daughters desperately sought her release.

with a cat-o'-nine tails. Remarkably, five days after this severe punishment, Emanuel faced Houghton again, this time for 'Disorderly conduct and improperly driving in the Streets of Launceston'. For this crime he was merely admonished.

Even though it was assumed the lash would break a man's spirit, Emanuel was not suited to slave labour. Resistance was common in the Australian colonies, where convict protest took a number of forms such as physical or verbal attacks, malingering or self-mutilation to avoid work, withdrawal of labour as a form of bargaining for better conditions, retribution against a master's property or complaints to authorities about perceived invasions of rights.[9] One of Emanuel's contemporaries, William Day, had been assigned to 'a downright tyrant' who kept his convicts on starvation rations. Filled with resentment about receiving no better rations at Christmas, Day confessed that:

> I loosened the stonework from the oven [and seized] ... a Yorkshire pudding—bubbling away ... and [a] nearly cooked bullock's heart ... and ... hastened with my prize to the hut, where I and my mates soon put out of sight the best meal we had had for years.[10]

Compared to other convicts, Emanuel's rebellion was less subtle. A month after being lashed, he appeared before Houghton again for 'Gross Insolence and threatening to Strike his Oversear [sic]' on 6 May 1835. By now Houghton had had enough. He sentenced Emanuel to twelve months' imprisonment with hard labour for his defiance. Part of this sentence appears to have involved time spent in a chain gang on Buckingham Island. Such islands were popular forms of 'secondary punishment' in the colonies and meant gruelling work, isolation and physical and mental pain.[11]

Despite this punishment, Emanuel continued to rebel. On 29 September 1836, he was again convicted of disobedience of orders and sentenced to ten days' solitary confinement, which was meant to encourage a convict 'to commune with his conscience'.[12] For Emanuel it compounded the injustice of his conditions, which now included minimal food and constant darkness in the convict-built Launceston Gaol. He was then returned to the care of the Government, 'his Master declining to take him back on acct [*sic*] of his sulky ways'.

On 17 June 1837, when Emanuel was absent without leave, he was admonished, although for whom he was working is unknown. Six days later, it seems Emanuel had shifted from outright resistance to more cunning methods since he was punished for 'representing himself to be free' with seven days on a J Wheel. This may have been a reference to Launceston's treadmill, an alternative to the lash and a dreaded punishment because of its exhausting monotony. Treadmills were used to drive the stone mill wheels for grinding wheat into flour. Residents could bring their grain to have it ground at these convict-powered mills for a fee charged by the government.[13]

An 1825 description of how the treadmill in Sydney worked captures the punitive nature of it:

> It is a large wheel whose horizontal blades are wide enough to allow a certain number of men to position themselves, each next to the other, on the outside ... [N]aked from the waist up ... they ... [hold] on to a wooden crossbar ... attached at the height of the chin, [and] climb without stopping from one blade to the next ... forty minutes without a break; the men rest for twenty minutes, then they start up again, and so on for the whole day.

Not only was it monotonous and tiring, convicts worked in fear of 'missing the blade and having [their] legs mutilated'.[14] This ingenious punishment had its intended effect on Emanuel since it was another year before he was brought before a magistrate—this time for an act of retribution. After working in a flour mill for at least a year, on 5 June 1838 he was convicted of 'wilfully or carelessly breaking his Master's Mill to the Damage of £2'. For this he was 'kept to hard labour on the roads' for two months and returned to Government. His assignment to a road gang meant a return to the harsh life of living and working outdoors in chains, as well as the indiscriminate punishment of the convict superintendent.

On 19 September 1838, Emanuel was imprisoned for using abusive language and received another two months' hard labour. But eventually

Sarah's father conformed to the convict regime, since he spent the rest of his penal servitude with no further convictions. He was granted his 'free certificate' in 1840, which permitted him to return to Britain or remain in the colony. Although Emanuel stayed and became a free settler, his rebellious and angry temperament remained, having a lasting effect on the girl who would become the infamous Sarah Makin.

An emigrant lass

Sarah's mother and Emanuel's wife, Ellen Murphy, was born in Limerick, Ireland in about 1816 and migrated to Launceston from London on the *Branken Moor*, arriving as a free settler on 4 April 1843. Although the local newspaper reported the names of the most important passengers, Ellen Murphy was not named, only the fact that the ship had arrived with 100 emigrants who were available for the job opportunities promised in the colonies. On 10 April, *The Teetotal Advocate* carried the following advertisement:

> Emigrants on board the *Brankenmoor* are open for hire on board
> the said vessel, from 10 o'clock till 3, every day, Sundays excepted.[15]

The female immigrants were in for a surprise because with news of a ship's arrival usually came:

> hordes of men ... assembl[ing] at the docks, waiting to claim their
> share of the imported goods. Employers seeking domestic servants
> had to battle with lustful men who had no intention of paying for
> the services they required.[16]

The local newspaper reported that female immigrants disembarking in Hobart in 1834 were subject to a gauntlet of men who jeered at them, using 'the most vile and brutal language' or 'stopped [them] by force' and addressed them in 'the most obscene manner'.[17] For Ellen Murphy, relief at having arrived safely in an unknown land may have been replaced by worry as she waited on board a cramped ship in the hope that someone would want to make use of her skills as a straw hatmaker and servant,[18] but was greeted, instead, by a crowd of men jostling and yelling obscenities, and peppered by proposals of marriage.

The colonists of Launceston were spoilt for choice that day with a range of workers and other precious goods available in the harbour. A variety of 'winter goods' which had arrived on the *Branken Moor* were also advertised to the 'Ladies of Launceston', including silk, satin and satinetts, an assortment of furs (sable, musquash and squirrel), scarves, shawls and French stays all in 'the newest style and fashion'.

Ellen, aged about 27, may have met Emanuel, aged 30, on the docks that day. With his certificate of freedom, Emanuel would have been in the market for a wife. Whether he was a brute with a foul mouth or whether he offered a gentlemanly proposal of marriage is hard to say.

Ellen and Emanuel married almost a year later on 20 May 1844 in Launceston during an economic downturn which led to cut-backs in public works and employment in the private sector. As jobs disappeared, many free convicts and ticket-of-leave holders became unemployed. Because the number of convicts in Tasmania had been increasing since transportation to New South Wales had been suspended in 1840,[19] Emanuel was now in competition with the newly arrived slave labourers. In this climate, he and Ellen decided to start afresh. They arrived in Sydney on the *Palmyra* on 26 October 1844. Mr and Mrs Sutcliffe were listed as two of the six passengers who arrived from Launceston along with grain, potatoes and other foodstuffs.[20]

Sydney Town in 1844

Sarah's parents would have been astonished by the sights that accosted them after sailing from the backwater village of Launceston. Sydney Town had expanded rapidly in the 1830s and 1840s as the main port for the export of the colony's produce, notably wool. Although the early settlement 'clung to the shores of Sydney Cove',[21] by 1844 the city had expanded inland along a narrow strip of land from Circular Quay to the cemetery (where the present Town Hall stands), although it was still the size of a small English town on the edge of a vast continent—a pimple of so-called civilisation on an untamed giant with the settlers oblivious to the ancient Aboriginal culture surrounding them.

The city struggled for a sense of order with a system of planned, grid-like streets to overcome its early days in the area known as the Rocks, which retained its narrow lanes and alleyways along with its reputation for crime and other 'irresistible attractions'[22] such as the popular *Sheer Hulk*. This sly grog shop represented all that was loose and licentious about the Rocks—carousing male voices blended with laughing, drunken women in 'a large, low dilapidated, half-lit room' filled with tobacco smoke and gamblers and convicts who had managed to escape the nearby barracks by bribing the night watchmen. Described by one patron as 'a perfect frenzy of drunken vociferation', it was the arse-end of Sydney Town.[23]

As the Sutcliffes walked down the gangplank of the *Palmyra* into the Rocks, they found a port abuzz with convicts and carts loading and offloading the flotilla of arriving and departing ships against a backdrop of convict-built warehouses. While this was the 'real' Sydney, a commercial city dependent on imports and exports and its underbelly of licentiousness, the newspapers and periodicals of the time were keen to show off the colony's literary pretensions.

The *Colonial Literary Journal* began its life on 27 June 1844 to supply literature to those who must meet 'the pressing calls of business, or of duty'.[24] In the month the Sutcliffes arrived, the journal contained liberal doses of ancient history, poetry, chemical philosophy, tips on waterproofing walls along with some useful maxims for new, hot-headed arrivals:

> Attempt not to fly like an eagle with the wings of a wren.
> The fool is obstinate, and doubteth not; he knoweth all things
> but his own ignorance.[25]

It also carried a long essay on the 'endless variety and degrees of intellectual capacity, by which some [men] are prompted to higher undertakings' while others had to content themselves with the 'humbler occupations'.[26] This meant there was a place reserved at the bottom of the social ladder for ex-convicts like Emanuel Sutcliffe.

But when Mr and Mrs Sutcliffe disembarked from the *Palmyra* in October 1844, all was not well in the New South Wales colony. Although it was only 56 years old, commerce was stagnant:

> Commercial transactions of the past week have been few and unimportant, the markets generally remain languid, as noticed for some time past, and in the absence of all speculation sales are confined to immediate requirements and cash payments.[27]

A five year drought from 1837 to 1842 had caused 'a catastrophic fall in land sales' which plunged the colony, like a cold water splash, into an economic depression, reducing the demand for labour. Because the Governor of New South Wales, Sir George Gipps, believed 'the depression was a result of excessive speculation', he was not prepared to assist private enterprise through an injection of government funds because 'he thought thrift, not more capital, was necessary'.[28]

The governor's caution had profound effects on hundreds of Sydney-siders, including the newly arrived Sutcliffes. On 5 October, *The Guardian* reported the results of a parliamentary inquiry into 'the state of distress alleged to exist amongst' the unemployed in Sydney. *The Guardian* was not impressed by the inquiry or its findings, criticising it as a sop to employers and calling it a 'farce' with inadequate solutions.[29] To the newspaper editors, the problem was simple—'superabundant labour' with insufficient jobs and 'cruel' rates paid for labour. According to *The Guardian*, the true rate of 'distressed operatives in the city' was 2000 families dying of starvation which was worsened by an influx of people from the country. The newspaper also criticised the government's evasion of its responsibilities by refusing to undertake various public works as a way of soaking up the excess labour.

'House-rent' was a particular form of distress, indicating that times were not good for new arrivals like the Sutcliffes, who merely exacerbated the rental crisis since Sydney was overpopulated by 5000 to 6000 people.[30] Assisted immigration brought more and more British settlers to the colony and town people were reluctant to move to the country. No-one acknowledged the fact that Sydney society was still dependent on convict labour, which meant that many employers were unable or unwilling to employ free settlers for a living wage.

The problems were eloquently expressed by Mr Adam Smith, a recent arrival to the colony from Ireland with his large family, in a letter to *The Guardian*:

> [Employment] is the thing that is wanted, let us get permanent work, good and honest masters, and we shall ask *little else* ... [B]ut we would if it were available, ask a little more. We would claim equal wages with what allured us from our homes ... [N]ot only have I not bettered my situation by my adventures, but have hardly got anything to do since I came out.

Unlike many other new settlers, Mr Smith did, in desperation, try his hand in the country as his money ran out. He travelled more than four hundred miles, stopping at various settlements and stations on the way where he had to beg for food:

> On returning to my wife and children I found them in great poverty, and their anxiety was at its height ... *when I had no relief to give them.*[31]

Finally, the governor was forced to offer inducements to the unemployed to work on the roads leading out of Sydney[32] in order to relocate families inland and 'eradicate the desire' to stay in Sydney.

As new immigrants from Tasmania, it is possible the Sutcliffes found themselves in a similar situation to Mr Adam Smith. Although they stayed in Sydney for at least fourteen months until the birth of their first child, Sarah Jane, they eventually left the high rents of Sydney. One of the main public works outside of Sydney included the new line of road to the Illawarra in the south-west on the way to Camden, the small town in which the Sutcliffes settled. Emanuel was an ideal employee given his experience in the convict road gangs of Launceston. Since the Legislative Council had requested the governor to put aside £160 for repairs to the bridge over the Cowpasture River where Camden was located,[33] this may have been the reason why the Sutcliffes set out in a horse-drawn coach or wagon into the wilds of the Australian countryside.

A family tragedy

For 30 years, Camden Park's 28,000 acres was the largest farm in the colony. It was owned by John Macarthur, the son of a Scottish draper, who is known as the father of Australia's wool industry—one of the ironies of Australian history since it was his wife, Elizabeth, who was largely responsible for the development of the Macarthurs' sheep breeding project during the eight years Macarthur spent in England between 1809 and 1817.

Although Macarthur refused to cede any of his huge parcel of land for the creation of a town for workers, after his death in 1834 his two sons subdivided 50 acres which were sold in lots of half an acre for the creation of Camden Town in 1840.[34] Six years later, the Sutcliffe family—Emanuel, Ellen and baby Sarah—travelled 65 kilometres south-west from Sydney to Camden, which was a blossoming town with two churches, a school, an inn, a post office and a courthouse. Ellen Sutcliffe gave birth to a boy, George James, on 26 October 1847, exactly three years after she and Emanuel had arrived in Sydney.

Nothing more is known about the Sutcliffes until five years later when they were living in the District of Maitland in the Hunter Valley, about 160 kilometres north of Sydney. The bridge over Wallis Creek on the outskirts of Maitland had been another badly needed public work.[35] It is possible Ellen and her children found themselves living in this distant rural outpost as Emanuel followed the road building work available in the colony.

The next to be heard of Emanuel Sutcliffe comes from an advertisement in the local paper on 24 July 1852 when he offered a reward for a lost filly that had strayed from a farm near the Paterson River where the Sutcliffes were living:

> Ten Shillings reward will be given for her recovery, on delivery to the undersigned, at Mr. Nicholson's mill.[36]

While road building may have taken the family to the Hunter Valley, Emanuel had found work in a local mill in West Maitland. Three years later, the family's social and economic status had improved, with Emanuel becoming the proprietor of a flour mill. On 16 March 1855, Emanuel was charged with malicious injury 'by destroying a certain dwelling house, valued at £10, the property of Patrick Doolan ... at Black Creek'. But he had good reasons for doing so. He had pulled down a slab hut about a quarter of a mile from the mill he operated since he had a four year lease over the land on which the slab hut had been built. Since Emanuel's lease, dated 1 April 1854, pre-dated the sale of the land to Mr Doolan on 1 June 1854, the court dismissed Doolan's case against Emanuel who, as lessee, was entitled to possession.[37] He had shown Doolan who was in charge.

However, more neighbourly discord was to follow. On 29 July 1855, Constable Joseph Davis was charged with assaulting Emanuel 'by wresting a gun from him'. One Sunday evening, when Emanuel was riding on the road near Black Creek, he fired a shot which caused Mr William Monk's horse to run off. Monk called Emanuel a 'blackguard' who replied in kind. Half an hour later, Monk turned up at Emanuel's house with Constable Davis while Sutcliffe was taking the powder out of his gun. Davis challenged him, 'Will you repeat the words again?' When Emanuel refused, Davis 'rushed on him and wrested the gun out of his hand'.

At his trial for assault, Constable Davis defended his actions because Emanuel was 'in the habit of going about with a loaded gun, and many of the neighbours had complained of him'. Although he had seen Emanuel with the gun on the road earlier, he took the gun from him 'at his own door' because he regarded Emanuel as a dangerous person. But the magistrate was not happy about an individual being attacked in his own home. Instead, Davis 'should have taken the gun from [Emanuel] when he saw him on the street with it'.[38] For this lapse in judgement, Davis was fined five shillings, with four shillings and sixpence costs awarded against him. The ex-convict had won a battle against authority.

After this incident, it seems that Emanuel's neighbours took their revenge. One year later, he advertised a reward of £10 in the local paper:

STOLEN or STRAYED from Black Creek, on the 29th October, 1856, one large STRAWBERRY BULLOCK, branded RB near side on rump.

If stolen, the above reward will be paid on conviction of the thief, and recovery of the bullock; if strayed, £1 reward will be paid for such information as will lead to recovery.[39]

Since Emanuel waited until 25 November to place his advertisement, he may have received information that his bullock had been stolen, a piece of do-it-yourself justice in a small rural community against the man with the loaded gun.

In January 1857, Emanuel placed another notice in the local paper which suggests he was in financial trouble or planning to quit the mill:

All parties INDEBTED to me are requested to pay the amount of their bills on or before the 16th of this month; if not, they will be handed over to my solicitor for recovery; and all persons that have claims against me will please forward them at once for liquidation.
EMANUEL SUTCLIFFE
Black Creek Steam Mills[40]

This ad confirms that Emanuel was running a flour mill, using the skills he had learnt as a convict. But 1857 was not turning out to be a good year for the Sutcliffes, with Emanuel experiencing further losses and offering a huge reward in the local newspaper at the end of January:

STOLEN or STRAYED, from the Mill Paddock, Black Creek, THREE HORSES, of the following descriptions and brands ...

If strayed, One Pound reward will be paid for each of them; and if stolen, Fifty Pounds will be paid on conviction of the thief or thieves and the restoration of the horses to me at Black Creek.[41]

Perhaps the missing horses amounted to another form of local payback against the temperamental ex-convict who had upped the stakes by offering the extraordinary sum of £50, equivalent to £4305 or $6504 today. But the ad appeared to have no effect since Emanuel was still advertising the reward one month later.[42]

On top of these losses, worse was to come. To end a year that had begun badly, a family tragedy was reported in the local newspaper. On 22 December 1857, the Sutcliffes' son drowned at the age of nine years. While the details of George's death were reported, there is only imagination to document the grief of Sarah's parents upon the discovery of their son's body in Anvil Creek and during the inquest held on Christmas Eve:

> An inquest was held before the coroner ... at the house of Emanuel Sutcliffe, Black Creek on the body of George James Sutcliffe ... On Tuesday morning he had been seen bathing in a water-hole in Anvil Creek, where horses were usually watered. In the evening he was missed, and on searching the water-hole next day his body was found. It was supposed that he had been drowned in trying to catch a goose belonging to him which had been seen in the water-hole.[43]

At the age of 12, Sarah witnessed her grieving parents, as well as suffering the loss of her brother, the family's only son. As the older sister, had it been her responsibility to look after her brother? Did Emanuel take out his grief on her? In later life Sarah was known for her own violence and quickness to anger, as she followed in the footsteps of her unruly father, who rode around the neighbourhood with a loaded gun and a chip on his shoulder. With a father who had suffered the brutality of the convict system, perhaps it was inevitable that Sarah would suffer a punishing childhood.

After the death of their son, more misfortune visited the Sutcliffe family. Despite his success as a mill owner, Emanuel continued his wild, gun-toting ways. On 20 January 1858 he appeared in the Maitland Quarter Sessions Court where he was:

> indicted for wilfully presenting fire-arms, to wit, a gun, at the person of William Schofield, at Aberdeen ... with intent to alarm

him. A second count charged the prisoner with unlawfully producing fire-arms, near to the person of William Schofield, with intent to alarm him.

The jury returned a verdict of not guilty, the prosecution case having collapsed because a key witness failed to appear.[44] Yet again Emanuel's predilection for pointing loaded guns at people had gone unpunished.

By the 1860s, Emanuel and his family had quit the Hunter Valley and moved back to Sydney, although the reasons are unknown. Perhaps their departure was due to more neighbourly discord, financial failure of the mill or failure of the new landowner, Mr Doolan, to renew Emanuel's four year lease, which lapsed in 1858. As the *Colonial Literary Journal* had warned in 1844, 'Attempt not to fly like an eagle with the wings of a wren'.

Sarah and the ship's captain

Sarah's life with her parents ended at the age of 19 when she married Charles Edwards in Sydney on 29 April 1865 by special licence at the Reverend Dr Fullerton's, in Elizabeth Street, Sydney. Because the marriage was not in a church and under a special licence, there may have been urgent reasons, such as pregnancy, for the ceremony. Charles Edwards was a 26-year-old from Dundee, Scotland and was described as a master mariner in the marriage notice in the newspaper.[45] Only one child was born after Sarah married, a girl named Minnie Josephine, in either 1866 or 1867, although her birth was not registered.[46]

Very little is known about Sarah's first husband or how long the marriage lasted. There are a number of references to a Captain Charles Edwards in the newspapers over three decades in the mid to late 1800s. Unfortunately, there were two Charles Edwards in Sydney around the same time, both mariners, making it impossible to determine which Charles Edwards was the commander of the various ships which sailed the coasts of north-east Australia and New Guinea during this time, including the first scientific voyage to New Guinea. In 1875, Captain Charles Edwards was appointed commander of an exciting expedition to collect animal and plant specimens from what was considered to be the last great frontier. Setting out on the *Chevert* on 18 May 'with a fair wind', Captain Edwards commanded a ship full of naturalists, zoologists, taxidermists, botanists, a complete armoury of weapons and items of trade to 'facilitate friendly intercourse' with the natives. The ship was given a huge farewell by the public, the premier and his ministers, members of Parliament, government officials and 'other influential residents of the city'.[47]

Did Sarah and her daughter, Minnie, read about the exciting adventures of this Captain Charles Edwards? Had Sarah's mariner husband been 'converted' into a captain through wishful thinking? Unfortunately, there are no hints in the historical material to indicate either way. All we know is that by 1886 Sarah's first husband was dead since Minnie's marriage notice stated that she was the only daughter of the late Captain Charles Edwards.

Sarah's parents: inglorious endings

While Sarah's parents lived long lives, their endings were inglorious. At the age of 72, Sarah's father entered the Liverpool Asylum in October 1885. Less than a year later, in August 1886, Emanuel Sutcliffe died from paralysis. Liverpool Asylum provided refuge for infirm and destitute men in an era when nursing homes and government assistance for the elderly were unknown. A small daily wage was paid to those who were able to work in the Asylum's farm and workshop.[48] For the old and infirm, however, the asylum provided very basic living conditions in overcrowded wards with underpaid workers.

Five years after the death of her husband, Sarah's mother, Ellen, died at the age of 77,[49] two years before Sarah's baby-farming activities were discovered. After Sarah and John Makin were arrested, John revealed an interesting snippet of family history—that Ellen Sutcliffe had been a midwife or ladies' nurse and Sarah had learnt the craft from her mother. If so, Ellen's skills may have supplemented the Sutcliffes' income in rural New South Wales.

Ellen Sutcliffe met her end in the Newington Asylum in Rydalmere, where she died from senile debility and diarrhoea.[50] She was blind when she died and was given a pauper's burial at Rookwood Cemetery, suggesting that Sarah had little contact with her mother at the end. There was no love lost between Sarah and her mother since John Makin's sister-in-law had once witnessed Sarah 'knock her own blind mother down with a chair'.[51] Somewhere along the way Sarah had learnt that violence was a legitimate way of dealing with conflict.

❧

CHAPTER THREE

John Makin: son of the middle class with a past
26 April 1824–23 June 1872

John Makin was born on 14 February 1845 in Dapto, a small coastal
town south of Wollongong in New South Wales. He was the fourth of
eleven children born to William Samuel Makin, a publican, and his wife
Ellen Selena, née Bolton (or Boulton), also known as Eleanor. William
married Ellen on 23 January 1837 at St Philip's Church, Sydney. Not
much is known about the origins of John's father who, according to family
history, was an 'elusive' man, a sawyer by trade who may have been from
London and whose mother's name was Agnes.[1]

There were two William Makins who arrived in New South Wales as
convicts. The first, an army deserter, arrived on board the *Lloyds* in 1833
after being sentenced to seven years' transportation with 400 lashes. He
was 32 years of age when he arrived, making him just about the right age
to be the 35-year-old William Makin who married John Makin's mother
in 1837. However, this William Makin was working in a chain gang at
Berrima at that time and did not gain his certificate of freedom until 1842.[2]

The second William Makin arrived as a convict on board the *Earl Grey*
in 1836 with a certificate of freedom granted in 1843. However, the only
person with a similar name listed in the 1837 Convict Muster is William
Macken, who arrived on the *Earl Grey* aged 16 years, making him far too
young to be John Makin's father. There are no free settlers by the name
of William Makin listed in the immigrant passenger lists for New South
Wales although a Samuel Makin arrived from Liverpool, England via
Hobart on 1 April 1833.

William Samuel Makin's elusive origins are also reflected in the different information contained in the family trees which contain John Makin as one of their descendants.[3] In one family tree William Makin was born in 1815 in Ireland to an Agnes Makin. Three other family trees state that he was born in 1812. Yet another says he was born in 1815 in Birmingham to a mother called Agnes and an unnamed father, suggesting that John Makin's father was illegitimate. Even when William died on 20 January 1887 in Wollongong from 'diarrhoea and debility', his granddaughter (the informant for his death certificate) did not know the name of his father or the surname of his mother who was only known as Agnes. While William may have started out life with dubious working-class origins, he became a well-to-do hotel owner and agent for the Illawarra Steam Company, having lived for 60 years in New South Wales when he died at the age of 85.

Much more information is known about the origins of John Makin's mother, Ellen, whose father, William Bolton, was transported to Van Diemen's Land for the two unrelated crimes of sacrilege (theft of a bible and a prayer book from Shenstone Church) and coining. Born in 1772 in Birmingham, he had married Mary Tysall on 19 October 1795 at St Martin's Church in Birmingham. Mary, born in 1774 or 1775, bore six children before William disappeared from her life.[4] Since the making of counterfeit coins amounted to treason against the king, it carried the death penalty. It was also William Bolton's second conviction for such treasonous acts. Convicted on 15 March 1821 in Stafford,[5] William Bolton was one of many whose death penalty was converted to transportation for life. He arrived in Hobart on 26 December 1821 on the *Lord Hungerford* to serve his sentence at the age of 49.

Compared to the convict father of Sarah Makin, William Bolton was a well-behaved man with his gaol report stating his character was 'not vicious' and his hulk report praising him for being 'orderly'. During his sentence he acquired only two misdemeanours against his name. The first was on 28 November 1826 when he was convicted of having a pair of government shoes on his person and not being able to account for them. For this crime he spent two months in a chain gang.[6] At the time, William had been assigned to Dr Adam Turnbull, a young Scottish surgeon who had settled on a property at Winton on the Macquarie River.[7] On his conviction, John Makin's grandfather swapped the comfortable environment of the Kirklands for the harsh labouring work in a chain gang on one of the local road or building projects in the area. It was a cruel punishment for a man 54 years of age. It is unknown where he was assigned after his two months in the chain gang. However, on 28 April 1828, he was found absent from the evening muster 'until half past 8 o'clock on Wed last'. His punishment this time was 'to labour the whole of successive Saturdays for Govt'.

Unlike most Australian convicts, William Bolton did not see or taste freedom. After nine long years in Tasmania, the Convict Muster of 1830 states that John Makin's grandfather was 'Found dead May 1830'. These records were always short and to the point with no explanation about how William died or where he was buried. Perhaps nine years of hard labour had worn him out at the age of 58. His death would have been unknown to the family he left behind—a family which ironically was living just a few hundred miles north when he died.

Ellen Bolton's journey to New South Wales

William's transportation in 1821 had left a family of seven without a father, husband or income. It would have been no surprise to the Georgian authorities that, three years later, the whole Bolton family would find its way to infamous Botany Bay, as the New South Wales colony was known in Britain.

Women with children who were left to fend for themselves after their husbands were transported depended on local charity, prostitution or crime to survive. But some did not. Jane Ryan was a native of Dublin living in Chelmsford, England when her husband was sentenced to transportation for life. Since a parish only assisted those who were native to the area, Jane Ryan petitioned the Duke of York, stating that she was in a 'state of starvation' with no 'claim on any Parish to protect her and her infant child' and begging 'the first possible passage' to New South Wales to join her husband. The petition was refused: 'John Ryan laboured alone "for the term of his natural life" in New South Wales while his family starved to death in Chelmsford'.[8]

John Makin's maternal grandmother, Mary Bolton, was luckier. Left alone with her children after William was transported, she turned to crime since her trade as a laundress was insufficient to provide for six children between the ages of one and eighteen years. Worse still was the stigma of a husband's conviction, which was an embarrassing impediment to 'securing honest employment'—the 'respectable' view persisted that Botany Bay was nothing more than 'the receptacle for the scum, the sweepings of the gaols, hulks and prison'.[9]

Mary Bolton was convicted on 26 April 1824 in Birmingham for receiving stolen goods, namely, three pairs of boots, three pairs of shoes and 25 yards of binding. The previous year she had been before the courts on a charge of larceny but was found not guilty.[10] Paradoxically, her conviction ensured that she and her daughters would at least be fed and clothed, placing them one step up from destitution during their imprisonment and transportation.

Sentenced to seven years' transportation, at the age of 50 Mary set out on her long sea voyage on the *Grenada* on 25 September 1824 with 81 other female convicts, arriving four months later in Sydney Cove on 23 January 1825.[11] Four of Mary's daughters were also transported with her: Anne aged 19, Eliza aged 12, Helen (known as Ellen) aged 8 and Sarah aged 6.[12] It is not known what happened to Mary's eldest children, William and Mary.

When married women were transported to the Australian colonies they arrived 'without the protection of a husband, father or family and, to all intents and purposes, [were] single women'. Mary was allowed to travel with her four children, which was unusual because there was an official reluctance to allow convict women to take their children on board the transport ships. This was based on the need to keep 'colonial expenditure' to a minimum 'with no room for pity for the women or concern for the fate of children left behind'.[13] Since many petitions to allow children to accompany their mothers to Botany Bay were refused, Mary Bolton was one of the fortunate few who, exiled from her native land, was able to leave England's shores with her heart intact.

In this way, John Makin's mother, Ellen, began her early life as the daughter of a convict. She was probably imprisoned with her mother before sailing the seas for four months to arrive in a strange colonial outpost on 23 January 1825. Even though they had won the right to travel with their mother, upon their arrival Ellen and her younger sister, Sarah, were separated from the family and placed in the Female Orphan School in Parramatta. The reason was simple—convict women were considered to be a 'disgrace to their sex', 'filthy in their persons, disgusting in their habits, obscene in their conversations'[14] and a bad example to their children.

Children of the streets—a colony's shame

Since 1788 there had been considerable concern within the colony about the 'growing numbers of neglected and destitute children ... who were to be found eking out a living in the streets of the main settlements'.[15] These children were the offspring of convict women and their various couplings with male convicts, soldiers and sailors. While sex was popular in early Sydney Town, child care was thin on the ground.

When Philip King arrived to take up his appointment as governor on 15 April 1800,[16] Sydney's street kids were estimated to number about 1000 in a population of just over 5000 men and women.[17] They were vulnerable to exploitation and abuse in a colony where men outnumbered women by almost three to one. The degree of child neglect in the 12-year-old colony must have been stark since Governor King set about establishing an orphan school within months to teach abandoned girls skills appropriate for their station in life, together with obedience and morality:

> Soon after I arrived here the sight of so many girls between the ages of eight and twelve, verging on that brink of ruin and prostitution which several had fallen into, induced me to set about rescuing the elder girls from the snares laid for them, and which the horrible example and treatment of many of their parents hurried them into.[18]

Nonetheless, the number of orphans and neglected children continued to grow. By 1806, there were 1832 children in the colony, of which 1025 were illegitimate. Not all were abandoned since marriage was uncommon amongst convicts, soldiers and ex-convicts. While King had been prepared to ignore the marriage problem, Governor Macquarie's arrival in January 1810 signalled a firmer approach to the 'lower orders' since he was gravely concerned about their lack of morals, especially 'the common practice of ... cohabitation' and its effect on their children.[19]

Macquarie's answer lay in building a larger Female Orphan School, for which he laid the foundation stone on 13 September 1813 on the banks of the Parramatta River. Although the building took five years to complete, it was an architectural wonder, becoming the colony's first three-storey building. With 'a charming vista to the river across park-like lawns',[20] it was modelled on Mrs Macquarie's family home in Scotland and had:

> all the necessary out [sic] offices for the accommodation of 100 female orphans, and for the master and matron of the institution, having an extensive garden and orchard and a grazing park or paddock for cattle ... the whole of the premises enclosed with a high strong stockade.[21]

While this description evokes a charming rural retreat for the city's orphaned girls, the cattle in their 'grazing park' probably had a much easier life than the 100 inmates. On 30 June 1818, the female orphans from the old Orphan School in George Street were taken by government boats up the Parramatta River to their grand, new accommodation. Far away from the temptations of Sydney Town, they were to be educated 'only in view of their present condition in life and future destination, namely as wives or servants'.[22]

The school represented the best and worst of institutionalisation where all rights were forfeited, moral regeneration was the overall goal, contact with the outside world was restricted and life was ordered and regimented.[23] Punishment was severe for any transgressions, as young Sarah Patfield experienced in October 1821 when she was accused of stealing the caps and shirts she had given her visiting sister. As a deterrent to the other girls, Sarah was forced to wear a wooden collar marked 'thief' day and night. Her head was shaved in the presence of the other girls and she was held in solitary confinement for a month, fed only on bread and water.[24]

With claims that the old Female Orphan School had produced too many girls who returned to their former prostitution ways, Macquarie wrote the new school's constitution with rules and regulations that set out its objectives, curriculum, and admission and apprenticeship procedures. Age limits were imposed to restrict admission to girls between the ages of five and eight years since 'the moral reclamation' of older girls was not considered to be possible,[25] because of the unstated belief that older girls were corrupted by the sexual habits of men.

The new curriculum ensured that inmates were not educated above their status but would receive sufficient instruction to improve 'their economic potentialities'. In February 1810, the *Sydney Gazette* carried the following announcement:

> Plain Needle-work will be taken into the Orphan House and executed by the Girls under the inspection of the Matron, on moderate terms, to be paid for when delivered.[26]

In this way, the aim of the first orphanages in Sydney was to produce a reliable servant class who would fit into the colony's well-ordered class system. Ironically, it was this system that produced the problems Governor Macquarie was keen to eradicate—children were abandoned not only because of a 'lack of family cohesiveness among the humbler classes' but also because of the desperation of the poor within colonial society.[27]

Inmates of the Female Orphan School were apprenticed out as servants, without pay, at the age of 13 to 'Families of Good character' for a five year period or until they married. Marriage entitled a former female orphan to the gift of a cow from the school's herd of cattle 'but only if she ... had a good record as a bound apprentice'.[28] This meant that she had to be careful to survive any number of claims on her female character during her apprenticeship either by her master or other male members of the household to which she was apprenticed.

The relief and grief of arriving in Sydney Town

A few months after their arrival on 23 January 1825, John Makin's mother, Ellen Bolton, and her younger sister, Sarah, faced a painful separation from their mother. While Mary Bolton was sent to the Female Factory in

Parramatta as a newly arrived convict, this institution was not considered to be a suitable place for children. Although the whole family had survived the prison system in England and the dangers of a four month sea voyage, Mary Bolton no longer had any legal right over her daughters.[29]

In the year of the Bolton family's arrival, another convict, Ann Kelly, described how her daughter had been 'wrested' from her 'without her consent' in a petition to the Female Orphan School seeking to have the girl returned to her care and providing a brief description of the distressing scene when female convicts were separated from their children.[30]

Ellen and Sarah were admitted to the Female Orphan School on 10 May 1825. After being taken by boat up the Parramatta River to one of the most picturesque places in the colony, Ellen and Sarah Bolton would have seen the imposing, three-storey Female Orphan School as the boat drew near, perhaps overwhelmed by its sheer, prison-like size. The first thing to greet them as they entered the ground floor hall would have been the noise and sight of so many other girls dressed in identical clothing. Perhaps the Matron, Mrs Walker, reassured them as they held onto each other, and she presented them with the plain uniform which represented their new 'Condition in Life': 'a blue gown, white apron, and tippet [or cape] with a white cotton or straw bonnet'.[31] All of this would have been a vast improvement on the clothing they were wearing after four months at sea. They would soon learn that the best part of the school was the food: a daily diet of two pints of milk, three-quarters of a pound of bread, half a pound of meat with vegetables and a pudding one or two days a week.[32]

At the ages of six and eight, Sarah and Ellen were meant to learn how to read and write from 9 a.m. till noon so they would be able to understand the 'Holy Scriptures'. The rest of their day was spent learning all the domestic tasks required of a servant and wife, including needlework, washing, spinning and carding, managing a dairy, baking and gardening. Their days were topped and tailed with Bible readings and prayer which took place every morning and evening while Sunday was reserved for church. With hard work and constant moral instruction, the authorities expected that Ellen and Sarah would not repeat the immoral behaviour of their convict mother. But when Ellen later married John Makin's father she was only capable of writing her 'X' mark on her marriage certificate rather than her name, suggesting that the Orphan School had been more focused on producing servants than educating convict children.[33]

The religious instruction of the school was in the hands of a Methodist missionary, the Reverend William Walker, who had arrived with Mrs Walker in early 1825. Soon after his appointment, Reverend Walker found that things were not to his Methodist standards since the departure of the original master and matron:

> Since the departure of Mr Hoskings, [the children] have had no religious care extended over them. When we first came ... the children were wearing clothes that had not been washed for three weeks or a month before, and these so ragged as to make them no less indelicate than our wild aborigines. Numbers of the children had never been to church for months!! ... The master that was here before me made several attempts to prostitute the girls ... plac[ing] an indelible stain of unfitness upon his character.[34]

This letter illustrates the religious atmosphere that was established in the school in the very month that Ellen and Sarah arrived, perhaps making a great impression on two little girls who had lost their family. But Walker proved to be an inadequate master with no ability to institute proper administrative procedures and a tendency to attend political meetings rather than his duties.

In an inspection of the school in June 1825, the inmates were found to be 'covered with the Itch and Scald heads' and suffering ophthalmia (inflammation of the eyes), causing the children to abandon their work and studies. It is likely this affliction also affected Ellen and Sarah, since the school's assistant surgeon provided 491 treatments for ophthalmia between 25 March 1825 and 14 October 1826. Other reported medical complaints included mouth and scalp ulcers, diarrhoea, constipation, abscesses, dysentery and tinea, which were spread easily between children living in close quarters in dormitories and exacerbated by a poorly constructed sewerage system.[35]

After Reverend Walker was removed from his position, Ellen and Sarah and the other inmates came under the control of Reverend Charles Wilton and Mrs Wilton, who took over in April 1827. It seemed that the moral state of the 108 girls was an ongoing and irrepressible problem because the new master made complaints to the school's committee that were similar to those made by Reverend Walker two years before:

> I write ... to say that it is <u>totally impossible</u> for me to prevent <u>immorality</u> in the Servants of the Institution, or to protect the <u>morality</u> of the children, many of whom are growing up to be young women.[36]

The problem was the 'improper persons ... talking to the females through the <u>palings of the Institution</u>' which the school's constable was unable to control. However, the Reverend Wilton was very much out of his depth, his words underscoring the shock he felt about the situation he had landed in, fresh off a ship from England. Time proved that he was a man of 'little judgement', even less experience and unfit for his duties. Mrs Wilton was also not up to the task, declaring that 'she could not bear the smell of the children or the house, and would not reside in it'.[37]

During the time that Ellen and Sarah lived in the Female Orphan School, the number of its inmates grew each year, from 104 in 1825 to 145 in 1831. Their lives were a mixture of hard work and religiosity amidst overcrowded and diseased conditions. But with a matron who expressed her distaste for the children, a master unfit for the job and only an assistant matron in charge, there would have been opportunities for the girls to escape authority whenever they could. But only for a short time, since the colony embraced the idea of the Female Orphan School as a source of labour. Applications by colonists for orphaned girls were so common the school acted 'as an agency' for domestic servants. Under the apprenticeship system, girls were supplied to 'respectable settlers and government officers' with very few applications refused. In a period of labour shortage, they 'performed an important function for the colonial economy'.[38]

Ellen's and Sarah's mother might have asked for her daughters to be returned to her but any reunion was impossible until her sentence had been served. Even visits by relatives had been severely restricted after the 'theft' by Sarah Patfield in 1821, suggesting that the girls did not see their mother for many years. However, a number of other parents and relatives applied to have their girls returned to them. These applications had to be recommended by a religious minister or a magistrate[39] and while they were not always successful, the trustees of the Female Orphan School looked favourably on the applications made by Ellen and Sarah's family.

Family applications were usually made when the circumstances of a girl's family improved. Recommendations which stated that a mother was of good or moral character smoothed the way for mothers and daughters to be reunited. Some petitions were granted conditionally when children were returned to parents or relatives as apprentices. In 1828, after spending three years in the Female Orphan School, John Makin's mother was apprenticed to Edward Raper, who had married Ellen's eldest sister, Anne Bolton, in 1826.[40] On 19 March 1827, Edward Raper wrote to the Reverend Archdeacon Scott:

> My wife, Anne Raper, has two sisters, Ellen and Sarah Bolton at present in the Female Orphan School, whom she is desirous to remove from that Institution, and to receive ... under our own Guardianship, and Protection: because, as we are both free persons, & able to maintain these Children, we are unwilling that they should continue a burthen on a public Charity ... We therefore respectfully entreat, Reverend Sir, that you will be pleased to direct their discharge from the School.

The letter was signed by a Justice of the Peace who certified that Edward and Anne Raper were married and had the means to support Ellen and Sarah. After this letter was received a note was scrawled by Charles Cowper, Clerk of the Church which ran the School Corporation, to a Mr Harington:

> Edward Raper per Tottenham wants a Girl out of the Female Orphan School. He says he is free but that he has lost his Certificate

[of Freedom] ... [W]ill you let me know whether what he says is correct.

Harington Esquire then made a notation in the elegant script of the times:

Edwd Raper per Tottenham obtained a Certificate of freedom on No. 79/2088 the 15 April 1824.

Tottenham was a reference to the convict ship on which Edward Raper had arrived in October 1818 after being convicted in North Riding, Yorkshire on 15 April 1817 and sentenced to seven years' transportation, although his crime is unknown. As a result of this correspondence, Anne and Edward Raper were successful in gaining the guardianship of Ellen but not her sister, Sarah, who at the age of nine was left to fend for herself in the Female Orphan School.

Nine years later, at the age of 20, Ellen Bolton married William Makin, 35, on 23 January 1837 in St Phillips Church, Sydney and began her 22 year career of childbirth.

After Ellen was released from the Female Orphan School, it took three years and more letters for her sister, Sarah, to be given her conditional freedom.[41] On 26 February 1831, Sarah Bolton was apprenticed to Mr Francis O'Meara, a Conductor of Police, who had married the second eldest Bolton daughter, Eliza, in 1828.[42] When Eliza O'Meara wrote on 4 February 1831 seeking her sister as an apprentice, her request was approved, although the terms of Sarah's release into the O'Mearas' care were strict and the subject of an indenture. This contract required Sarah to faithfully serve 'in all lawful Business, according to her Power, and Ability; and honestly, orderly, and obediently, in all Things, behave her self towards her said Master'. Today we might be appalled at the thought of a 12-year-old child being indentured as a servant but in 1831 the colony needed cheap labour. The trustees of the Female Orphan School also needed free settlers to take children off their hands in order to be relieved of the cost of their day to day care. The indenture system was a system of slave labour for a limited period of time during which the trustees had to hope that the child's master and mistress would not neglect, abuse or prostitute the young girls assigned to their care.

Serving her seven year sentence—Mary Bolton's moral regeneration

Back in January 1825, at the age of 50, John Makin's grandmother had been sent to the notorious Female Factory at Parramatta where all newly arrived female convicts were held either to work within the Factory or until they were assigned to provide free labour to the colony's middle class.

With her first assignment, Mary Bolton, four feet, ten inches tall with a dark complexion, black hair and chestnut eyes, was fortunate to end up in the household of an eminent free settler, Dr Patrick Hill, who had accepted a position as surgeon at Liverpool Hospital in January 1821 and obtained a land grant at Liverpool on 17 May 1825.[43]

Mary Bolton stayed with Dr Hill for over two years, probably being responsible for all the chores in his bachelor household. But it appears she was no longer needed after Dr Hill married Mary Throsby at St Luke's Church, Liverpool on 12 July 1827.[44] Although a free woman, Dr Hill's newly acquired wife replaced Mary Bolton, convict, in supplying his household needs. In this way, Dr Hill was a perfect example of the opportunities and privileges accorded to male free settlers—free convict labour, free land (courtesy of the local Aborigines) and a wife who provided more free labour.

Soon after his marriage, problems surfaced in Dr Hill's household. On 5 December 1827, Mary Bolton appeared in the Court of General Sessions accused of being 'useless in her service'.[45] Her punishment was listed as '1st Class at the Factory one month'. A bachelor living alone with a middle-aged female servant suggests there may have been some territorial rivalry between Mary, who had previously been in charge of Dr Hill's household, and his new wife.

Within the Female Factory, the convicts were divided into three classes. The first class consisted of women who had just arrived from England, those who had been returned from assigned service but with good character reports and second class women who had been moved up because they 'had sustained six months' good behaviour'.[46] These women were eligible

for assignment, as well as marriage. Second class women were on probation, often having been sent back to the Factory because they had become
pregnant while on assignment. The third class consisted of women who
had been punished for breaking the law or misbehaved on the voyage to
Australia.[47] Each class of woman was distinguished by her dress, with first
class women much better dressed than their lower class companions, while
the third class had their hair cropped 'as a mark of disgrace'.[48]

Although she had 'misbehaved' Mary was probably returned to the first
class because Dr Hill wrote her a glowing reference. While this punishment does not sound terribly onerous, the Factory was notorious for its
overcrowded conditions and lack of basic comforts. Local men had a habit
of visiting new arrivals with liquor in hand 'for the purpose of forming
a banquet *according to custom* … as a prelude to excesses which decency
forbids to mention'.[49]

In the year of Mary's return, the Factory was brewing rebellion. Not
only did the female convicts have to endure damp, overcrowded and unhygienic conditions, but insufficient food and forced hair shaving combined
with solitary confinement had also taken its toll. For unknown reasons,
the rations of tea and sugar and other victuals for the third class convicts
had been reduced by Matron Raine. In fact, salt had been substituted for
sugar in the morning porridge. This caused 'a general spirit of discontent
… and a determination to have revenge on the retiring Matron' who was
rescued by a party of constables after the women 'assailed' her in one of the
Factory's rooms.[50] To make matters worse the new matron, Mrs Gordon,
stopped the bread and sugar 'allowances' completely as punishment.

On 27 October 1827, Australia's first industrial action took place with
a mass escape involving more than 200 women from all classes. At first,
the women took over the yard of the Factory, ejecting a constable and
allowing no-one to enter. Although there were attempts at conciliation, the
frustrated women 'assailed the [wooden] gates [of the Factory], with pick-
axes, axes, iron crows' then 'poured forth thick as bees from a hive' into
the surrounding neighbourhood. When about 100 women swarmed into
town, the bugles sounded to call the military to arms, with about 40 soldiers
'flying in all directions with fixed bayonets' to quell the uprising. Many of

the local bakers, rather than be taken over, 'threw into the street whatever loaves the women required'. Another group of women, shouting 'Starvation', attacked a raw quarter of beef hanging outside a butcher's stall.

But the women, described as violent 'Amazonian banditti', stood up to the soldiers. Eventually, with threats to shoot and hunger satisfied, many were brought into line and conducted back to the Factory under military escort, 'shouting as they went along, and carrying with them their aprons loaded with bread and meat ... after the manner of a conquering army'. Back at the Factory, the Superintendent of Police ordered the ringleaders to be singled out and confined 'but so determined were the rioters' they managed to overcome the soldiers and rescued their companions, 'declaring, that if one suffered, all should suffer'.

When Mary Bolton returned to the Female Factory in December 1827, she may have found a very different atmosphere as a result of improved rations and emboldened women who had stood up to authority. After her one month sentence in the first class, Mary was assigned to Stephen Owen, a government official who was responsible for paying the contractors who supplied provisions to the colony's road gangs.[51] Mary served Mr Owen for the rest of her sentence.

While still in the service of Mr Owen, Mary Bolton received her ticket-of-leave on 16 July 1829, a reward for good behaviour which enabled her to work for wages, although she was still subject to curfews at night, mandatory attendance at church on Sundays and was not allowed to travel without permission.[52]

On 9 May 1831, Mary petitioned the School Corporation, seeking the return of her daughter, Sarah, something she must have longed for during her six years of servitude:

> Your petitioner being now free, and naturally anxious to have her youngest daughter, Sarah, (who from her tender years, and inexperience require her more particular attention) under her own immediate care ... prays, that the ... School Corporation will restore her daughter, Sarah, to her (Francis O'Meara ... being agreeable to forgo any claim which he may have to her services).

The petition was 'signed' by Mary's mark (a cross) and witnessed by Stephen Owen, who wrote a glowing reference for her:

> I certify that Mary Bolton was recommended to my notice by Patk
> Hill Esqu, Col Surgeon, Liverpool, as a very decent woman, and an
> excellent servant … that she has been in my service for six months,
> during which periods she has fully maintained the good character
> awarded her by her former master.
>
> I, further, consider, Mary Bolton, capable of maintaining her
> daughter, and … that she will not be inattentive to the moral &
> religious obligations which devolve upon her.

Finally, on 13 September 1831 Mary Bolton received her certificate of freedom. As an emancipated convict, she was now able to take custody of her youngest daughter, Sarah, and become a full participant in the British experiment to tame the great southern land. But it was not to be for long since she died on 5 October 1836 at the age of 62 years.

Ellen Makin, mother and survivor

The family history of Ellen Bolton, John Makin's mother, suggests she was left with her fair share of emotional scars. She had lost her father, experienced the uncertainty of a long sea voyage when very young and, soon after arrival, was separated from her mother and older sisters. In the Female Orphan School she was subject to the regimentation of a school tasked with imprinting morality, obedience and servitude into the very fibre of its inmates.

What effect did the Female Orphan School have on Ellen as a mother? Was she overly strict? Religious? Unloving? Was it inevitable there would be a black sheep in her very large family of eleven children? As one of more than 100 children in the Female Orphan School, which was sometimes diseased and dirty, she would have needed a great capacity for survival, something she would rely on as her fertile body produced a child every two years. When John Makin was born in 1845, Ellen had four children under the age of seven. By the time he was two years old, another son had arrived; by the time he was four, there was yet another and by the time he was six, he had a baby sister. John Makin, middle child, may have been relatively invisible in a household filled with babies and a mother preoccupied with nappies and breast-feeding. When John was eight, his younger brother, William, nearly died after falling into a pot of boiling water.[53] With severe scalding, William's recovery increased the heavy childcare burden on Ellen Makin. As John grew older, every two years, another child was born until there were eleven in 1860 when he was 15 years old. By this time he may have been sick of the sight of young children. As John later revealed during several coronial inquiries and his trial, he was a man who showed little emotion, displaying no empathy towards mothers, babies and his own children.

Despite their less than salubrious origins, John Makin's parents created a respectable middle-class family in Wollongong, a coastal town 84 kilometres south of Sydney. While John moved to Sydney, most of his brothers and sisters remained in the region, reproducing a huge clan of more than 50 grandchildren. John's father, William, became the holder of general publican licences during the 1850s and 1860s for the Illawarra Steam Packet Inn in Corrimal Street, Wollongong. The family also owned the old Royal Hotel in Wollongong, which was purchased in April 1882 for the sum of £1250.[54] But John gained a reputation for being a foolish young man, in and out of trouble, who could not be trusted with money. Was rebellion the only way to catch the attention of his preoccupied parents?

John Makin—black sheep and sheep thief

John started early as the black sheep in the family since, even before his name appeared as a notorious baby farmer, there are several references to him in the newspapers over a 20 year period. The first is on 25 February 1864 when he pleaded guilty to stealing a harness and was sentenced to Parramatta Gaol for six months with labour.[55] The entry for John Makin in the New South Wales Gaol Description and Entrance Books, 1818–1930, states, incorrectly, that he was born in Wollongong in 1844 and was an inmate of Darlinghurst Gaol in 1863, possibly on remand, with the prison number 2109. While there is no record of the crime he committed, this entry shows that John Makin from Wollongong was in Sydney in the early 1860s. The notation on the record of his admission to Darlinghurst Gaol stated that he was a blacksmith with brown hair and blue eyes, was five feet, six inches tall and that he could read and write. This description accords with the one made after John was arrested and held on remand for murder in 1892.

On 4 January 1871, *The Sydney Morning Herald* reported a long list of 108 men and two women whose estates had been sequestrated (seized by bailiffs or sheriffs) at the end of 1870.[56] John Makin of Wollongong, a clerk, was one of them. How John fell into debt is unknown, although it may have been in one of the many gambling saloons that operated at the time. His liabilities were listed as £22 12s 10d with assets of only £2. The cause of his insolvency was the 'pressure of creditors', perhaps the type of creditors whom his well-off family refused to pay. It was a small debt compared to that of many others on the list, some of whom owed thousands of pounds to their creditors. One was Henry Parkes, later the Premier of New South Wales, whose merchant business failed at the end of 1870 when he owed the enormous sum of £35,036.[57]

John Makin appeared in the Insolvency Court in Sydney on Tuesday 2 November 1870 and surrendered his assets of £2 to Mr Semphill, the official assignee of his debt. A month later he appeared at a meeting of creditors in Wollongong[58] where he promised to pay his outstanding debt.

Less than a year after his appearance in the Insolvency Court, on 27 August 1871, John Makin, aged 26, married Sarah Jane Edwards (née Sutcliffe), aged 25, at 41 Burton Street, Sydney in the Free Church of England. For some reason there was no notice in the Sydney newspapers of their marriage, unlike the marriage of John's younger brother, Daniel, in 1878 and unlike Sarah's first marriage, six years earlier.

Sarah and John met in John's home town, since their marriage certificate reveals that Sarah's place of residence was Wollongong at the time.[59] John was a commercial clerk whilst Sarah's occupation was recorded in the elegant handwriting of the day as 'Lady', although she was actually a barmaid working in a local hotel, most likely the one owned by John's father. When Sarah married for the second time, she used her married surname of 'Edwards' even though she was described as a 'spinster' on the marriage certificate, rather than a widow or divorcee. Perhaps she was a bigamist, something that was relatively common in the 1800s given the frequency of desertion by husbands and the difficulties with obtaining a divorce.

But both of them had a past. John was still dealing with his debt in 1872 when he applied for a certificate from the Insolvency Court on 23 June to show that his debt had been paid.[60] This was just in time, since there were ballooning expenses about to arrive in the newly created Makin family.

CHAPTER FOUR

The deadly secret in Sarah Makin's body
2 August 1872–8 November 1888

Almost a year after John and Sarah married, their first child, William Sutcliffe Makin, was born on 2 August 1872 in Wollongong. At the time of William's baptism, John was a publican[1] which suggests he was working in the family hotel business.

Two years later, on 27 August 1874—the Makins' third wedding anniversary—Blanche Ellen Gertrude Makin was born at Phoenix Wharf, Shelley Street, Sydney, where John was working as a wharfinger.[2] Sarah must have become pregnant soon after the birth of Blanche because less than nine months later she gave birth, prematurely, to a second daughter, Florence Eileen Elise Makin on 16 April 1875 in Sydney. She now had three children under the age of three years.

Seven more children arrived over the next 16 years. Clarence Ethel May Makin, known as Clarice, was born on 26 February 1878 at the Clarence River, New South Wales, and baptised in Wollongong. Sometime in 1879 or 1880, Percy Frederick Makin was born although his birth was not registered. Two years later, Daisy Makin was born on 23 October 1881 at 190 Goulburn Street, Sydney. By the end of 1881, Sarah had six children, all of whom survived into adulthood.

But 1881 was not a good year for the Makins since the newspapers reported that John Makin and Thomas Strange were charged with stealing a lamb from one John Brierly on 11 October. John confessed to taking the lamb when picked up by the police but said 'he did not think that Brierly would say anything about it'.[3] At the time, John was employed as a livestock delivery man by Thomas Ellis, a livestock auctioneer in George Street South, close to where the Makins were living in Goulburn Street.

On 6 October, John Brierly had purchased twelve lambs from Mr Ellis which were held in two pens at the saleyards. Another employee of Ellis', James Rochford, testified that he saw Makin 'throw a lamb over the fence at a time when Strange was in a cart close by' although he could not swear it was one of Brierly's lambs. He thought nothing of it until he later noticed one of the lambs from Brierly's pens was missing.

Robert O'Halloran testified that 'he conveyed a lamb in his cart from Ellis's yard to Hay-street [at Makin's request], where Strange, who was with Makin in the yard, took charge of and carried it away'. The lamb was then killed by Makin.

Makin's lawyer told the court there was no evidence the lamb was owned by Brierly and that Makin had made no attempt at concealment, arguing 'there had been no felonious taking'. Nonetheless, both Makin and Strange were committed to stand trial in the Court of Quarter Sessions. Although both were given bail, the charge of stealing probably meant that John was now unemployed.

While the Makin family had had a hearty meal of lamb chops, Sarah must have worried about the outcome of the trial since she was due to give birth to her sixth child. On 31 October 1881, both John and his companion in crime pleaded not guilty before Judge Dowling in a Darlinghurst court-room. Their lawyer, Mr Roberts, mounted a novel defence by arguing 'it was customary for a sheep, or a pig to be taken, in the way Makin had taken the lamb', the custom apparently allowing payment to be made afterwards. Although Roberts urged the jurymen to accept there was no felonious intent, they appear not to have heard of this sheep-borrowing custom, finding John Makin guilty and Mr Strange not guilty. For this petty theft, John received three months' gaol with hard labour. The prison record for John Makin confirms that the sheep-stealing and the baby-farming John Makin were one and the same, stating that he received three months for stealing on 1 November 1881.

The sentence would have been a terrible blow to a family with six young children, the youngest just eight days old. How Sarah survived without

John's income is unknown but his incarceration may have prompted her to begin baby farming or another well-known profession that was conducted on the docks. If she had already learnt the art of baby farming from her mother, Ellen Sutcliffe, it was a short step from starvation to the purchase of the next edition of the newspaper where unnamed mothers advertised for 'kind ladies' to adopt their unwanted babies.

It seems John's work insecurity continued to be an issue even after his release from gaol. Just before Christmas 1882, John was working for Mr Frederick Stuart, who had improperly used the water bottles of a company called Summons and Co. which was in the business of selling tonic and soda water to hotels and shops.[4] These bottles were the property of the company and bore their registered trademark, 'The Crystal Fountain Company'. Summons and Co. sued Stuart for breach of trademark since he appears to have been in the crafty business of refilling their empty bottles with 'lemonade and other liquors', aided by one John Makin.

Makin testified in the proceedings that he had 'delivered the bottles when filled to different publicans', collecting the empty bottles at the same time. To the frustration of Summons and Co., there was insufficient evidence to prove the trademark breach and the case was dismissed. Nonetheless, the case may have heralded the end of another career path for John Makin, who had given evidence against his employer.

There are two more references to Mr Makin in the newspapers in the late 1880s before his name became synonymous with baby farming after his arrest in 1892. In 1889, a man named Makin hijacked a horse at the Liverpool races and would only return it to the owner for a cheque for £20.[5] There is no way of knowing whether or not this story involved our John Makin, although the subsequent presentation to another person of the cheque, which Makin knew had been dishonoured by the horse owner,[6] sounds very much like the underhand dealings of John Makin, baby farmer. In November 1889, a John Makin was also charged with fraudulently converting a sewing-machine he had borrowed from Thomas Feather.[7] The newspaper report states that John Makin was 36 years old at the time, which does not match the age of John Makin, baby farmer, who was 44 in 1889. Nevertheless, law reporters did not always report the correct facts.

If these two incidents involved the baby-farming John Makin, it suggests the Makin family was supplementing its income through petty crime with too many hungry mouths to feed. Unexpectedly, extra costs arrived that many families had to bear because of high infant mortality rates.

Sarah's seventh child, Leslie Roland Joseph Makin, was born on 2 November 1883 off Bourke Street in Redfern. He died just after his first birthday on 13 November 1884 at 47 Oxford Street, Darlinghurst from convulsions caused by syphilis. Today this disease is known as congenital syphilis. According to the doctor who last saw him, Leslie had been suffering convulsions for five weeks. He was buried in Rookwood Cemetery with John and a friend as witnesses, Sarah apparently not in attendance. At this time, John was working as a clerk.

One year after Leslie's death, a girl, Linda, was born on 20 November 1885 at 26 George Street, Redfern. Eight months later, on 27 July 1886, she also died from convulsions from which she had apparently suffered for two weeks according to Dr Markby, who saw the baby the day before she died. At this time, John was working as a delivery man while the family was living at 207 Wells Street, Redfern, the suburb which would become their favourite haunt.[8]

Linda was buried at Rookwood Cemetery with John and Minnie Helbi, Sarah's married daughter, as witnesses. Again it appears Sarah did not attend the funeral. Given Linda's young age, her cause of death and that of her brother two years earlier, it is almost certain that Eveline Linda Makin (the name on her death certificate) also died of congenital syphilis. Another boy, Harold Campbell Makin, was born on 5 August 1888 at Bullanaming Street, Redfern. At the age of three months, he died on 8 November from infantile atrophy. The doctor who signed the death certificate said the baby had been suffering from infantile atrophy for two months, a clear sign Harold had failed to thrive, another symptom of congenital syphilis. With John still working as a delivery man, the Makins were living at 26 Dale Street, Chippendale when the baby died.[9]

The tenth and last known child of the Makins, Cecil Montague Makin was born in 1890. His birth was not registered, perhaps because Sarah and John expected that he too would die. Against the odds, he survived into adulthood. It was rumoured that Sarah had another six children[10] although there is no evidence of their births or their deaths. But dead babies were to become a speciality of the Makins, with surreptitious burials late at night and thoughts of registration the furthest thing from their minds.

Sarah and syphilis

Because one of Sarah's newborn babies died of syphilitic convulsions, Sarah herself was infected with syphilis, since the only way a baby can contract congenital syphilis is from its mother in the womb. How and when Sarah Makin contracted the disease is a mystery, but it is an event that affected her mental and physical health in the baby-farming years to come.

Sarah may have contracted syphilis from her first husband, who was a mariner, given the well-known affiliation between seamen and women of 'accomodating [sic] morals' whilst in port after long voyages at sea. Syphilis had formed deep roots in Australia with the disease being traceable to the country's convict origins and the 'basic nexus between poverty, prostitution and venereal disease'. Even before the First Fleet set sail, Governor Arthur Phillip was aware that many of the female convicts on board suffered from 'venereal complaints'.[11]

Sexual liaisons on the First Fleet between female convicts and seamen were common, although ships' officers and surgeons did not necessarily condone the behaviour of the 'depraved' women whose lust seemed to be uncontrollable and who bore the brunt of the moral censure. Upon arrival, the colony's first orgy apparently took place[12] and the promiscuous relations between convict men and women of the colony continued, much to the disgust of Governor Phillip, who tried to encourage convict men and women to marry. Yet there was very little privacy in a tent city. The challenges of camping in a strange land with strict food rationing meant that sex and drinking 'were among the few pleasures available'. In fact, '[t]he imbalance of the sexes produced by the convict transportation system encouraged promiscuity and in turn a marked incidence of venereal disease'. This means that sexually transmitted diseases were as much a part of the colony's early history as were settlement, exploration and rebellion. As early as 1789, Governor Phillip had formed the view that 'venereal disease "has gained such a footing in this settlement that I doubt if it will ever be done away"'.[13]

By 1808, one-quarter of the deaths of soldiers was due to syphilis and gonorrhoea and by 1819 venereal disease was the third most common illness treated at the Sydney Hospital. By 1834, it was reported that syphilis had spread 'over the whole of the Australian continent', including the Aboriginal population.[14]

If Sarah Makin had been infected by her first husband, it meant she contracted syphilis when she was about nineteen. If so, she would have had the disease for about six years by the time she married John Makin, making it highly likely that some of her first six children would have been affected by congenital syphilis. Since this did not occur, and for medical reasons discussed later, it is more likely she contracted syphilis sometime after the birth of her sixth child, Daisy, who grew into adulthood and as far as we know was not affected by the disease. Because Sarah's seventh child, Leslie, was her first to die from the disease, Sarah probably contracted syphilis between 23 October 1881 (Daisy's date of birth) and February 1883—nine months before the birth of Leslie.

When John Makin was sentenced to gaol for sheep-stealing on 31 October 1881, Sarah only had two options for paying the rent and filling the bellies of her six children: prostitution or baby farming. The remarkable coincidence of John's imprisonment in November 1881, the loss of his wages and the date of birth of her first baby with congenital syphilis sixteen months later suggests that Sarah became a 'lady of the night'.

Prostitution was common among working-class women in the 1800s in both Britain and Australia as a part-time way to boost inadequate wages or during periods of unemployment. Married women also supplemented family incomes with part-time prostitution, sometimes with the assistance of their husbands. It was usually 'a temporary phase' in a woman's life rather than a career. In the 1880s, the services of prostitutes were in high demand in New South Wales, since less than 50 per cent of men aged 20 to 30 years were married and 'significant proportions' of older men were bachelors, although married men were one of the largest groups of clients.[15]

With John Makin in prison and her eldest child, William, placed in charge of his younger sisters and brother, Sarah may have begun her lonely trade working the streets close to Darling Harbour where the family was living at the time, with plenty of randy sailors looking for 'horizontal refreshments' and leaving a tip in the form of syphilis. It is also possible that John Makin infected Sarah after he contracted syphilis in Darlinghurst Gaol.

Since the discovery of penicillin, most people have very little knowledge or experience of syphilis. Today its prevalence is highest in developing countries, although outbreaks of syphilis occur in developed countries with high immigrant populations and high rates of HIV infection.[16]

It is possible to get a sense of how common congenital syphilis was in the 1880s when Sarah lost her three babies by looking at the data from countries where sexually transmitted diseases are harder to control. In sub-Saharan Africa, the extent of syphilis in the population is similar to its prevalence in the USA in the early 1900s, with conservative estimates ranging from 3–18 per cent of the population. In some African countries, 24 per cent of all stillbirths and 30 per cent of infant deaths soon after birth are caused by congenital syphilis.[17]

Like the situation today, women who contracted syphilis in the nineteenth century were more likely to be young, unmarried, poor, or engaged in prostitution.[18] Once Sarah was infected by the worm-like, spiral-shaped organism (*Treponema pallidum*) that causes syphilis, she would have developed a chancre from 3–90 days later.[19] This is an unsightly but small ulceration or sore (sometimes multiple sores) which develops on a person's genitals and represents the primary stage of the disease. Because it is painless, Sarah Makin may not have known she was infected, especially if the chancre was located inside her vagina or cervix. In any case, it would have lasted about four to six weeks then disappeared without treatment.

In the secondary stage of the disease, Sarah would have experienced some or all of the symptoms that mark this stage—headaches, low grade fever, muscle aches, tiredness and loss of weight, a rough, lumpy, reddish-brown rash on the soles of her feet and palms, swollen lymph glands, sore throat, patchy baldness on her scalp, mild hepatitis and a kidney disorder which may have caused swelling around her eyes, feet and ankles. Because some of these symptoms are associated with other illnesses, like the flu, Sarah may not have known that her symptoms were connected with her genital sore.

In the late 1800s, the treatment for syphilis included mercury with salt or hydrochloric acid, a poisonous potion that was often ineffective.[20] People also sought remedies from herbalists, quacks or chemists who advertised their 'cures' in daily newspapers, guaranteeing relief from syphilitic disorders. Even without treatment, Sarah's symptoms would have disappeared, marking the latent stage of syphilis during which the infection remains without a person experiencing any symptoms, sometimes for decades.

Only about one-third of those infected will develop tertiary syphilis, which involves damage to the heart, blood vessels, brain, eyes and the nervous system, resulting in blindness, shooting pains, emaciation, loss of muscular coordination, incomplete paralysis, chronic dementia and, ultimately, death. A most unpleasant way to die, Elisabeth Kehoe describes how Lord Randolph Churchill, the father of Sir Winston Churchill, 'lay dying in the final stages of syphilis, his mind slowly yet inexorably slipping into madness' and how he 'groaned and screamed with pain' which was only relieved by strong doses of morphia.[21]

By the time Sarah was arrested in October 1892, she had had the disease for at least ten years and may have been in the initial stages of tertiary syphilis. As she sat through weeks of coronial inquiries and then her trial, her behaviour became more and more erratic. Although she was known for her 'fiendish' temper before she married John, the disease may have exacerbated an already fragile mentality, suggesting that Sarah was not of sound mind when she was tried for baby farming in March 1893.

The legacy of congenital syphilis

Because Leslie Makin's death certificate states that he died of syphilitic convulsions, Sarah would have known that she had syphilis by 1884, if not earlier, since baby farmers and midwives were well acquainted with the symptoms and cause of congenital syphilis. While a foetus can contract the disease as early as the ninth week in utero, this will depend on how long the mother has had syphilis.[22] If a woman has untreated early syphilis of four years or less, she is more likely to give birth to a stillborn child or a child who dies soon after birth. Transmission of the disease to the baby is highest when women are in the primary and secondary stages (70 to 100 per cent), although this risk drops off to 40 per cent in the early latent stage and 10 per cent in the late latent stage.

Between November 1883 and August 1888, Sarah had three children who died from the symptoms of congenital syphilis: syphilitic convulsions and infantile atrophy. This suggests she was in the early stages of syphilis and contracted the disease between October 1881 and February 1883 before she became pregnant with Leslie. She could also have become infected *during* her pregnancy with this baby. By the time Sarah had her last child, Cecil, in 1890, she was in the latent stage of syphilis and was less likely to give birth to a child with congenital syphilis. Cecil was the fortunate baby who survived to adulthood.

As common as the disease was in the nineteenth century, it was a terribly sad legacy since babies with congenital syphilis suffered from a range of serious medical problems. Often these symptoms did not develop for some weeks and months after birth or even as late as two years of age. Occasionally, symptoms did not manifest until puberty. But Sarah's three babies, Leslie, Linda and Harold, all had symptoms in their first year of life.

They may have been born premature and underweight, possibly with respiratory distress. They would have had a rash of raised, round, copper-coloured eruptions filled with fluid on their palms and soles, although this unpleasant rash can sometimes occur over the whole body. These skin lesions seep fluid and form a crust which causes scarring. Because they had symptoms within their first year of life, Leslie, Linda and Harold probably would have had the characteristic fissured or cracked lesions around their nose, mouth and genitals which also cause scarring as they heal.

Because of complications like gastroenteritis, babies with congenital syphilis fail to thrive and have a wizened, 'old man' look due to starvation which causes the skin to turn yellow-brown. Harold's death certificate says he died of 'infantile atrophy', which is another way of saying he suffered from marasmus, the medical term for starvation or wasting away. Sarah's babies may also have developed meningitis and an abnormally enlarged head, which would have caused the seizures or convulsions that led to the deaths of Leslie and Linda. They may have had inflamed bones and cartilage, especially in the arms and legs and ribs, which would have caused paralysis of their limbs. Other tell-tale symptoms include jaundice, an enlarged liver or spleen giving the baby a swollen abdomen, an unpleasant mucus, pus and bloodstained discharge from the nose (called snuffles), patchy hair loss on the scalp, anaemia, blindness, no eyelashes or eyebrows and abnormal fingernails. Before they died, Sarah's three babies were not only very ill but a shocking sight—bald, wizened and wasted before their time.

Leslie died in 1884, Linda in 1886 and Harold in 1888. During these years, Sarah's life would have been filled with sickly babies, all with similar, distressing symptoms, and their untimely deaths. How she and John reacted to their deaths can only be guessed at, although guilt, grief and shame is a potent mixture. Did Sarah and John harden their hearts, becoming indifferent to young children?

When Sarah contracted syphilis, John would have become infected as well, turning the family into the economic victims of the disease. John did not work from Christmas 1891, although the Makins gave no explanations to neighbours or the police about the reasons for his 'idleness'. Was he too sick to work as the disease took hold? Or did he merely exploit Sarah's skills to compensate for his disinterest in work? Either way, the family became completely reliant on Sarah as a 'ladies' nurse' and the revolving door of mothers and babies that characterised their lives from at least 1888 onwards.

PART II

❧

DIGGING UP THE BABY FARMERS' SECRETS

CHAPTER FIVE

The baby trade

Sarah was imprisoned and John died 'for the sake of getting three pounds from a "poor girl"'.[1] This paltry sum—which bought a bale of fresh hay in 1892[2]—was the money they received from a young, unmarried barmaid who believed her baby had been taken to live in the country air of Hurstville, some distance from the nefarious activities of city-dwellers and her own tainted life.

The questions that intrigued everyone at the time were, when did the Makins become baby farmers and why did they switch from being poor to taking advantage of the poor around them? Possibly, they began baby farming after the death of their third baby in November 1888 when a third lot of doctors' bills, undertaker's costs and cemetery fees had brought them to a new low. Along with the bills spread out on the table in their sparsely furnished kitchen, perhaps John scanned the columns of advertisements for work in the daily newspapers. An interesting advertisement by a scientific reader of cards and teacups may have momentarily caught his eye. John's finger stopped at a small ad which asked for a 'kind person' to adopt a young baby. A small premium is offered. John and Sarah have six children to feed and a landlord demanding rent.

With his quill and ink and a clean sheet of lined paper, John scratched the first letter to the first, unsuspecting mother who would gratefully hand over her baby to the man with a gift for stories and his unassuming wife. Maybe Sarah looked over John's shoulder as she thought about how a little baby would take her mind off her own dead babies. As John signed the letter, he used a false surname. Perhaps it was 'John Hill', one of his many aliases which would protect the family time and again from demanding landlords and curious mothers. But the risk was worth it. Unlike John's previous jobs, baby farming ensured a guaranteed stream of babies and pounds with little intrusion from the authorities.

Some evidence for when the Makins transformed into baby farmers comes from the birth and death certificates of their three dead babies, Leslie, Linda and Harold. These show that the Makins were moving frequently between late 1881 and 1888, preferring the inner city of Sydney where rents were cheap. As the Makin family increased in size each year, they also increased the pace of their nomadic lifestyle. Altogether, they lived at at least 16 different addresses between 1880 and 1891.[3] Sometimes the Makins moved to avoid paying unpaid rent, although by 1888 the frequency of their house moving had increased.

Relocations at regular intervals of a few weeks or months were characteristic of baby farmers in the nineteenth century. For the Makins, packing up was an operation of little difficulty because they had hardly any furniture, despite having six children. But each move meant they needed money to pay rent in advance for their new premises. A new batch of babies would be needed. The old batch would soon disappear.

To most people the term 'baby farming' is unknown, while to others it is a quaint term from a simpler time. During the 1800s it evoked great concern among the medical profession, politicians and social reformers.[4] But what was baby farming? One of the best kept secrets of the nineteenth century was the trade in the life and death of children. Bought and sold like cats and dogs, an illegitimate child was a commonly available 'commodity' with no oversight by government authorities in Australia until the 1890s when the *Infant Life Protection Act* was enacted in Victoria in 1890, followed by the *Children's Protection Act* in New South Wales in 1892.

For thousands of unmarried mothers, the baby trade was a necessary evil, since illegitimacy was a moral transgression condemned by the church and the law. An unmarried pregnant woman was trapped by the twin gatekeepers of financial ruin on one side and moral ruination on the other. The thin space in between was occupied by the baby farmer, holding out a helping hand. Perhaps it is no surprise that illegitimate children had a much higher mortality rate than those born within marriage.[5] Baby farmers like John and Sarah played a crucial role in contributing to this mortality rate.

Baby farming in Sydney was a lucrative trade because particular demographic factors made unwanted pregnancy a major problem for New South Wales women in the 1880s and 1890s. Marriage was an uncommon event, with Sydney and its suburbs having 'the highest rate of spinsterhood in Australia', due to the shortage of men in the city and the older age at which they married compared to women. While Sydney was a 'poor marriage market' it was not necessarily a poor sex market.[6] Unmarried men could easily obtain sex without marriage and married men could easily obtain sex on the side from young, cheap prostitutes who gave birth to some of the city's illegitimate babies.

But most illegitimate babies were born to servants. Domestic service was the most common form of employment for single women in cities and usually involved living-in, with all the implications that evokes.[7] Female servants were frequently the subject of their employers' attentions or those of the male servants in the household since female servants worked long hours and had little free time for outside amorous adventures. Unmarried domestic servants under the age of 25 gave birth to most of the annual number of registered illegitimate births which, in New South Wales, was 2000–3000. Although these births amounted to about 12 per cent of babies born between 1880 and 1899 in New South Wales, this was an underestimation because illegitimate babies were not always registered.[8] An unmarried, pregnant female servant faced dismissal and homelessness, which ensured an ongoing market for the farming of babies. Low rates of marriage, no state regulated adoption scheme and lack of effective and affordable abortion all meant that unmarried pregnant women had two options—infanticide or baby farming.

If an unmarried mother was lucky she might be able to conceal her growing belly beneath the skirts of her domestic service. If luck was still her friend, she would give birth in secret in an outside privy or stables as she struggled to swallow her cries and push out the new, insistent life. Perhaps an older servant who knew the tricks for suppressing an infant's first cry assisted by turning the healthy newborn into a blue stillborn whose death would not attract police attention. Sometimes the child would be smothered or the umbilical cord would not be tied so that it bled to death.

A lonely walk late at night with a small wrapped bundle deposited in the nearest drain or watercourse meant the child became another statistic for the Coroner and the mother remained unknown. Between 1881 and 1939, 864 dead babies were discovered in public places in Sydney, while 614 police cases of infant corpses were reported between 1885 and 1914 in Victoria.[9] Perhaps the most desperate women chose to abandon their babies in this way. Other mothers with a little money to spare hoped the baby farmer offered a better solution.

The underground trade in babies often began with a midwife who delivered an illegitimate baby in her home. She would place an advertisement in a local newspaper, seeking a 'kindly lady' to look after the infant, using a discreet address such as the newspaper office for replies. Other times a young mother would pay for her child to be nursed by her midwife for a few weeks or months before being forced to place an advertisement herself. For the women who gave up their babies to the Makins, some went to great lengths to hide the pregnancy, the baby and their identities.

The Makins danced with fate by answering advertisements from all the daily Sydney newspapers which were unwitting vehicles for the baby trade, although this trade included much older children as well:

> WANTED Lady to adopt pretty little GIRL two and a half months old, fair, large blue eyes, no premium given. Address: Mrs Greves, G.P.O., Sydney.
> ADOPTION—Will kind LADY ADOPT fine healthy BABY (boy). Address Mrs Bland, P.O., William-st.
> WANTED, Protestant Lady to adopt healthy Girl aged 7. 519 Elizabeth-st, South, Sydney.[10]

These ads appeared in the classified advertising section where all manner of items—dogs, cats, horses, second-hand clothing and old coppers—were advertised for sale. In 1892, the year they were arrested, the Makins might have answered any one of them.

The language of the ads was always in code, reflecting the expectations of the mother and the baby farmer. If a one-off payment, called a 'premium', was offered or the word 'adopt' was used this meant the child was to be sold, although some unmarried mothers hoped the occasional visit would be part of the adoption plan.

Even after legislation was passed in the colonies to regulate the activities of baby farmers, adoptions were rarely reported to the authorities, although occasionally a written agreement was signed by the mother and the baby farmer. Midwives involved in the baby trade, if not the mother herself, would have known that the premium was actually a fee for disposing of the child. The premium was usually in the range of £2 to £5, more if the unmarried mother was well-to-do. Anonymity and discretion were usually understood.

If a weekly payment was offered or the words 'no premium' were used, this indicated the mother's hope that the arrangement was temporary and she would have ongoing contact, perhaps being able to reclaim her child if her situation changed. A weekly payment also meant her child would live longer and be better looked after since weekly visits meant the baby farmer had to keep up appearances.

Most baby farmers took in more children than they could possibly afford to care for, either in time or money. Many kept a mixture of children— those they adopted outright for a fee and those they kept for a weekly payment. When the premium ran out or weekly payments dropped off, some baby farmers sold adopted children on to other baby farmers for a lower sum, pocketing the difference. This made way for another batch of babies and a new injection of money and left someone else to deal with the problem of disposal.

Others subjected their premium children to weeks of neglect and starvation. Hidden in the slums of Sydney, baby farmers effectively operated as kennels for babies to be 'put down'.

Crimes and punishment

All of those involved in the baby trade took risks, since the law punished reproductive crimes severely in terms of the sentences imposed. Infanticide was punishable by death while anyone encouraging the murder of an infant was liable to life imprisonment. Concealment of the birth of an infant found dead attracted a penalty of four years' gaol while a mother or midwife who harmed a baby during its birth could be jailed for fourteen years. Abandonment of an infant was an offence punishable by five years' gaol.[11]

Although these crimes were rarely detected and prosecuted,[12] the severe response of the criminal law to reproduction outside marriage meant that baby farming was the far safer solution. Baby farmers filled the gap between abandonment and infanticide by carrying out the killings that some unmarried mothers could not bring themselves to do.

Even though reproductive crimes were rarely prosecuted, historian Judith Allen concludes they were *the* most commonly recorded crimes committed by women in New South Wales. Between 1880 and 1899, 80 per cent of murder charges laid against women were for infanticide, while another 6 per cent were for abortions leading to fatalities. Women who killed babies constituted the largest group of people, men or women, in the late nineteenth century who committed murder in New South Wales,[13] a fact that will surprise many since most murder is committed by men today.[14]

While the crime of murder was more commonly committed by women than by men in the late 1800s, it had a specific focus:

> [although] new-born infants were less than 3 per cent of the population, their murder occurred at fifty-five times the rate of the murder of adults.[15]

The activities of baby farmers were hidden by 'the smokescreen' of high infant mortality among illegitimate children. They were also aided by a lack of regulation of those involved in birthing, including both qualified and unqualified midwives like Sarah Makin. Doctors were rather too willing to attribute baby deaths to 'separation from the natural mother rather than inadequate substitute care' and lax standards existed in relation to reporting unnatural deaths by both midwives and undertakers.[16]

In the late 1800s infanticide was not a priority for the police, who frequently failed to investigate an abandoned baby's death. Cases were only pursued when there was clear evidence of foul play. Not only was there a lack of police interest in women disposing of their children in high numbers, but infanticide was also tacitly condoned by judges and juries with convictions hard to come by.

Because a high infant mortality rate was normal in the nineteenth century, a 'certain fatalism accompanied the death of babies rather than the moralism, shock and suspicion often apparent by the late twentieth century'. The lack of specific state regulation of baby farming until the 1890s meant that it was accepted that infant deaths were 'women's business, to be managed by them as best they could'.[17] This attitude made it so much easier for baby farmers to step in and become the sole regulators of this particular type of women's business, with few questions asked. It also helps explain why the Makins were able to practise under the police radar for so many years. Until they became a little too careless.

❦

CHAPTER SIX

The Macdonaldtown discoveries
29 June–13 October 1892

On Monday 27 June 1892, John Makin took a lease on a house in Macdonaldtown for 17 shillings per week. At the time, he and his family were living at 109 George Street, Redfern. Since their rent was in arrears, their landlord had become a far too frequent visitor. The last time he called, he caught the Makins hiding and whispering while he knocked on the front door. A few days later, they outsmarted him when they moved on a dark and rainy night, leaving through a rear lane, hurriedly, secretly. But there were other reasons for the hasty move—they had left behind a backyard of graves and some mothers whose curiosity they were keen to avoid.

From 29 June to 16 August, Sarah, John and three of their daughters, Florence, Blanche, Daisy, and son Cecil (known as Tommy), lived in a two-storey house at 25 Burren Street, Macdonaldtown, one suburb away from Redfern. Their new home was in a quiet, dead-end street which runs parallel to the railway line. The name of the street comes from Burren Farm, the land granted to Nicholas Devine, who took up the post of Principal Superintendent of Convicts in 1790. This appointment put him in charge of the day to day administration of the colony's convicts. Like many new landowners, Devine named Burren Farm after his native birthplace, which was in Ireland.[1] One hundred years later the name would become synonymous with death, and the crimes of the descendants of two convicts.

Macdonaldtown is a tiny suburb squeezed between Newtown and Erskineville in the inner west of Sydney, although it is part of the Newtown precinct. This area was a thriving commercial centre which was first established by Government Gazette on 12 December 1862. By the early 1890s, King Street, Newtown had the longest shopping strip in Sydney with various types of tradesmen and shopkeepers making up 75 per cent of the suburb's working population.[2]

The day after his family moved into Burren Street, John Makin visited one of the chemist shops in King Street to buy a potent elixir after a bad night with the baby who cried too much. He also visited the local printer's shop that day. Back at their new home, Sarah and her three daughters busied themselves with unpacking and acquainting themselves with the local shops and hawkers. They may have heard the call of the 'rabbitoh' who pushed his cart, strung with rabbits, through the narrow streets and back lanes, calling out 'Rabbitoh, rabbitoh'. Two rabbits cost sixpence, a cheap meal for a family of six. Helpfully for housewives like Sarah, the rabbitoh chopped off the rabbits' heads and skinned them on the spot.

If Sarah needed a long stick to prop up the clothesline, she would have to wait until the clothes prop man called out 'props today—props today' when she could buy 'a sapling eight or ten feet long with a fork in the end … to prop the line up'. She could buy bags of fuel from the wood and coal man for the fuel stove in the kitchen and the copper which needed to be heated for washing. When the milkman called morning and afternoon, Sarah might have sent Tommy out with a halfpenny for a bottle, although there was competition between everyone on Sundays when the milko called out 'Milk for the babies and cream for the ladies and lay-ay-ty' since cream topped off the Sunday pudding.[3]

When John returned from his shopping trip to King Street on 30 June, he brought home a bottle of the mixture, made up by every local chemist, called Godfrey's Cordial, the babies' elixir that contained such a high concentration of opium it was guaranteed to quieten or kill crying babies. His visit to the printer's meant he could now advertise Sarah's skills in their new suburb using cards printed with her name:

> Mrs. Makin, qualified midwife and ladies' nurse,
> 25 Burren-street, Macdonaldtown.[4]

When John acquainted himself with his new neighbour, Mr Hill, he would have realised he and Sarah had moved up a notch on Sydney's social ladder since Burren Street was 'inhabited chiefly by working men of a good class'.[5] Most lived in single-storey cottages which comprised a front room, a bedroom, a small dining or sitting room, a lean-to for a kitchen and an outhouse, the quaint description for the backyard toilet.

The house at number 25 was a little more prosperous in appearance than the neighbouring houses, with two bedrooms upstairs, two rooms downstairs and a bathroom in the rear. The upstairs bedroom had French doors which opened onto a wooden-floored verandah enclosed with decorative iron-lace work. It had been built in December 1890 for Patrick Mulvey, a storeman in the employ of Tooheys, the local beer brewers. The Mulvey family had lived in Burren Street until 5 June but moved out on the advice of Mr Mulvey's doctor, who was treating him for a chest complaint. Although the houses in Burren Street have since been renumbered, the free-standing house still exists as a sober reminder of its infamous history.

The backyard was a modest 16 by 35 feet and backed onto the railway line. It had a shed and an outhouse at one end with a brick path running down the left-hand side of the yard to the outhouse. An open, shallow drain ran down the middle. The whole yard was enclosed by six foot high wooden fencing on top of which was another four feet of wire so that entry was only possible through the front of the house or a locked side gate.[6]

The prosperous Mr Mulvey also owned a vacant lot at 27 Burren Street and was the landlord of number 29, which was occupied by Mr and Mrs Hill, the couple who acted as his agents in letting the house at number 25 to the Makins. The Makins arrived in a hurried, clandestine fashion on the night of 29 June. They left the same way a mere six weeks and six days later.

The first discoveries

Most baby farmers were never suspected, let alone investigated, charged or convicted. For the few who were reported to the authorities, usually there was insufficient evidence for the police to lay charges. But the Makins had been particularly careless. After they left Burren Street on 16 August, Mr

Mulvey tried to let the house again with no success since applicants for the house complained about an unpleasant smell and said 'the drains appeared to be in a bad state'. To fix the problem, Mr Mulvey hired two local men to lay new drainage pipes.

On the morning of Tuesday 11 October 1892, James Mahoney and Patrick Cooney began to dig a trench from one end of the long, rectangular backyard at number 25. After some time, Mahoney came across a bundle that had been buried six inches below the ground. Thinking it was merely the remains of a cat he removed the bundle and reburied it near the trench.[7]

The next day, Cooney dug up a similar bundle which had been buried in a direct line about a metre away from the first. These two bundles are represented by the crosses marked 1A and 2A in the sketch of the Burren Street backyard that was printed in *The Evening News* of 10 November 1892. Struck by the coincidence of finding a second, Cooney inspected the bundle and found to his great surprise the decomposing remains of a baby. The two drain-layers hurried to Newtown police station about a kilometre away.

When Senior Constable James Joyce and Constable Alexander Brown arrived in a horse-drawn police van, they discovered the bodies of not one but two decomposing babies in the well-wrapped bundles. After delivering the remains to the South Sydney morgue, Constable Joyce made inquiries with Mr Mulvey and his neighbour, Mrs Elizabeth Hill, who told him about the short stay of the Makin family two months before. It is easy to imagine Mrs Hill's shock when Joyce knocked on her door in quiet Burren Street. Perhaps she repeated her tale to another neighbour, Mrs Parry:

> *I've never been so surprised in all my life when the constables stood on my doorstep and announced two dead babies had been dug up in Mr Mulvey's backyard. They wanted to know if Mr Mulvey and his wife had any children and I assured them the babies could not belong to them. Likely as not, I said, it must've been the Makins because she called herself a midwife and ladies nurse. Mind you, I only ever saw them with one baby, about three months old. But it wasn't theirs. Mrs*

Makin was nursing it for a young couple I saw two times when they
visited. They seemed a decent enough pair, neatly dressed. One time
when I asked about the baby Mr Makin told me the young couple had
taken it away. At any rate, I didn't see any other babies although they
left in a bit of a hurry in August. At this the constables became quite
excited though I couldn't tell them where the Makins had gone.

With this information, Constable Joyce had the lead he needed to
commence his investigations. The Makins had been doubly careless—not
only had they become used to the smell of decaying bodies, but they had
also used their real surname when they rented 25 Burren Street.

The day the police arrived

By mid August 1892, the Makins had returned to live in Redfern, the
suburb in which they moved from house to house as sneakily as the local
rats. It was also the suburb in which Constable Joyce discovered them just
as they began to buy more babies.

On 12 October 1892, the Makins were living at 6 Wells Street, their
fourth address in four months. It had not taken long for Constable Joyce
to track them down, most likely using tenancy records, because by four
o'clock on the afternoon of Wednesday 12 October he had arrived at Wells
Street to conduct his inquiries.[8]

The door was opened by an 18-year-old girl. When Joyce asked her
whether the Makins lived there, she said they were not in and gave her name
as Priscilla Edwards. Joyce said he would wait for the Makins to return,
taking a seat in the front room. 'Priscilla' waited with him, batting back his
many questions. Were there any infants in the house? She admitted there
were three upstairs with their mothers. Joyce then wondered if she was
related to the Makins but she replied she was only a friend. Joyce pressed
on, curious about how long she had known the family. The girl faltered.
She confessed she was fibbing and that her real name was Blanche, the
eldest daughter of the family. It would not be the only time Joyce caught
her out as she calmly practised the Makin family trait of artful lying, a skill
her parents would later rely on.

At 6.30 p.m., John Makin arrived to face the unexpected—the ominous presence of a well-built police officer in his house. With the bravado he would later become known for, he readily admitted he had lived at 25 Burren Street for about two months but denied that he and his wife were in the habit of taking in children to nurse. As Joyce pressed him for details, John agreed that during their stay at Burren Street his wife had nursed one baby for ten shillings per week, more than half their weekly rent, although it was the only child they had ever taken in since they had enough children of their own. According to his improvised story, the baby had been returned three weeks later to its parents, Mr and Mrs Wilson, who said they were going to live in Melbourne.

Constable Joyce reappeared at the Wells Street house about ten o'clock that night to interview Sarah. It must have been a tense scene since Joyce stayed until midnight, pestering the family about Sarah's whereabouts. Joyce's persistence and odd work hours provided the first hint that he was a police officer who did not rest. Already he had enough evidence to suggest the Makins moved frequently and could easily do a late night runner. When Joyce returned early the next morning, he was in for disappointment. In her interview on 13 October, Sarah Makin's answers were identical to her husband's.

At the end of his interview with Sarah, Joyce was puzzled by a number of things. Although the Makins denied being in the business of nursing babies, they had three babies in their home in Wells Street and demonstrated the peripatetic behaviour of baby farmers by moving frequently. Yet their story about only having one child in their care was confirmed by Mrs Hill, their former neighbour.

When Joyce attended the morgue later that day he examined the material in which the two dead babies had been wrapped, as well as their garments. As he was doing so, he noticed that a flannel worn by the first baby unearthed in Burren Street had been sewn with black thread. He realised the sewing was remarkably similar to the stitching he had seen on a white apron worn by Blanche Makin when he was at Wells Street.

The Makins must have felt the cold hand of the law tightening around them when Joyce returned to Wells Street a fourth time. He searched the house and the backyard and removed the white apron with the black stitching. Even by the standards of today, Joyce was an observant detective. It was his obsession with the case and its ever growing number of loose threads and bits of clothing that explains why the Makins, out of the dozens of baby farmers operating at the time, found themselves facing the law's piercing blue eyes as Joyce pried into their furtive world.

CHAPTER SEVEN

༺ঌ৩༻

To catch a baby farmer
1892

Eighteen ninety-two was a busy year for the Coroner's Court in Sydney. Apart from the usual murders and suicides, the newspapers reported the regular discoveries of dead infants who had been abandoned on the streets of Sydney Town. So frequent was infanticide that *The Evening News* carried a weekly column entitled 'How the Babies Go', which reported on the number of dead babies found in the city each week.

Previously, infant deaths had attracted little police attention. But things changed with the enactment of the *Children's Protection Act* in New South Wales on 31 March 1892 after a Parliamentary Committee Inquiry decided that legislation was needed to protect the colony's children from rapacious baby farmers. During the inquiry, sensational evidence was presented by the president of the New South Wales Society for the Prevention of Cruelty to Children. He revealed that the Society had tested the extent of baby farming in Sydney by placing a false advertisement in *The Evening News* asking for a 'kind mother to adopt child for life'.[1] The Society received 80 replies with most baby farmers requesting lump sums from £3 to £30, although one asked for £50. Seventy-five replies promised the child would never be heard of again.

When legislation was subsequently introduced into the New South Wales Parliament to ban the payment of premiums to baby farmers, the sponsor of the legislation, Mr Neild, argued that these payments were nothing more than 'an incentive for contract killing':

The plain fact is that these unfortunate, helpless creatures are taken for a sum of money in order to be put to death by the most miserable, the most cruel ... the most hellish means it is possible for human beings to conceive.[2]

Parliamentarians debated how widespread this type of murder was in New South Wales, with one member stating that it was 'a slur on the character of Australians to say ... that wholesale murder has been taking place among them'. With little understanding of the prevalence of poverty in New South Wales, some believed there was no excuse for infant deaths because, compared to Europe, '[h]ere we have bright homes, better chances of life, and a more robust life'. But parliamentarians were unable to account for the approximately 6000 deaths of children under the age of five years each year in the New South Wales colony. Others realised that New South Wales differed little from Victoria, where 7500 children under the age of five years had died the previous year, with baby farming 'greatly responsible'.[3]

Only one enlightened member of the Legislative Assembly thought that the government was the proper authority to deal with unwanted babies. Instead of legislation, he argued a properly funded foundling hospital should be established, since registration of baby farmers would not prevent people taking children for the sole purpose of making money.[4]

Although it was too late for controlling the activities of the Makins, who continued their 'contract killings' until October 1892, the aim of the *Children's Protection Act*[5] was to regulate people who took children into their care. The Act set up a compulsory registration scheme although it did not make baby farming illegal. All persons who took a child under the age of three years to adopt or nurse for a payment could only do so with a written order of a Justice of the Peace. This, in turn, required inspectors to assess houses as being suitable and the owner had to show she was of good character and had the means to maintain the children. Inspections could take place at any time while refusal of an inspection was a criminal offence.

The Act also limited how much could be paid to a baby farmer in order to stop the payment of one-off premiums. Any money paid had to be in the form of periodical instalments and could not exceed the sum of twenty shillings. Baby farmers were also required to register a child within seven days of receiving it at their local Births, Deaths and Marriages Register. They were not allowed to move house or relinquish the care of a child without notifying the District Registrar.

There were lots of sanctions under the Act. If a person failed to register a child she could be fined up to £50 with or without imprisonment for six months. It was also an offence to pay a lump sum payment to have a baby adopted or to adopt a child without written permission. If it could be proved that a baby farmer had wilfully and without reasonable excuse neglected to feed, clothe, provide lodging or medical aid to a child, she could be fined or imprisoned, making it much easier for the law to prosecute wilful neglect cases.

Unfortunately, this new registration scheme was not widely enforced or policed. Between 31 March and October 1892, only 71 houses and 74 infants had been registered. Two days after the first babies linked to the Makins were dug up in Burren Street, a newspaper reported that 'cases of child murder and heartless desertion of infants have of late been unusually frequent', which was thought to be due to the greater restrictions placed on baby farming by the Act.[6]

By 1899 only 59 breaches of the *Children's Protection Act* had resulted in charges and most of these merely resulted in baby farmers being fined.[7] All of these cases were from the inner city of Sydney where the network of midwives, dodgy doctors and baby farmers continued to trade in, and dispose of, the unmanageable problem of illegitimate births. Even registered baby farmers continued to greet death frequently, a fact that was sometimes excused in coronial inquiries on the grounds that a midwife took in weak children who other baby farmers had refused.[8]

Sometimes the inspection system introduced under the *Children's Protection Act* made interesting discoveries about the baby-farmer trail. In one case, Emily S's baby son, Roy, passed through the hands of three baby farmers with each woman paying a smaller premium than she had received for the baby boy, who was never located by the inspector seeking his whereabouts.[9] What the inspector found were unregistered adoptions, unregistered houses and six dead babies. Although five bodies were found buried in the backyard of one baby farmer's house, there was insufficient evidence to prosecute her for murder or manslaughter. She was merely fined for failing to register the adoption of Baby Roy. In another case, eight infants were found packed away in boxes in the ill-ventilated underground room of a baby farmer who was known to the police.[10]

In the year the Makins were arrested and the *Children's Protection Act* was passed, these discoveries show that mothers and baby farmers continued to practise underground. Although it was now an offence under the Act to fail to register the birth of an illegitimate baby, unmarried mothers continued to conceal their babies' existence, since registration did not bring them any benefits—only state scrutiny.[11] Baby farmers were also unlikely to advertise *their* existence by registering their homes. The business of birth and death remained hidden by women's voluminous skirts and the furtive appearances and disappearances of baby farmers.

CHAPTER EIGHT

❧❧❧

The first inquest: two babies called A and B
14 October–28 October 1892

Because of the *Children's Protection Act*, the Coroner now had to investigate the suspicious deaths of children, particularly in the circumstances where on 12 October two surprised plumbers had discovered two infants buried in a backyard. These babies, a boy and a girl, were known only as Babies A and B because no-one came forward to claim them during the inquest into their deaths, perhaps because the discoveries did not attract much public attention. While they were the gossip *du jour* of quiet Burren Street, the local newspapers gave little space to the findings, with just a small paragraph squashed between other legal reports on the back pages.

The inquest was opened by City Coroner Mr Woore two days after the babies' discovery although he did not hear most of the evidence until 26 October.[1] Unlike coronial inquiries today, a jury of twelve men was sworn in to consider the evidence and hand down a verdict as to the cause of death of each baby.

On the morning of 14 October, John, Sarah and their daughters Blanche and Florence adjusted their derrières on the hard, polished cedar benches of the public gallery in a high-ceilinged, cedar-lined courtroom in King Street, Sydney. The Coroner sat at the judge's bench directly in front of them while the twelve jurors were seated in two rows to their right. Constable Joyce took his place in the reserved seating for the police to the left of the Makins while two or three curious court reporters lounged on the benches in between Mr Woore and the jury.

After taking the oath, plumber Patrick Cooney was the first witness for the day. As he stood, cap in hand, in the witness box, he told the court about his discovery of the female baby, Baby B, on Wednesday 12 October and how his boss had dug up a similar bundle the day before that they thought was a cat.

Constable Joyce then entered the witness box to describe his arrival at Burren Street and his inspection of the two bundles. He also gave evidence about the black stitching found on a flannel worn by Baby B that was similar to the stitching on a pinafore owned by Blanche Makin. At the bench, Mr Woore scratched a note about this particular evidence with his quill pen.

With a sense of the familiar, Dr Frederick Milford stepped into the witness box as the government pathologist. A man with a great, sweeping moustache which joined his broad sideburns, he was also known for his efficient and skilful surgical performances.[2] He informed the Coroner that Baby B had been stillborn, although at a later inquest he revised this opinion, saying the child had been eight to fourteen days old when she died. Because she had been buried between three and six months earlier, the degree of decomposition of the body meant he was not able to give a cause of death. Neither could he do so in relation to Baby A, who he estimated had been buried for the same length of time. Initially, Dr Milford thought this child was about five to eight months old based on his examination of the thigh bones, an estimation he changed at a later inquest to eight to fourteen months. He stated that no trace of any poison had been found in the intestines of either baby, although Baby A had a fractured skull which could have been sustained before or after death.

Mr Patrick Mulvey and Mr and Mrs Hill were the next witnesses called to give evidence. Mr Mulvey told the court the Makins had been the only tenants at 25 Burren Street while Mrs Hill testified she had only seen one baby in their care. It was a girl in long clothes, an indication of her young age, who, to her, looked healthy and well looked after. She had twice seen a man and a woman visit the house and was later told by the Makins they were the parents of the baby. Crucially, she said she had not seen any other babies taken into the house during the Makins' stay.

As Mr Hill stood in the witness box, he gave the tantalising evidence that John Makin had borrowed a shovel then a pick during his stay in Burren Street. He also mentioned the Makins had a baby in arms the night they arrived at Burren Street in their horse-drawn van.

When Blanche Makin was called to give evidence, one can only guess at the emotions sweating the underarms of her parents as she swore 'to tell the truth, the whole truth, so help me God'. Perhaps their shoulders gradually relaxed as Blanche confidently revealed that, when her family moved to Burren Street, they did not have any babies with them, contrary to what Mr Hill had told the court. Her mother had nursed one child, about a fortnight old, which was the only child she had ever taken in. In fact, Blanche lied that her mother had not taken in any children until they went to live in Burren Street. She also denied sewing the black stitches found on the flannel of Baby B.

When Florence took the stand and gave identical evidence, the Coroner may have become suspicious that the two girls had been coached by their parents. He was disturbed by Blanche's denials, particularly those to do with the black stitching on Baby B's flannel. After obtaining unsatisfactory answers from Blanche, Mr Woore interrogated Florence about the black stitching on Blanche's pinafore:

Coroner: You see it is a peculiar stitch.
Florence: She said she sewed it in a hurry ... but she sews differ-
             ent sometimes.
Coroner: Look at that child's garment. Did you ever see that
             before?
Florence: No, sir.
Coroner: You see that the black cotton stitch is like that on the
             apron.
Florence: It is something like it, but the stitches are longer.
Coroner: Is that your sister's sewing?
Florence: I do not know.

Dissatisfied, the Coroner brought the inquest to a close for the day, no doubt aware that there was insufficient evidence to implicate anyone in the deaths of the two babies. Despite the unsatisfactory day of evidence, the morning had been much more exciting, since Sarah Makin had revealed some of her many character flaws which became more alarming and entertaining for the public and the court reporters alike as more babies were found and more inquests held. On that morning, Sarah had intercepted Mrs Hill outside the court in a 'great rage': 'I have a good mind to "ribbon" you, limb from limb. How dare you come up to give evidence against me? You don't know me; you have never spoken to me. It was your child, and you put it there. You took drugs'. She then 'raised her umbrella and attempted to strike Mrs Hill'.

When the inquest resumed two days later, it was time to hear from Sarah and John Makin themselves. Every eye was on the intimidating Mrs Makin as she stepped into the witness box, her hair covered by a wide-brimmed hat, her thin-lipped expression avoiding the eyes of Constable Joyce. As the Coroner began to question her, he gradually realised that Sarah was someone who could deny that black was black and white was white:

Coroner:	What is your occupation?
Mrs Makin:	A ladies nurse.
Coroner:	Look at that printed card. Is that your name and occupation?
Mrs Makin:	Yes, but my husband had them printed. I don't know anything about it.
Coroner:	But that is the card you had distributed.
Mrs Makin:	No, I never distributed any of those cards.

In the face of further questions, Sarah admitted her family had moved to Burren Street at night because 'we were poor, and were in arrears in the rent'. But she swore the only persons who moved on the night of 29 June were herself, her husband and four of her children. As a result of a newspaper advertisement, she had received a baby girl to wet nurse for the sum of ten shillings per week the evening after arriving in Burren Street.

Sarah said she cared for the child for three or four weeks before the parents, Mr and Mrs Wilson, returned to take the child away, although they left no forwarding address other than to say their destination was Melbourne. But Sarah was happy to be rid of it: 'It was a very cross child, and I was very glad when the parents took it away'. When pressed further about whether she was in the habit of taking in children to keep, Sarah swore that the baby girl was the 'first and only one'. Again the Coroner worried about the black stitching on Baby B's flannel but Sarah replied she could not recognise Blanche's sewing on it or her apron.

When John was called into the witness box, he gave evidence identical to that of his wife. Giving nothing away, he swore that the baby girl they received on 30 June was the only one 'ever kept by my wife or any member of my family'. Although the Coroner would not realise until later inquests, the Makins were highly practised in the art of deception, making it effort- less for Sarah and John to craft the evidence they gave. But it was the only time they gave evidence, declining to do so at the next 11 inquests and their subsequent trial.

When it was time to sum up the evidence, the Coroner informed the jury the case was 'surrounded by suspicion' because there was no doubt the bodies had been buried secretly. Besides that, the jury had little to go on. Evidence given by the Hills that John had once borrowed a shovel and pick had come with the innocent explanation that Mr Makin had wanted to plant some ferns. Apart from circumstantial evidence that a baby's flannel found on one of the dead babies had black stitching on it that matched the stitching on an apron owned by Blanche, there was no other evidence implicating the Makins in the deaths and burials of the two babies. In any case, no crime had been committed if one of the babies was stillborn.

Based on Dr Milford's evidence, the jury returned a verdict that Baby B had been stillborn. Because they were not able to say when Baby A died or how his death came about, the jury returned an open verdict.

By the end of the inquest, Constable Joyce had not heard any new infor- mation to direct his investigation. Baby B, apparently stillborn, and Baby A, a male child, could not have been the female baby the Makins had been caring for. Mrs Makin had testified that the parents had reclaimed the child while Mrs Hill confirmed she had seen a couple visiting the Makins. In this way, the Makin's story appeared to stack up.

The same day, an inquest into the death of another baby-farmed child, a two-month-old boy named Harold Bertram McLennon, also resulted in an unsatisfactory verdict.[3] Because a doctor had given evidence that Baby Harold was thin and sickly with not long to live when he was adopted by Mrs Griffin, who lived in a brothel with her lover, the jury accepted that his 'very much wasted' body was due to 'natural causes'. Both cases heard that day in the Coroner's Court illustrated how difficult it was to gather enough evidence to lay charges against those involved in the baby-farming trade.

Due to general ignorance about what caused young babies to die, together with a society used to high infant mortality rates, particularly those of illegitimate children, the Makins and Mrs Griffin were able to slip back into the dingy streets in which they lived to continue their surreptitious activities, dependent as they were on baby farming for an income. And there the Makins would have remained but for a 43-year-old senior constable from Newtown police station. What was driving Australia's unknown James Joyce?

Decomposition

Decomposition is a grisly subject but a necessary part of this tale. Without the sophistication of DNA testing and with no other means of identifying the bodies discovered in the Makins' former backyards, estimates of decomposition given by Dr Milford were used as evidence against the Makins in all subsequent inquests. A detective reinvestigating these deaths today would want to know how accurate these estimations were in 1892. If they were inaccurate, Sarah and John might well be innocent.

While forensic scientists today use the degree of decomposition of a body to determine how many days, weeks or months a person has been dead, such estimations in the 1890s were based on a doctor's experience rather than scientific studies. In the Burren Street inquest, Dr Milford had estimated that Babies A and B had been buried for three to six months.

He would have known that decomposition takes place in stages and varies according to the time of year. The rate of decomposition will also differ depending on whether a body is left in the open or has been partially or fully buried, and on a number of interrelated factors including air temperature, access by insects, cause of death, a body's size and build, the amount and type of clothing, as well as rainfall and ground water level.[4] The most important factor is air temperature, since decomposition occurs much faster when a body is exposed to the air—about twice as fast than if a body is immersed in water and about eight times faster than a buried body.[5] This means that decomposition occurs at different rates during summer compared to winter and in cold climates compared to the tropics. Aside from temperature, the other most important factor that slows decomposition is lack of, or decreased, insect activity. Burial slows decomposition by restricting the access of insects[6] since most soft tissue destruction is caused by feeding insect larvae. If a body is buried, the degree of decomposition will also depend on the amount of moisture in the soil and its acidity, as well as the depth of burial.

While the degree of decomposition of Babies A and B meant their facial features were no longer recognisable, their internal organs had not yet decomposed, since samples taken from the contents of the two babies' stomachs and intestines were analysed by the Government Analyst. The relatively slow rate of decomposition of Babies A and B was due to the formation of a substance called adipocere, also known as grave wax, which, as strange as it may sound, is actually soap. Because adipocere is resistant to bacteria,[7] its presence on a corpse decreases the rate of bacterial decomposition that causes the internal organs to liquefy, a process called putrefaction.

Depth of burial affects not only the rate of decomposition but also the rate of formation of adipocere. It is more likely to form when a body is buried in some type of wrapping or clothing as was the case with the tightly bundled bodies of Babies A and B. Such wrappings reduce the access of percolating rainwater coming into direct contact with the body, which increases the conditions for soap formation.[8]

Adipocere is a white-yellowish, greasy, waxy substance that forms on a dead body when moisture in the soil reacts with the fats on the cheeks, buttocks, chest, stomach and legs in the presence of bacterial enzymes, turning the fatty parts of the body into 'a shapeless mass in which the original structure can no longer be discerned'.[9] This means that Babies A and B had undergone a process called saponification, a chemical reaction that many people will have created in chemistry classes at school by making soap from fat. Dr Milford gave evidence that Babies A and B had been buried in clay soil which created a moist earth bath and the rapid formation of adipocere.[10]

The amount of grave wax on a body provides clues about the rate of decomposition, while forensic scientists can tell if a body has rapidly or slowly decomposed based on the consistency of the adipocere. If there has been rapid decomposition the grave wax will be hard and crumbly while slow decomposition produces grave wax that is soft and paste-like.[11] Generally, adipocere will form within a month after death, depending on the amount of moisture in the soil.

Another factor that would have affected the rate of decomposition of Babies A and B was their time of burial. In the somewhat macabre discipline of forensic science, experiments have been conducted to compare the rates of decomposition of bodies buried in summer and winter. After six months' burial, all the internal organs of a body buried in summer have turned into a thick, sticky mass compared to a body buried in winter, in which the internal organs are still discernible.[12] Because some of the internal organs of Babies A and B were still intact, this suggests they had been buried in winter when the soil temperature was at its lowest, which coincides with the Makins' residence in Burren Street. While a cause of death can be determined in cases of winter burial for up to a year, the method by which the Makins despatched their baby-farmed children eluded Dr Milford.

The rate of decomposition of buried bodies is also related to the *depth* of burial because soil temperature fluctuates with depths up to 0.3 metres (one foot). At depths of 0.6 and 1.2 metres (two and four feet), however, practically no daily fluctuations occur due the insulating effect of the soil.[13] Soil temperature is slightly higher at 0.3 and 0.6 metres compared with a depth of 1.2 metres, although soil temperature at all depths is lowest in winter.

Because bodies are hotter closer to the surface, they decompose faster due to bacterial activity. This in turn causes the production of heat in the surrounding tissues which is higher than the surrounding soil. At a depth of 1.2 metres, a body buried for a year will show a remarkable level of preservation. Similarly, a body buried at 0.6 metres for a period of six months will also show little decomposition with skin and hair on the skull and moderate amounts of adipocere on the chest and legs. By comparison, a body buried at 0.3 metres for three months will be extensively decomposed, with arms and legs in a skeletal state, no skin or hair on the skull and no internal organs.[14]

Paradoxically, a body that has been buried deeper and longer may show less decomposition that a body buried at a shallower depth for a shorter period of time. Thus, the depth of burial is crucial for linking the degree of decomposition with the time of burial. Because Babies A and B were in an adipocerous state with their internal organs intact, they were relatively well preserved. If they had been buried at a shallow depth of six inches, as estimated by the two plumbers who dug them up, they could not have been buried for very long. But if they had been buried closer to the depth at which later discoveries were found (18 inches), the babies could have been buried for up to a year.

Without knowing the precise depth of burial, the best guess is that Babies A and B were buried in the winter months of July or August when the Makins lived in Burren Street. Sydney's summer temperatures had not yet set in when they were discovered in October and the six inch covering of soil, together with their wrappings, had kept the babies from greater decomposition. As the spring temperatures started to warm the ground, the rate of decomposition would have gradually increased. This created the unpleasant smell that had hung around the backyard of 25 Burren Street when Mr Mulvey tried to rent his house to unimpressed prospective tenants.

❦

CHAPTER NINE

Constable James Joyce: Joycean fictions and the art of deceit
6 January 1849–14 May 1912

The man who pursued John Makin into an early grave and was almost single-handedly responsible for uncovering the stench of the baby-farming trade in Sydney was born on 6 January 1849 in Surry Hills, Sydney to John and Jane Joyce.[1] He appeared to lead a conventional married life with several children and a successful police career. But Joyce became so obsessed with the Makin case that he may have influenced witnesses to give particular testimony. Was Joyce the type of man to massage the evidence?

Joyce joined the Sydney Metropolitan Police Force as a probationary constable on 18 February 1879 at the age of 30 after some time spent as a stonemason, his father's occupation. Very little is known about Joyce before he joined, although he was living in a small town near Armidale, New South Wales when he married. He returned to Surry Hills, his place of birth, sometime in 1877.[2] With receding dark hair, light blue eyes and a handlebar moustache, he was thickset and five feet ten inches tall, just the right height and build required for catching the thieves and conmen of the inner city and frightening unsuspecting baby farmers when he knocked at their door.

After three months on probation, he became an ordinary constable. He was promoted to first class constable on 1 August 1881 and then senior constable on 1 June 1885. On 1 January 1902 he was promoted to sergeant. All up, he was a police officer for 30 years before his retirement on 18 February 1909 at the age of 60, when he was discharged on a police pension. Three years later he was dead.

The Newtown police force was once described as a 'first-class set of men, obliging, full of zeal, and actuated by the one desire to do their duty'.[3] Although this comment was written in 1912, the year that Joyce died, it is a fitting epitaph to the obsessive man who brought the Makins to heel.

At the age of 43 and the pinnacle of his career, James Joyce stumbled upon his most famous case the day he drove to Burren Street to inspect the drain-diggers' discoveries. However, his name often appeared in the newspapers in relation to various chases and arrests. In one article headed—

SENSATIONAL CASE OF

SHOOTING

A WOMAN SHOT AT PETERSHAM

AN EXCITING CHASE

POLICE USE THE REVOLVER

THE WOMAN'S HUSBAND ARRESTED

—Joyce was lauded for his bravery when he captured James Maslin who, after shooting his wife three times in an upstairs apartment in Petersham, escaped with a crowd chasing him for close to a mile. But he 'was brought to bay with a revolver fired' by Joyce when Joyce cornered Maslin, still armed, in a cow paddock in Annandale. In a few seconds, however, Joyce turned from threatening Maslin's life to protecting it when Maslin 'was rushed by the crowd' and both were almost overwhelmed in the onslaught.[4]

Family secrets

Like the Makins, Joyce had secrets. Rather a lot, as it turned out. A chance glance at one of the many family history trees of the descendants of James Joyce led to the discovery of his secret family life.[5]

On 31 December 1869, James Joyce, a 20-year-old labourer, married a very young Miss Margaret Connor, who was aged either 13 or 14 years. They were married in the house of Mrs Mary Connor in Bendemeer, a town about halfway between Armidale and Tamworth in northern New South Wales. Mrs Connor gave her permission for the marriage to take place, although the marriage certificate incorrectly stated that

Margaret was 16. Pregnancy is the likely reason for the marriage of a 13- or 14-year-old girl to a 20-year-old man, although no birth certificate could be found for a child born to James and Margaret in 1870.

It appears that James and Margaret's first child, Elizabeth, was born in 1872 in Grafton, New South Wales while a son, James, was born in Tenterfield in 1873. Another son was apparently born before 1880 but no record of his birth could be found. From 1880 to 1899 Margaret gave birth to eight more children when she and James moved to Sydney; all except one were born in Newtown: Thomas (b.1880); Mary (b.1883, d.1884); William (b.1886, d.1886); Milbra (b.1887); Walter James (b.1893); Harry Herbert (b.1894); Rita Doris (b.1897) and Ella Agnes (b.1899). As the informant for all these births, Joyce had a poor memory, variously reporting his wife's age as 37 in 1893, 40 in 1894 and 42 in both 1897 and 1899.

Newspaper reports show that Joyce served at Newtown police station from at least 1881, when it was reported he was assaulted by Thomas Donohue in the execution of his duty.[6] Local census directories reveal there was a James Joyce living in Newtown from 1882 to 1907, while the birth records of his children state they were born to James Joyce, police constable, and Margaret Connor.

However, other family history trees revealed that, at the age of 43 years, James Joyce married Miss Agnes Bath on 30 September 1892 at the Wesley Parsonage, 81 Pitt Street, Redfern. At the time, Agnes was 35, a domestic servant born on 21 April 1857 in Walcha, New England, the daughter of Priscilla and William Bath, a labourer. Walcha is 50 kilometres from Bendemeer, the birthplace of Margaret Connor, Joyce's first wife. Strangely, Agnes' and Joyce's marriage certificate states that the usual place of residence for both bride and groom was New England. It stated that James Joyce was a labourer even though he was serving as a constable at Newtown police station at the time of this marriage, about to begin the biggest investigation of his career. Was he also involved in a shady, cover-up job of his own?

It is possible that the James Joyce who married Agnes Bath was a different person to the man who had married Margaret Connor. However, before their marriage Agnes and James had produced three children between 1877 and 1882: Jane Evangeline (b.1877) and Annie Dolly (b.1879) were born in Surry Hills while Mary Minnie was born in O'Connell Street, Newtown in 1882, close to Newtown police station. Jane's birth certificate states her mother was Agnes Beath, aged 21 and born in Bendemeer, while her father, James Joyce, was a 28-year-old labourer, the same age as Constable Joyce. Annie's birth certificate states that her mother was Agnes Barth, aged 24 and born in Walcha, and her father was James Joyce, a 30-year-old stonemason. Mary's birth certificate reveals her father was James Joyce, a 32-year-old police constable and her mother was Agnes Connor, aged 29 and born in New England.

The certificates of these three children also state that Agnes and James were married, although no marriage certificate could be found for Joyce and Agnes Bath until 1892. Since Joyce was the informant for each of his children's birth certificates, it appears he was covering up his illicit liaison with Agnes Bath by pretending they were married and by changing her name to Connor on Mary's birth certificate.

While two men by the name of James Joyce could have been living in Newtown at the same time, the household census taken every year in Newtown reveals only one, a constable, who was living in Newtown between 1882 and 1899. James Joyce lived in a number of streets in Newtown until he finally settled at 29 Australia Street in 1892, the year he married Agnes.[7] It does not appear that Agnes Bath and Margaret Connor were the same person since birth certificates exist for each of these women. It is also doubtful that one woman could have given birth to a child called Mary Joyce on 6 December 1882 and, seven months later, to another child called Mary Joyce on 2 July 1883. Even after Agnes' marriage to James Joyce in 1892, four of his children with a mother called Margaret Connor continued to be born between 1893 and 1899.

Twelve days after Agnes and Joyce married, Agnes' new husband would become embroiled in the most infamous case of his career, although something more surprising was in store for the new Mrs Joyce. When Joyce married Agnes in September 1892, he stated he was a widower. But Margaret Connor was very much alive and well. So alive and well that Margaret Joyce bore a son, Walter James, eight and a half months after James and Agnes married. The birth certificate for Walter, born on 19 May 1893, states that his father, Senior Constable James Joyce, aged 44 years, was married to Margaret Connor and gave the more or less correct date of their marriage (29 December 1869). At the time, he and Margaret were living in Fitzroy House, 29 Australia Street, the same street as the Newtown police station. The most curious evidence linking James Joyce with *both* Margaret Connor and Agnes Bath comes from the birth certificate of Joyce's son Harry, who was born in 1894. While his birth certificate states that Margaret Connor was his mother, online records of his birth state that Agnes Bath was his mother.

It seemed it would be impossible to resolve this mystery until a search of the 'in memoriam' notices of Joyce's demise at the age of 63 on 14 May 1912 revealed more intriguing information. When Joyce died suddenly in his home in Livingstone Road, Marrickville, he appears to have left a trail of children who grieved for many years after his death. In 1912, there was, however, only one death notice:

> JOYCE—May 14, at his residence, Brooklyn, Livingstone-road, Marrickville, James, beloved husband of Agnes Joyce, aged 63 years.[8]

Although there was no mention of his surviving children that year, in the years that followed many 'in memoriam' notices were published. One year after his death, on 14 May 1913, five such notices appeared in *The Sydney Morning Herald* including:

> JOYCE—In loving memory of our dear father, James Joyce, who departed this life on the 14th May 1912. Inserted by his loving daughter and son-in-law, Dolly and Louis O'Neill.
>
> JOYCE—In sad but loving memory of our dear father, James Joyce, who departed this life 14th May 1912. Inserted by his loving daughter and son-in-law, Milbra and Ted Nickless. Fondly remembered.
>
> JOYCE— In sad and loving memory of my dear father, who departed this life May 14, 1912, aged 63. Inserted by his loving daughter and son-in-law, Jennie and Ernie.

JOYCE—A tribute of love to the memory of my dear father, who departed this life on May 14, 1912. Inserted by his loving daughter and son-in-law, Tom and Minnie.

A glance at these notices reveals a surprise—while Dolly, Minnie and Jennie were the daughters of Agnes, Jennie being the nickname of Jane Evangeline, Milbra was the daughter of Margaret.

In 1914, only one in memoriam notice appeared, from Milbra and her husband Ted,[9] while in 1915 five more notices appeared,[10] as if the rest of the family had been stung into action by Milbra's lonely notice from the year before. They included ones from 'his loving wife, Agnes, and daughters, Rita and Ella', 'his loving son and daughter, Harry and Minnie', 'his loving son, Walter', 'his loving daughter and son-in-law, Milbra and Ted Nickless' and 'his loving daughter and son-in-law, Jennie and Ernie'.

These notices reveal that Rita and Ella, whose mother was Margaret, were living with Agnes and considered Agnes to be their mother while both Harry (the son of Margaret) and Minnie (the daughter of Agnes) referred to themselves as the son and daughter of James Joyce. For the first time, there was also a notice from Walter, Margaret's son who was born eight and a half months after Joyce's marriage to Agnes.

In 1917, the final in memoriam notices appeared from 'his loving sons, Walter and Harry (on active service)', 'his loving daughter and son-in-law, Milbra and Ted Nickless, and children' and 'his loving daughters and son-in-law, Rita, Minnie and Ted'.[11] All of these notices suggest that some of the sons and daughters of James Joyce saw themselves as one family, with Rita, Harry and Walter being the children of Margaret while Minnie was the child of Agnes. With no evidence that Joyce had divorced Margaret before he married Agnes in 1892 and with children born to Margaret after Joyce married Agnes, Constable James Joyce, a Roman Catholic, was a bigamist with two wives and nine children living with him, a somewhat expensive enterprise on a constable's salary.

All of this information does not even begin to tell the more intriguing story of when the two wives found out about each other, their reactions when they did and how they apparently tolerated living in the same house with the same husband, since Margaret's last three children were born in the Australia Street house in Newtown in which Agnes was living. It is possible that Margaret died after the birth of her last child and Agnes agreed to bring up her youngest children, Walter, Harry, Rita and Ella. But no death certificate could be found for Margaret Joyce. Perhaps Constable Joyce had his own missing person's story to tell.

Through the moralistic eyes of the 1890s it would have been necessary for Agnes and Joyce to pretend they had been married for longer than they were and for Margaret's children to refer to Agnes as their mother. When Margaret's children Milbra and Walter died in 1918 and 1919 from the influenza pandemic that swept the world, their death certificates stated that their mother's name was Agnes Bath, suggesting that Margaret was also dead by this time. In 1920, the year that Harry married, Agnes took the extraordinary step of applying to have his birth certificate amended to delete 'Margaret Connor' as his mother and insert the name 'Agnes Bath'.

Agnes lived a long life with her and her husband's secrets, dying at the age of 95 years on 21 June 1952 and outliving most of her and Joyce's children.

CHAPTER TEN

More digging and the strange behaviour of the Makins
2–3 November 1892

When Constable Joyce investigated the Makins in 1892 he was newly married to Agnes Bath. By this time he had several children of his own, although he had lost a daughter in 1884 and a son in 1886 when the babies were very young. Perhaps it was these losses that drove Australia's unknown James Joyce, his own grief remembered as he unwrapped the bundles containing the first two babies found in Burren Street. But with open verdicts pronounced by the jury in the inquest into the deaths of Babies A and B, it was not possible to lay any charges against the Makins. Spurred on, Constables Joyce and Brown continued to work 'assiduously in the matter',[1] an understated way of saying the two men were obsessed with the case.

Joyce was disturbed by the evidence given by the Makins at the inquest. He probably recognised a pair of practised liars in Sarah and John Makin and heard the hollow sound of coaching in the evidence of Blanche and Florence. The presence of three babies in 6 Wells Street told him that the Makins were 'professional' baby farmers. So when the young, unmarried couple who called themselves Mr and Mrs Wilson turned up at Newtown police station, this was the break that Joyce needed. Rather than being in Melbourne with their baby as the Makins had testified, they were living and working nearby but without their daughter.

On 4 November 1892, *The Sydney Morning Herald* reported that the police had received some information which justified their return to

Burren Street. The information almost certainly came from Mr and Mrs Wilson who had read newspaper reports about the discovery of the two babies in Burren Street. In fact, one newspaper stated that the police had acquired a 'mass of information' from the public and tantalised readers with the teaser that there were some details that 'it would be manifestly improper to mention at this stage'.[2]

Presented with key pieces in the Makin puzzle from Mr and Mrs Wilson, Joyce sought permission from Mr Mulvey to re-examine the backyard of 25 Burren Street. He was also keeping his eye on the Makins, because he knew that, early on the morning of Monday 7 November 1892, the Makins moved from Wells Street to Chippen Street, Chippendale.[3]

The first dig at 25 Burren Street

On the afternoon of Wednesday 2 November 1892, when Constables Joyce and Brown arrived with shovels to begin their methodical dig of the Burren Street backyard, Mr and Mrs Mulvey, who had returned to live in the house in August, probably looked on nervously, praying for the best and dreading the worst. Starting at the rear of the garden, the two constables dug adjacent to the open drain at a depth of about 18 inches. At 5.20 p.m. they unearthed a bundle—a female baby, aged about fourteen months, wrapped in a piece of white flannel with red and blue stripes and dressed in a pinned napkin.[4]

The dig continued the next day, this time with a third constable, Thomas Conran. At 9.30 a.m. a male child, about six months old, was discovered three feet away from the baby found the previous day. He was dressed in a coloured shirt and wrapped in a napkin and a piece of white flannel stained with drops of blood. An hour later, a third baby, a boy about three months old, was found wrapped in white calico. When later unwrapped he was dressed in a white napkin which was embroidered with the letter 'F' in one corner.

Then at 11.30 a.m. a baby girl, about two months old, was found dressed in a fancy white flannel dress which was embroidered and scalloped. She was also wearing a striped pinafore and striped petticoat. Another baby girl was found at 2.45 p.m. in a grave closest to the outhouse, dressed in a flannel wrapper twisted tightly around her body and a piece of thick woollen shawl. When this baby was retrieved from the earth, the five shocking discoveries made a total of seven babies which had been found in the backyard of Burren Street, including Babies A and B.

The five most recently discovered babies had been buried in what had been a poultry enclosure in two straight lines about the same distance apart and at a depth of about two feet, indicating a very methodical approach by the grave-digger.

For the police, it was hot, sweaty and arduous work, made all the more difficult by the 'dreadful odour' when each grave was opened. They had uncovered more than enough evidence to make trouble for the Makins. Although the papers around Australia reported the horror of the 'Shocking Revelations' as 'Wholesale Infanticide in Sydney',[5] what they and the police did not realise was that these discoveries represented a snap-shot of what was happening to hundreds of babies in the Australian colonies.

While the digging had been taking place, a crowd of people gathered on the vacant lot next door (number 27). Like so many flies, they were drawn by the pungent smell of decaying bodies and the macabre spectacle unfolding in front of them. Nothing quite like it had happened in the colony before. By the time the last body was found, close to 100 people were jostling on the other side of the six foot fence, trying to remove the palings in order to get a better look, the people nearest the fence pushed and squashed by those behind.

There are many mysteries to this story and the questions are still tantalising today—if the Makins were responsible, how did the seven babies arrive in the Burren Street house with the neighbours none the wiser? Why had no-one heard the crying of seven babies in a street where the houses were so close together? Or heard the sounds of seven baby graves being dug?

With local reporters waiting outside, the police loaded the bodies, interred in small boxes, into a police van which took them to South Sydney morgue. The reporters had probably interviewed the locals and found out that the Makins had recently lived in Burren Street for nearly seven weeks. Had they buried seven babies in those short six weeks and six days? The reporters wanted information and, although Joyce gave a small press conference, it seemed he had other things on his mind. He told them he did not believe the Makins had been baby farmers for long before they arrived in Burren Street. But 'to make assurance sure', he and his men would search all the houses the Makins had lived in for the past 18 months. He also announced that when he first visited the Makins in 6 Wells Street, Redfern, he made 'a sensational discovery'—he had found a hole, freshly dug, in their backyard from which a most offensive odour came.

While Joyce was now a local hero, more importantly he had enough evidence for an arrest. But he needed more to ensure the Makins would be convicted. So he set about finding it.

The arrests

Constable Brown arrested Sarah Makin, aged 46, in George Street West at 3 p.m. on 3 November. The time of the arrest indicates that Brown was travelling in the horse-drawn police van with the four freshly dug bodies as he made his way to the morgue. Sarah would literally have received the shock that would change her life when Brown told her what he was transporting in the police van. It appears it was a mere coincidence that he had noticed her in nearby Parramatta Road not far from the Makins' new residence in Chippen Street, Chippendale where they had moved rather quickly after Joyce had interviewed them in Wells Street three weeks earlier.

Two hours after Sarah was conveyed to Newtown police station, Joyce and Brown arrested John, aged 50, in Chippen Street along with his two daughters, 17-year-old Florence and 18-year-old Blanche.[6] The only other Makin child who was living at home, Tommy, aged two, was left with a neighbour after his father was arrested.

When the rest of the Makins arrived at Newtown police station, John and Sarah were charged on suspicion of having caused the death of an infant, one of the bodies that had been found that day. Blanche and Florence were also charged. The shock of this produced 'a pitiful [scene] when the children found themselves and their father and mother taken into custody on such a suspicion, and the girls wept bitterly when placed in the cells'. But why were charges laid in relation to only one of the dead babies? Joyce had re-examined the Burren Street backyard because Horace

Bothamley, known as Mr Wilson, had contacted the police after reading in the newspaper that he and Minnie were said to have reclaimed their child from the Makins and 'to prove what the family asserted was untrue' by telling the police his child had died in the Makins' house at Burren Street.

Had their baby received the same funeral rites as the other buried babies—a hastily dug grave late at night in the Burren Street backyard?

The police interview

Today the old Newtown police station still stands in its Victorian splendour in Australia Street. It was built some time between 1884 and 1887 although the exact date is unknown. It may have been built at the same time as the Newtown Court House which was designed by James Barnett, the Colonial Architect, and completed in 1885.[7]

It was in this imposing building that the Makin daughters were interviewed, first on their own then in the presence of their parents. The scene must have been tense. Although John and Sarah were practised liars with numerous aliases and stories for unsuspecting mothers, this was not the case for their daughters. While they were accomplices, they were young with a healthy fear of the law, since the first thing they asked was whether they would be sent to gaol. Joyce replied, 'That depends upon whether you tell the truth or not'.[8]

At first Blanche denied all knowledge of her parents' baby-farming activities and the whereabouts of the child of Mr and Mrs Wilson:

> I don't know where they live. One afternoon, when I and my sister went out, the child was asleep, and when we returned the child was gone. I asked my mother what had become of it, and my mother said the parents had called and taken it away.

Constable Joyce then escorted John and Sarah Makin into the room. They would have been watchful, glancing from Blanche to Florence, praying their daughters had told as little as had been agreed.

Joyce repeated what Blanche had just told him and the information he had obtained from Horace Bothamley. He asked Florence whether her sister's story was correct. Florence agreed that it was. Then John Makin spoke up:

> There were no children that came to the house in my time. If any
> person says they gave me £2 for the purpose of burying the child
> and registering the death, they tell a falsehood.

Blanche sat across a table from her silent but vigilant parents, their eyes warning her. She had already been told she would be sent to gaol if she didn't 'tell the truth'. Joyce wanted to know if her mother had other babies in her care during their time in Burren Street. She was trapped. She looked at her parents. But their eyes were steadfast. She stared at Joyce as he repeated the question. She wanted to save her parents but she also wanted to save herself. So she did a bit of both. She confessed there had been three babies in the house at Burren Street and when *they* disappeared, her mother and father had told her the babies had been collected by their parents.

When asked whether this was true, Florence followed Blanche's lead and agreed. It was enough to satisfy Joyce even though it was a lie. Both girls knew the secrets that had accompanied them to Burren Street on a dark and wet night in June.

Joyce then wanted to know why Blanche had lied on oath at the inquest the previous week when she had said there had only been one baby that she knew of at Burren Street. Sarah and John probably sweated in their sombre dark clothes, willing Blanche to keep her mouth shut. Blanche was caught out, having just revealed that she had committed perjury. She needed to save herself so she confessed that her parents had 'told us to say we knew nothing about the infants found in the yard at Burren-street'.

At the end of the interview, Joyce took the Makins into the charge room. John and Sarah were charged on suspicion of causing the death of the illegitimate child of Minnie Davies and Horace Bothamley. Much to the disgust of Blanche, who had been told she would not go to gaol if she told the truth, she and her sister were also charged 'on suspicion with being concerned in the death of the said child'.

The next morning they were taken to Newtown Police Court where they were remanded in custody for the weekend. They were to appear in the City Coroner's Court on the Monday, the first day of the next set of inquests.

Peering into the Makins' souls

John Makin's prison card, prison number 5567, states that he was a butcher and labourer who was born in Camden in 1842, which may have been a lie to disguise his origins and protect his family. On his entry into the remand section of Darlinghurst Gaol on Thursday, 3 November, he weighed 160 pounds (just over eleven stone) and was five feet, six inches tall. With brown hair and a bald patch, he had a round scar on his left elbow bone and on the bridge of his nose.

Sarah Makin, prison number 5568, also lied about her age that Thursday, with her prison card stating that she had been born in Sydney in 1850, instead of her real birth date of 1845. She was five feet, four inches tall with brown hair and brown eyes. Her weight was not recorded. She could read and write but had no prior convictions and no special marks or features.

These facts and figures, however, do not reveal much about who Sarah and John were. Hungry for gossip, reporters from various newspapers interviewed ex-neighbours of the Makins at the many houses in which they had lived, all of which allows us to fill in the brief sketches from their prison cards.[9]

Even though John had told various neighbours he was a labourer who had not worked for the past six months, he was 'fond of boasting that he was a person possessed of private means', something that would have distinguished him from his working-class neighbours. While he may not have been believed, he received £4 per month under his mother's will. In today's money, this is approximately £344 or $512.

When Ellen (or Eleanor) Makin died on 2 March 1890, this daughter of convict parents who had begun her life in the colony at the Female Orphan School in Parramatta left an estate worth £2888. Today it would have been worth approximately £248,656 (or $375,519),[10] indicating she was comfortably middle class. Her will, made the day before she died, shows that she placed all her trust in her youngest son, George, who was the executor and one of two trustees of her estate. When she died, she was a widow who owned various properties in and around Wollongong, including 16.5 acres of land at Mt Keira, three shops and dwellings, a vacant allotment in Corrimal Street and a paddock in Market Street. Her will left her properties to be sold with the proceeds to be divided equally among her remaining children. However, John, the black sheep of the family, and one of his sisters, Emily, were the only ones to receive their inheritance by way of a monthly payment.[11] Perhaps John's bankruptcy and unstable work history meant his mother felt the need to control his spending from the grave.

In spite of John's income and their baby-farming activities, 'the family always seemed to be miserably poor'. What they did with the money from baby farming is something that puzzled reporters. According to some local knowledge it appeared that John did not drink. Sarah was described as 'a sober woman' while her 'daughters also bore the reputation of being well conducted, and dressed according to their station in life'. The only time John was 'observed under the influence of drink' was on the first day of the Burren Street inquests.

On the other hand, John 'was by no means an industrious man' and appeared not to have had any permanent job for a few years. While he had had regular work as a drayman for Mr Shortland three years earlier, 'in spite of this the roving propensity of the family was not to be checked' even as far back as 1888 or 1889 when they had remained in a house at 113 Bullanaming Street, Redfern for a mere five or six weeks and kept very much to themselves.

John was last employed as a drayman by Mr Bedford of Great Buckingham Street, Redfern shortly before Christmas, 1891. Mr Bedford, a livery stable proprietor and mail contractor, said he first knew John eleven years earlier when he was working as a drayman for a brewer and supplied Mr Bedford with stout. Bedford's recollections match the fact that John worked for Mr Stuart, delivering water and alcoholic drinks to hotels and shops during 1882. Although Bedford had employed Makin after John went to him seeking employment, Bedford said 'the man never appeared to have much heart in his work, and left suddenly in about six weeks'.

Former neighbours in Levey Street, Chippendale reported that the Makins 'kept very much to themselves' although John was often seen 'idling about in front of the house' while the family lived there for about two months in late 1891. Mysteriously, other neighbours in Levey Street said the Makins were never seen 'in front of the house in daylight' and 'when any of the family went out they usually went by means of the lane at the back', thus avoiding Levey Street. In a time when front doors were left open during the day, observant neighbours noticed that the Makins only opened theirs at night.

John was heard to say in the nearby hotel that 'he had a fortune coming to him from Wollongong, but that his sister, who was the executrix of the estate, would not give him the money until some person who had bequeathed him the fortune had been dead a certain time'. He also told fellow drinkers he was a lorry driver but had left his employment owing to a strike and 'did not know whether he would get any [work] again'.

John was the only one who mixed with the locals since neighbours said 'they only saw Mrs. Makin once or twice, and some had never seen her at all'. Several neighbours remembered the one time she was seen one evening after dark when Sarah and another woman had a 'particularly lively' dispute, with both women fighting 'like pugilists'.

Although the family attempted to lead a secluded and secret life, they would have attracted less attention had they tried to act normally, since they were considered to be 'peculiar'. It seems that neighbours kept a look-out for their mysterious comings and goings because it was known that 'Mrs. Makin was in the habit of leaving the premises by the back entrance every evening at about 8 o'clock, and not returning for some time'. Whatever Sarah was up to, either collecting babies or supplementing the family's income with casual prostitution, one neighbour said 'she had occasion to speak to Mrs. Makin one day, when she struck her as being "quite the lady"'. While none of the neighbours were suspicious about the Makins' activities, the family 'left in a mysterious manner one evening' with no forwarding address.

The police found it difficult to discover any information about the Makins while they had lived at 11 Alderson Street, Redfern 'due to the wandering habits of the people' in the locality. Eventually a Mrs Williams told Constable Joyce that the Makins had not been popular during their short stay from early December 1891 to late January 1892, having quarrelled with one family in the street. When Mrs Williams became involved in the quarrel, she was burned on the arm by a hot poker wielded by Mrs Makin. As Mrs Hill had also found outside a courtroom during the first Burren Street inquest, Sarah, like her father before her, was a person not to be trifled with.

Former neighbours of the Makins in St Peters described the Makin girls as rude, with more neighbourly discord when they lived on Cook's River Road in August 1891. During this time John was employed as a driver for Mr Whitehead, a parcel delivery agent, while a sign in their front window advertised Sarah as a ladies' nurse. There was quite a bit of tittle-tattle about Sarah, who was known to have been married to a seafaring man. Some neighbours believed she had had no less than 16 children while Sarah herself told other neighbours she had 13 children although one or two had died.

The Makins' eldest son, William, lived with them for a time in Cook's River Road but due to 'some disturbance in the house' he left home for good to live with John's family in Wollongong. Neighbours also revealed the Makins moved out of St Peters in a hurry with no notice to the landlord and their rent in arrears, something that was to become a habit of theirs. Their next door neighbour, in particular, reported 'many disputes with Mrs Makin, owing ... to the rude conduct of the children' and 'no-one was sorry when they left'.

When the family moved to Wells Street, Redfern, the house in which Constable Joyce discovered them, they found themselves in 'a much superior locality' in 'a cheerful thoroughfare, occupied by the superior class of working people'. Apparently aware of this move up the social ladder, John 'thought it necessary to apologise to his neighbours for the small amount of furniture he brought into the house'. Although he reassured them that more furniture would follow, 'that promise was never fulfilled'.

During their short stay in Wells Street, Mrs Makin 'was rarely seen' but John was 'always hanging about, and on occasions evinced quite a friendly disposition'. The neighbours in Wells Street frequently heard the sound of crying babies coming from the Makin house. While in Wells Street, one day John knocked on the door of a young lady and announced 'I have something to show you'. 'Have you?' the young woman replied, taken aback by Makin's jocular and 'unceremonious manner' but not wishing to be unneighbourly. Encouraged, John returned to his house then produced three babies, two of whom, he informed his surprised young neighbour, were twins.

These were the three infants who had just been born in 6 Wells Street when Constable Joyce first discovered the Makins. This story shows that the Makins were also running a lying-in house for women who were desperate enough to give birth in an establishment with little furniture and few material comforts. It also suggests they may have acquired babies in ways other than by answering ads in the daily newspapers.

It is hard to say what John's 'neighbourly' behaviour was about. No doubt he needed social contact, since he had once told Mr Hill of Burren Street that, 'Things are dull out here; I am sorry I came'. His extroverted personality included a tendency to brag, since he later introduced himself to another female neighbour to whom he boasted 'as references prominent persons in the town of Wollongong'. But when the woman replied she also knew these people, John 'dropped the subject and left hastily'. Still, the neighbours in Wells Street were generous enough to say that 'whatever are the Makins' faults he always appeared to be a singularly affectionate father, more especially to his little boy, 2 years of age'.

What did the Makins do with their regular income from baby farming and John's inheritance? As we will see in the next chapter, opium in the form of various elixirs was easily available and widely used by Australians. For John and Sarah, doses of opium would have been necessary to dull the pain of syphilis. An addiction to opium would also explain the Makins' constant need for money, John's irregular work habits, Sarah's volatile behaviour and John's mother's careful control of his inheritance.[12]

❧

CHAPTER ELEVEN

The next five inquests: the Makins' lives stripped bare
7–8 November 1892

Throughout the many inquests, the Makins' behaviour deteriorated. As the veil was lifted on their nefarious lives, they sobbed, collapsed, wailed, fainted, fought, threatened, shrieked and, in desperation, one of them undertook a little spying.

They employed a competent lawyer, Mr Williamson, who represented them at the next five inquests which investigated the deaths of the last five babies unearthed by the police in Burren Street. Williamson was clever and crafty, an ideal match for the Makins. But by the end of the final Burren Street inquest, the Coroner had had enough of him, refusing to let him speak. By this time, the greed and heartlessness of John and Sarah may have been all too hard to bear as the short lives of the five babies were exposed in the courtroom.

The inquests began on Monday 7 November 1892 in the Coroner's Court.[1] The infants were known as Babies 1, 2, 3, 4 and 5. The *Sydney Morning Herald* reported the opening of the inquest in its morning edition and a large number of spectators crowded into the court at 10 a.m. hoping to see the mysterious Makin family.[2]

The paper also revealed '[t]he public interest in the case shows no signs of abating' with large numbers of 'curiosity-seekers' visiting Burren Street on the weekend. This would have caused quite a stir in the narrow, dead-end street and rattled the unsuspecting Mulveys, with people crowding around their front garden, knocking on the door or trying to climb into their backyard to see for themselves the empty graves of the dead infants.

Also published the previous Saturday were the ages and sex of each child, along with a description of the clothing in which they had been buried. This information had been released by the police to encourage 'any person who can throw the slightest light on the subject' to come forward. The clothing worn by each baby was central to their identification, as well as connecting the Makins to the children, because decomposition meant the babies were unrecognisable.

After the jury was sworn in, the inquest visited the South Sydney morgue to view the bodies, whereupon 'the female prisoners became greatly affected'. The Coroner, the jurymen and the Makins then adjourned to the Coroner's Court in Chancery Square.

The first inquest concerned the death of Baby 1, who was 12–15 months old when she died, according to Dr Milford's examination of the length of her thigh bones. She had been buried for three to six months between May and August that year.

After Mr Mulvey took the oath, he told the court that when he returned to live in his house in August, no-one could have used his backyard without his knowledge because of its high fencing, the presence of two savage dogs and a locked gate which opened into the Hills' backyard. He described how he had had to deal with a family who did not pay their rent by visiting the house on 2 or 3 August to speak to John Makin. When the rent remained unpaid he sent a bailiff with a distress warrant for rent. By this time, the Makins had disappeared.

When Mr Hill gave evidence at the inquest after lunch, he revealed that he saw the Makins with a baby in arms on the night they arrived. This evidence contradicted John's and Sarah's police statements that they had acquired a baby for nursing the day *after* their arrival in Burren Street.

The question in everyone's minds was, did the Makins have any other babies with them when they moved to Burren Street? The newspapers reported that when the Makins moved there they had enough money to pay four weeks' rent in advance (£3 8s). Yet Sarah had told the previous inquest that the family left George Street because they were poor and could not pay the rent. Did they earn the rent for Burren Street by adopting more babies before they left George Street?

Mr Hill said that a few days after the Makins' arrival, John had asked to borrow a piece of timber from which he could make a signboard advertising Mrs Makin as a 'Ladies Nurse and Qualified Midwife'. Having no timber, Mr Hill offered John a piece of tin. A day later, John showed Mr Hill the sign he had painted on the tin and remarked, 'There's a good thing to be made out of these children'. He also revealed that Sarah's mother was a nurse who knew a lot about the business. Makin confided he had 'passed a rough night' with the baby in arms having kept him awake half the night, using such language that the newspapers could not print his comments. He asked to be directed to the nearest chemist.

The money to be made from Mrs Makin's skills as a 'ladies' nurse' appears to have been essential to the family finances, since Mr Hill testified that Makin was unemployed during his stay in Burren Street, although John had said 'on several occasions that he was going to get a job, or that he had been promised a job'.

As Mr Hill stepped down from the witness box, he told the Coroner he had not come willingly but had been summoned by the police to give evidence:

Mr Hill: [I]t's very hard upon me and my wife to have to hang round here loafing instead of earning 9s a day.

Coroner: You must not call it loafing.

Mr Hill: Well, I don't know what else it is, hanging round these verandahs. (Laughter.)

At the end of the first day of this inquest, the unhappy Makin family was taken back to Darlinghurst Gaol in the police cab. Florence and Blanche 'burst into tears and cried piteously' while Sarah 'looked very solemn and crestfallen' seated in the cab. But John was upbeat as he 'talked and joked callously about going to gaol again' while a large crowd watched them being driven away.

The next morning came the most interesting yet puzzling evidence heard so far. Miss Agnes Todd, aged 26, told the court she was a single woman living at 6 Dangar Place, Chippendale. She had given birth to a baby girl, called Elsie May, on 1 January 1892. She had known Makin as Mr Leslie after entering into a written agreement with him on 27 June to adopt her child for £3, five days before the Makins moved to Burren Street. The formal agreement was produced in court:

> Redfern, 27/6/92
> I hereby agree to take and adopt a baby girl six months old from Agnes Todd, for the baby, name Elsie May, for a compensation of £3. I hereby agree to take her for life, and not to trouble the said Agnes Todd, either in sickness or death of the baby.
> J.H.Leslie.

In court, Agnes was able to identify a fragment of linen that had been found on Baby B, the second body discovered by the drain-layers. This was part of a shirt that Agnes' baby had been wearing when she was adopted by Mr Leslie. The Makins' lawyer, Mr Williamson, informed the Coroner that Agnes' evidence had nothing whatever to do with the present inquiry. The Coroner was forced to agree and explained to the puzzled jurymen that he had put Agnes in the witness box since 'he had been given to understand she was in a position to identify some of the clothing found on the body of the child' who was the subject of this particular inquest, Baby 1. That appeared not to be the case, although at this stage the Coroner was unaware that the Makins frequently swapped clothing between their baby-farmed children.

Unfortunately, the Coroner had failed to realise that Agnes had relinquished her six-month-old baby to the Makins five days before they moved to Burren Street. No-one seems to have wondered what had happened to Elsie May and whether she could have been Baby 1, 2, 3, 4 or 5. Such were the vagaries of coronial justice in the 1890s.

The evidence given in the inquest into the death of Baby 1 was entirely circumstantial and did not enable the jury to link the Makins to her death. No poisons had been found in the baby's intestinal contents by the Government Analyst and Dr Milford was not able to give an actual cause of death due to the degree of decomposition of the body. During the inquest, no-one came forward to claim Baby 1 although if Dr Milford's age estimation was correct, someone had nursed Baby 1 for about a year before deciding to give her up. As the Coroner told the jury:

> The case is a very suspicious one, indeed, but it is only a suspicion, and
> I will leave you gentlemen to consider your verdict. There is nothing
> whatever in the evidence which would enable you to say when, where,
> or by what means this particular child came by its death.

Dissatisfied that so little evidence had been called, a juryman asked: 'And there is no evidence, beyond what has already been given, likely to come out in the case of the other four bodies?' The Coroner told the jurors he could not say and then asked them to retire to consider their verdict. The next day, Tuesday 8 November, the foreman of the jury announced:

> We find that the said female infant ... was found buried, but when
> the death took place, or what was the cause thereof, the evidence
> does not enable us to say.[3]

The Coroner replied: 'That I fear, will be the difficulty in each of these cases'. The Makins could sleep a little easier for the time being in their new, rent-free home in Darlinghurst Gaol.

'Metaphysics are the Godfrey's Cordial of the mind with which old women talk young children to sleep'[4]

John Makin's comment to Mr Hill that he had 'passed a rough night' with the baby in the house and his inquiry about the nearest chemist take us down another dim and dingy lane into the widespread practice of using drugs to sedate children. It was common in the 1800s for mothers, midwives and baby farmers to drug children with patent medicines or elixirs containing opium, such as Godfrey's Cordial. In fact, new mothers were advised by an article in *The Sydney Morning Herald* to ensure they were 'never without a flask of Godfrey's cordial ... in the nursery'.[5]

Perhaps there was a universal need to dull the senses because of the harshness or tedium of life in the colonies since 'at the turn of the century Australia was the largest per capita consumer' of opium-based medicines in the world. White, middle-class women seem to have been particularly partial to opium, since they were the ones most likely to obtain an opium habit, albeit discreetly.[6] Many would have agreed that opium was indeed 'donum Dei', the name it was given: a gift of God.

The term 'Godfrey's Cordial' was a common part of the language during the 1800s and was used to refer to all manner of complaints, not just those of crying babies. When the 'whining' Australian colonies were considering their independence from Britain in 1851, the *Colonial Times* in Hobart remarked:

> the discontented Colonies are all to be cured of their miseries by Constitutions. Whether they will cure their miseries, or only operate as a Godfrey's Cordial to stop their whimpering ... may be a sad doubt to us.[7]

The lack of laws regulating drug use and the relaxed attitudes towards drugs in the 1800s meant that people treated their ailments with patent medicines which were 'available from chemists or grocers' shelves, without prescription, if and when the customer wanted them'.[8] These elixirs were also widely used because they were cheap—'about the price of a pint of beer'.[9]

In England, Australia and America, the most widely used elixirs for children had pleasant names such as Mrs Winslow's Soothing Syrup, Bonnington's Irish Moss, Ayres' Sarsparilla and Godfrey's Cordial, which was also known as Mother's Friend or 'comfort'. Despite its disarming name, Godfrey's Cordial 'was a sinister preparation' because of its high opium content, with one grain of opium for every two ounces.[10] Named after its inventor, Thomas Godfrey of Hertfordshire, this potent brew appeared in the early eighteenth century during Britain's cultivation of opium in India for trade with China and consisted of sassafras, opium, brandy or rectified spirit, caraway seed, and treacle.[11]

The cordial was advertised as a cure for a wide range of children's symptoms—from fretfulness to colic to diarrhoea. It was frequently used to sedate temperamental babies and many died from opium overdoses either by mistake or as a result of continuous use by 'nurses to keep infants ... in a deep state of sleep and thus of no bother'.[12] Although Godfrey's Cordial was definitely the baby farmer's friend, baby farmers were in common company since its liberal use by mothers and midwives meant that it was one of the major causes of infant deaths in the 1800s.[13]

Godfrey's Cordial was commonly used by the working-classes to prevent children from crying when they were hungry[14] and to pacify infants so that mothers could return to work in the factories immediately after giving birth.[15] Every chemist made his own potion and because the potency varied, overdoses were common. Even so, more children died from starvation than from opium overdose because drugged babies failed to cry for food.[16] Chronic use of opium meant that babies failed to thrive and were cheap to keep for baby farmers. If the Makins were using Godfrey's Cordial to silence their adopted babies, these infants may have ended up similar to Sarah's own babies before they died—wasted like 'wizened little monkeys'.

Inquests into the deaths of babies who had been poisoned by Godfrey's Cordial were common during the 1800s. On 25 August 1855, an inquest was held in Hobart into the death of Martha Mills, four weeks old, who, it was found, had been given an accidental overdose of Godfrey's Cordial after her mother had bought the elixir from her local chemist.[17] Other inquests testify to its frequent use either as a daily pacifier or possibly a way of disposing of unwanted children with one family losing five children to overdoses of Godfrey's Cordial.[18] Because of its widespread use, it was diffi-cult to prove that someone had killed a child deliberately using Godfrey's Cordial, with most deaths being recorded as 'debility from birth', 'lack of breast milk' or simply 'starvation'.[19]

The intemperate use of Godfrey's Cordial was a concern in England during the 1840s with an inquiry reporting that children were frequently brought to doctors 'benumbed and stupified with opiates' using Godfrey's Cordial. The inquiry found that the problem prevailed over much of England while some reported that babies were given Godfrey's Cordial from the day of birth with high numbers of infants perishing:

Those who escape with life become pale and sickly children, often half idiotic, and always with a ruined constitution.[20]

Because of the habitual use of Godfrey's Cordial for pacifying babies by parents and baby farmers alike, it is almost certain that on the morning of 30 June 1892, John Makin headed for the nearest chemist in King Street, Newtown to purchase a bottle for the baby that had kept him up all night, the baby Sarah Makin had described as being 'very cross' and one she was glad to be rid of.

The use of this 'soothing' mixture would explain why none of the neighbours reported hearing the sound of babies crying from 25 Burren Street. Godfrey's Cordial would have been an essential tool for managing a house full of babies, since suspicious neighbours would only bring unwanted police attention. But its use also means that the babies found in the Burren Street backyard could have died from opium overdoses or starvation as they lay drugged, slowly wasting away. Had the Makins intended to kill these infants or were they using Godfrey's Cordial as a pacifier because they were just too poor to feed seven hungry babies?

John's confession: truth or another bit of Joycean fiction?

After the unsatisfactory verdict in relation to the death of Baby 1, Constable Joyce and the Makins remained in the Coroner's Court to observe the next set of inquests, which began on the same day, Tuesday, 8 November.[21]

Babies 2 and 3 were 4–6 months old and 2–3 months old respectively when they died. Both were in an advanced state of decomposition, having been buried for four to six months with most of their internal organs decomposed. Dr Milford could not determine their cause of death, although spots of blood had been found on the piece of white calico in which Baby 2 had been wrapped.

Baby 5 had died when she was about ten days old. Her right arm was missing, although nothing was made of this. She had been buried for two to three months and was the least decomposed of the five babies discovered by the police. Dr Milford's autopsy found that she had a small puncture below her left nipple which had not penetrated her chest. Because her internal organs were not as decomposed as those of the other babies, Dr Milford revealed that her lungs had expanded to fill her chest cavity and overlap her heart. He informed the jury that this expansion occurs when someone has drowned, or been strangled or suffocated, as well as in cases of opium poisoning. When her other internal organs were examined, Baby 5's intestines were found to be empty, suggesting she had not been fed for some time.

At the inquest into the death of Baby 2, Edward Jordan gave evidence of a confession that John Makin had made while they had shared a prison cell at Newtown police station in the early hours of 4 November. Jordan had been arrested for the carnal knowledge of a girl under the age of 14. Although John had denied any knowledge of the Burren Street discoveries in his police interview, Jordan told the court that he and Makin had spoken of the 'troubles' that had landed them in prison. John had confided he was inside for baby farming, revealing that while seven bodies had been found, there was still one more yet to be discovered. He was worried that when that one was found 'I'll never see daylight any more', adding '[t]hat is what a man gets for obliging people'. Resigned to his fate, John told Jordan, 'I don't care for myself, but for my children, who are innocent'. Perhaps thinking of his options, John mused '[h]e could do nothing outside, as they were watching the ground too close'. But he was confident that '[n]o doctor can say he had poisoned any of the children'. Makin had been annoyed that although 'the parents of one of the infants promised me £2 to register the death and bury the body', they had not kept their promise. When pressed under cross-examination, Jordan also revealed that John had admitted to burying the seven babies in Burren Street.

The jury may have wondered whether Makin really did confess to a man he had only just met or whether Constable Joyce had done a deal with Jordan. The answer depends on what information Joyce knew and when. John's revelation about the parents of one child promising to pay £2 could only have come from Minnie Davies and Horace Bothamley. Horace had contacted the police before John was arrested since his accusations had informed Joyce's first interview with the Makins.

The Makins' lawyer complained to the Coroner that Jordan had been told by police that John was a baby farmer and to get as much out of him as possible. Williamson was suspicious because Jordan already knew a lot about the baby-farming John Makin before he entered Makin's cell. But Jordan explained he had overheard the police discussing the case and decided to tell Constable Joyce about the confession because he 'considered he would be quite as bad as [Makin] if he concealed' it.

The one hint that John's confession was real, rather than manufactured, is the third search of the Burren Street backyard by the 'energetic' Constable Joyce, as a result of the information that there was an eighth body yet to be discovered.[22] On the other hand, John was a talker who loved to brag and was probably a shrewd assessor of people's character. He may have summed up the snake-like Jordan, feeding him lies in order to send Joyce off on a 'wild baby hunt' which would have given him a small amount of pleasure.

If Jordan's evidence was true, John's admission that 'no doctor can say he had poisoned any of the children' suggests that Godfrey's Cordial was the Makins' preferred treatment for 'cross' babies. Although the stomach contents of Babies 2, 3 and 5 had been tested, no traces of poison were found. Without modern techniques for chemical analysis, opium would have been undetectable by the time the babies were discovered because of its rapid breakdown in the body when administered, as well as further breakdown after death.

Although Joyce had hoped that Jordan's evidence would persuade the jury to find the Makins guilty of the deaths of Babies 2, 3 and 5, the jury did not agree. Warned by the Coroner that 'the case was simply one of suspicion', the jury followed the Coroner's instructions by returning open verdicts. With no cause of death and no evidence to identify the bodies, there was little else they could do.

The Makins' luck was holding out.

❧

CHAPTER TWELVE

The longest, saddest inquest: clothing and other complications
10–15 November 1892

Since the inquests conducted by the Coroner had been fruitless in sheeting home responsibility to the Makins, various members of Parliament became concerned about the police investigation. On 10 November 1892, Mr Carruthers questioned the Attorney-General, Mr Barton, in Parliament about the failure of the Coroner to elicit 'anything that would enable the Government to fix the guilt for those acts on any person'. He reminded Mr Barton of a case in Parramatta where four or five children had met their deaths but 'the guilt had not been sheeted home to anyone'. Casting doubt on the adequacy of the police case he argued that a special public prosecutor was needed to assist the police in gathering evidence.[1] But Mr Carruthers need not have worried since it was the sixth and longest inquest—which investigated the death of Baby 4—that was to cause a sensation in what was now being called the 'great baby-farming case' and 'the most extensive and brutal system of baby farming ever heard of in Australia'.[2]

Despite having survived the inquisitive eye of five inquests so far, the sixth was to be the first nail in the coffin of John Makin and a permanent iron bolt in the gaol door for Sarah. Out of all the parents of the seven Burren Street babies, it was 17-year-old Minnie Davies and 19-year-old Mr Horace Bothamley who could not let go of their baby girl, Mignonette. Born on 10 June 1892, her birth was registered more than once and in different names, suggesting an anxious need to disguise her birth. The first registration stated that her name was Mignonette Lavinia Wilson and her father's surname was Wilson. She was finally registered in the real surname of her father, W H Bothamley.[3] Nonetheless, when the Coroner's inquiry was over, she was named Mignonette Lavinia Davies in the Register of Coroner's Deaths.

As Mr and Mrs Wilson, Minnie and Horace paid the Makins ten shillings each Saturday when they visited Burren Street. It is possible they did not marry when Minnie discovered she was pregnant because both were under the age of 21 and needed parental permission to do so. Since Minnie was a domestic servant, she would probably have lost her position upon marriage. While Horace worked for *The Daily Telegraph*, at the age of 19 he earned a wage that would not have covered the cost of rent and three mouths to feed. Whatever the reasons, it was essential that no-one should find out about the birth of their illegitimate daughter.

With each inquest, the public's fascination had grown. When the inquest was opened on Monday 14 November 1892, a large crowd waited outside the courthouse hoping to grab a seat in the public gallery, with spectators besieging the court throughout the day and gathering at the gates each afternoon to catch a glimpse of the Makins.[4] In a time with no movies, television or playstations, this was a murder mystery that people in the twenty-first century rarely witness—a real life tragedy which had its own Acts I, II and III.

The sixth inquest made up the end of Act I. While the jury had to produce a verdict, everyone in the public gallery would hear all the evidence as it unfolded and make their own judgments. The prisoners, Sarah, John, Florence and Blanche, were present. It was to be a long ordeal with more than 12 witnesses called to give evidence. Sarah appeared to be in 'ill-health' and had to be assisted into the court by John, with one report observing that she 'bore a very sullen look'. As had become her habit, she was dressed in black and kept her eyes cast down with either a shawl or handkerchief to her face, 'so that beneath her hat very little of her features' could be seen.

Those who could not fit into the courtroom gathered at the doorway. When Constable Joyce began his evidence the crowd pushed forward towards Blanche and Florence, who were seated near the door. Spooked, they jumped up and refused to sit until the police cleared the court. Sarah, who was seated in the dock, hid her face with her shawl 'as if she was crying' and fell to the floor in a faint. As she was carried out of court, Florence and Blanche 'cried bitterly'. The Government Medical Officer, whose office was located next door to the court, rushed to help, pronouncing that Sarah was suffering from 'general debility' as she was in 'an excited and nervous state' and unfit to attend court. He ordered her removal to Darlinghurst Gaol Hospital. The proceedings continued without her.

Constable Thomas Conran told the packed court how he had dug up the remains of an infant at 11.30 on the morning of 3 November in the backyard of 25 Burren Street. The infant had been buried at a depth of about eighteen inches and was wrapped in a piece of flannel. It was the fourth baby discovered by the police. From the lengths of the thigh bones, Dr Milford estimated that Baby 4 was six to ten weeks old when she died, an age similar to that of Minnie's and Horace's daughter. He thought the decomposed body was that of a girl since if 'the child had been a male there would have been some traces of the male organs'.

When Constable Brown testified, he said that portions of a shawl found wrapped around the bodies of Babies 3 and 5 had been identified by Minnie Davies as part of a shawl she had given to Mrs Makin. As the Coroner asked the jury to make a note of this particular evidence, Mr Williamson scraped back his chair and announced:

> I object to this being regarded as evidence. It has nothing to do
> with the body (No.4) upon which the inquest is being held.

He argued that the evidence about the other babies would 'have the effect of prejudicing his clients'. But the Coroner was unconcerned:

> I knew you would object to all this. ... But [i]t is my duty to get out
> every scrap of evidence that I possibly can.

The inquest carried on, with the Makins' anxiety increasing.

The descriptions of the clothing of each dead infant found in Burren Street had been published in the daily newspapers and had generated results even though the police investigations were said to be hampered by a rumour that they intended to prosecute the mothers of some of the children.

Joyce produced the clothing found on Baby 4, including a pair of pink and white woollen bootees. He had shown these bootees to a Mrs Sutherland, who had contacted the police and said she had been the midwife to an unmarried woman named Agnes Todd (whose evidence was heard in an earlier inquest). Since Mrs Sutherland had handed Miss Todd's baby to the Makins, she was able to identify the bootees from Baby 4 and the clothing found on Baby 1 as belonging to Agnes' baby.

When day one of the inquest came to an end, it left the chattering public curious but also unsure about how events would unfold in the following days. As the spectators shuffled out of court, they would not have recognised the Makins' youngest children, Daisy and Tommy, who had been brought to court by Sarah's married daughter, Minnie Helbi, for a visit. Taken into the jury room with the rest of the family, they 'cried very bitterly' when Florence, Blanche and John were taken back to Central police station.

Outside the court, the crowds had increased as the afternoon wore on, becoming excitable when the case was adjourned for the day. The police waited for the crowd to disperse but the spectators were more patient than the police. Eventually, the officers were forced to clear the courtyard and escort John, Blanche and Florence through another gate, away from the waiting hordes. But the crowd spied them as they crossed into Hyde Park. With more and more people from the surrounding streets attracted to the procession, the gawking, chattering crowd followed them all the way to the police station on the other side of the park.

Day two: the Makins' nosey neighbours

On day two of the inquest, Sarah had recovered sufficiently to take her seat in court alongside her husband and daughters even though she cried several times during the proceedings, hiding her face in her handkerchief. She heard Patrick Mulvey give the same evidence he had given in previous inquests but she did not even raise her eyes as two of her neighbours, Mrs Hill and Mrs Jane Parry, were called, one after the other, to take the stand.

Mrs Parry, who lived at 23 Burren Street, confirmed Mrs Hill's evidence when she testified she had only seen and heard one baby at the Makins' house, a baby girl whom John had described as 'sickly and cross'. Mrs Parry had also seen children's clothing drying on the line at 25 Burren Street that, in her opinion, was too much for one child. Given the ten foot high fence surrounding the yard at 25 Burren Street, Mrs Parry had been a keen observer of the goings-on in the Makins' backyard, perhaps between the palings of the fence. She had taken careful note of pieces of woollen shawl hanging on the line, including a piece that was burnt at the edge, as well as little flannelette shirts, petticoats and several pairs of bootees, including a pair of pink and white ones.

For the first time, evidence about the babies' clothing was beginning to implicate the Makins in the deaths of not only Baby 4 but other babies as well. Despite this, one court reporter was bored by the proceedings, commenting that the inquest 'was monotonously uninteresting', protracted and ridiculously slow. As if tempting fate, he was in for the time of his court-reporting life the next day. For the Makins, day two had been bad. But worse was to come.

A daughter turned Crown witness

The day before this inquest began Constable Joyce had discovered that John and Sarah had two other daughters, Daisy, aged 10 or 11, and Clarice, aged 14, both of whom were staying temporarily with Sarah's married daughter, Mrs Minnie Helbi, at 61 Garden Street, Alexandria. Perhaps through the gentle art of police persuasion, Joyce managed to convince Clarice to talk, although Daisy was so 'frightened and alarmed that little information could be obtained from her' after Florence had warned her at Newtown police station, 'You know nothing whatever about this business'.

After questioning Clarice and Daisy, Joyce was able to trace the movements of the Makin family and concluded they had been baby farming since they lived in Harbour Street, Darling Harbour at least three years earlier.

When Clarice gave evidence on the third day of the inquest, the court was 'densely crowded in expectation' that she would reveal all. She told the court she was a domestic servant at 128 Cleveland Street where she lived-in. During Clarice's examination, Blanche and Florence 'were much agitated, and were continually muttering' while 'Mrs. Makin turned her head away, and sobbed convulsively' as betrayal hung in the air. They were being forced to watch as their statements to the police were exposed as a confection of lies. This emotional display did not stop Clarice from timidly informing the court she had lived with her parents at 109 George Street in June 1892 and that her mother took children into care.

> Coroner: Shortly before they moved did your mother take in a
>   baby to care?
> Clarice: Yes, sir …
> Coroner: Well, did your mother get one before that?
> Clarice: Yes. She had one then.
> Coroner: Was it a boy [or] a girl?
> Clarice: They were both girls …
> Coroner: Have you any idea how old [the first one] was?
> Clarice: About 6 or 7 months.
> Coroner: Do you know how your mother got that baby?
> Clarice: My father got it from a woman.
> Coroner: Do you know the lady?
> Clarice: Yes, sir.
>   (Mrs Sutherland [the midwife of Miss Agnes Todd]
>   was here brought into court.)
> Coroner: Is that the person?
> Clarice: Yes.

Clarice remembered that another female baby about two weeks old had also turned up in George Street. This was a healthy looking baby who had been visited by Horace Bothamley. Although Clarice said she accompanied her parents on the late-night move to 25 Burren Street, she left three days later to take up her live-in position as a servant. The next part of her evidence was damning:

> Coroner: Did your father take any other children to Burren-
>   street?

Clarice:	They took two altogether.
Coroner:	Were they in the house when you left?
Clarice:	Yes, sir.

When she visited her parents a week later the two babies were still in the house, including Minnie's and Horace's baby who 'seemed to be quite well'. Although she saw the two babies again the following week, that was the last time she saw them. On this occasion, Clarice told the court she remembered that Baby Mignonette was wearing 'a little pink dress' and pink and white bootees. When she was shown this clothing, Clarice turned away and 'burst into tears and it was some time before she could resume her evidence'.

As Clarice continued her tearful testimony, she said she could not remember seeing the particular bootees shown to her nor other any clothing found on Baby 4. The Coroner then asked, suspiciously:

Coroner:	Has anyone said anything to you about the case?
Clarice:	No, sir, nobody.
Coroner:	Has Mr. Williams spoken to you?
Clarice:	No, sir ...
Coroner:	Will you swear that?
Clarice:	Yes, sir.

A curious juror then interrupted:

Juror:	Had you any particular object in not visiting your parents very often while in Burren-street?
Clarice:	No, sir. I was not very fond of home.

Clarice's evidence was explosive because it was the first crack in the cone of silence surrounding the Makin family. During the luncheon break, Sarah, John, Florence and Blanche were held in the jury room, from which 'sounds of continued wailing and sobbing could be heard ... and occasionally the voice of Mrs. Makin rose shrilly above the weeping anathematising some one'. Attracted by this racket, a crowd gathered outside the jury room window, where Clarice was seen talking to some of the women in the crowd. On catching sight of her disloyal daughter, 'Mrs Makin rushed to the window and exclaimed, "A mother's curse! A mother's curse on you! You've all been swearing lies"'.

After lunch, when Sarah was led into the courtroom past Clarice, who was seated in a passageway, she raised her hand and 'hissed', 'May the curse of God Almighty rest upon my child'. This was a prelude to more dramatics. As Sarah, Florence and Blanche took their seats, they put on such a performance and 'sobbed so hysterically' that the inquest was delayed for a considerable time until they calmed down. Although they intended to send a message to Clarice, 'her evidence was not shaken'. She told the court that 'her mother had cursed [her] terribly, all because she had told the truth, and added passionately "I came here to tell the truth and I am going to tell it"'. While a few of the jurors called out, 'Hear, hear', Blanche 'burst into violent sobs, and repeatedly shrieked out that her sister was telling lies'.

No doubt the Coroner, the jurymen and even the Makins' lawyer had never seen anything like it. One journalist described it as 'one of the most remarkable scenes that has ever taken place in a court in the colony'.[5] But the Makin family was standing on the edge of an abyss. Desperate measures were called for. Because Mr Williamson had been unsuccessful in restricting the evidence that could be heard in the inquest, these tactics were the only defence the Makin family had at its disposal.

Despite her mother's threats and her sisters' sobbing and shrieking, Clarice bravely continued her testimony, although she cried throughout, determined to tell the truth. When she was shown the clothing found on Baby 3, she recognised the napkin by the letter 'F' in the corner and revealed she had seen it and the baby's shirt in her mother's possession in George Street, along with the piece of shawl in which Baby 3 had been buried.

Mr Williamson rose to his feet to begin what was to become a highly emotional cross-examination.

Mr. Williamson: When did Senior-constable Joyce see you?

Clarice: On Sunday morning last ...

| Mr. Williamson: | Did he make any promise or hold out any inducement that he would see that you be all right? |
| Clarice: | No, he did not. He simply told me to tell the truth and not tell lies, and I have spoken the truth. |

Sarah and her daughters again descended into tears, with Sarah 'moaning painfully' while Blanche cried out that Clarice was a liar. Clarice sobbed, producing a 'most painful' scene. A juror, disturbed by what he saw, spoke up:

Juror:	I think, your Worship, that steps should be taken to protect the young girl. She is in a very unpleasant position.
Mr. Williamson:	I don't think the jury have a right to take cognizance of what takes place out side the court.
Juror:	Well, it's a great shame the way the girl has been treated.

Since Clarice was spooked by her mother's and sisters' dramatics, why did she betray her parents, unlike Blanche and Florence, who had sought to protect them? At the age of 14, she must have been terrified about giving evidence in front of her stern father and volatile mother. Somehow Joyce had managed to reassure her, perhaps sensing in Clarice a vulnerability or resentment not evident in the Makins' eldest daughters.

One hint comes from the moment when Clarice 'burst into tears' as she was shown the clothing in which Baby 4 had been found. Perhaps she had bonded with Baby Mignonette, who at two weeks old was the youngest baby in Burren Street and the most bothersome, a child who 'always seemed to be peevish, because it was incessantly crying'.

When Clarice signed her deposition and walked back to her seat in the body of the courtroom, Blanche called out: 'I hate the dress you've got on your back'. This insult and the rest of the family's antics give us clues as to why Clarice was not fond of spending time at home. About a week later, Clarice attended Sydney Hospital to have her right arm dressed after she came out in painful white blisters the day after she gave evidence, the strain of giving evidence taking its toll in other agonising ways.

After Clarice stepped down from the witness box, the Coroner called Daisy Makin. This was an excuse for even more family dramatics. As Clarice left the court to collect Daisy, 'Mrs. Makin and her eldest daughter were greatly affected, and when [Clarice] returned leading her youngest sister who was crying, a terrible scene occurred'. According to one newspaper account, Daisy sobbed as soon as she saw her mother. Sarah then:

> stood up and exclaimed, 'Oh! my child, my child, bring her to me,'
> and attempted to rush across the court towards the child. She was
> held back by the constables, but struggled violently as if in a fit,
> and then fainted. The girl cried piteously, and exclaimed, 'My poor
> mother. Let me go to her. She is dying.'

Florence and Blanche shrieked and screamed at the sight of Daisy, who was crying loudly, 'My mother will die'. The scene was so 'heartrending' that everyone in court was unnerved, including the jurymen, who were so affected 'that a dry eye was scarcely visible'. For a few moments no-one seemed to know what to do, transfixed by the wailing Makin women.

According to another newspaper, *The Maitland & Hunter River General Advertiser*:

> Mrs Makin jumped up and called 'Come and take me out.' The
> girls Blanche and Florence clasped each other and wept most
> bitterly, calling out 'Oh, my mother' and threatening their sister
> Clarence. Mrs Makin was removed from court very ill. Her daugh-
> ters Florence, Blanche and Daisy followed crying most distressingly.

Perhaps this dramatic scene was another ruse by the Makins to divert the court's attention, since Daisy, a girl who could not read or write, would have been particularly vulnerable to the Coroner's probing questions.

Another journalist's description of the scene suggests the Makins' behaviour was akin to amateur theatre since 'Mrs. Makin at once threw up her arms with a loud shriek, and fell upon her husband's shoulder in a faint', which was 'the signal' for Blanche and Florence to begin their 'pitiful wailing intermingled with shrieks that their mother was dying, and with threats against Clariss [sic]'.

John Makin played his part by remaining mute; he sat 'without uttering a word', his face white and his head bent down. When Sarah, Blanche and Florence were removed from the court along with Daisy, a juror asked the Coroner, 'The scene which just occurred was a most painful one. Could you not postpone the child's evidence? I am sure she must be unnerved. I know we are'.

The Makins won the day since their antics persuaded the Coroner not to call their youngest daughter to give evidence.

Another daughter gives evidence

Instead of Daisy, the next witness was Mrs Minnie Helbi, Sarah's daughter from her first marriage. Not much is known about Minnie, including her exact date of birth or whether she had been part of the Makin family after Sarah and John married in 1871.

On 9 March 1886, at the age of 19, Minnie Josephine Edwards married Carl August Helbi, aged 30, an acrobat from Germany, at St Luke's Church, Sydney. The marriage notice stated Minnie was the only daughter of the late Captain Charles Edwards.[6] Since Minnie was under the age of 21, Sarah had given permission for the marriage.

Now aged 25 and a married woman with four children and a husband who worked for the government, Minnie was able to give her evidence without interference, since her mother and sisters had been removed from the court. She told the Coroner she had not been on friendly terms with her parents since an argument three years earlier. She was not the only child to have been on bad terms with John and Sarah; their eldest son, William, had left home after an argument in August 1891.

Minnie had not seen her parents again until 15 or 16 August 1892 when the Makins had moved hurriedly from Burren Street to 55 Botany

Street, Redfern. She had not seen any children at the Botany Street house, although when her mother had been living in Wells Street, she had visited her daughter one evening 'in a very excited state', saying there 'were men in her house'. While the conscientious Constable Joyce was patiently waiting to interview Sarah on the afternoon and night of 12 October at 6 Wells Street, it is likely Sarah stayed the night at her eldest daughter's home in the nearby suburb of Alexandria.

Minnie also revealed that, at the time of the inquests into the deaths of Babies A and B, Florence had visited one evening with a bundle of babies' clothing, telling Minnie to keep the clothing or burn it. Her mother then turned up, 'very angry', saying the clothing belonged to her two-year-old son. Strangely, a few days later, Sarah sent Florence along with more babies' clothing and the message that Minnie could keep it for her own children. But was Minnie telling the truth with her simple, non-incriminating tale or did she know more about her parents' baby-farming business than she was willing to admit?

When Minnie finished her evidence, the court adjourned until the following day, concluding what had been the most remarkable day of evidence so far. A large crowd of about 200 people was waiting outside, hoping to catch a glimpse of the Makins. This time, Constable Joyce was keen to ensure that his prisoners were not 'ill-used'. He ordered his junior constables to clear the courtyard and close the gates then waited for the crowd to disperse. But they were were not so easily dismissed.

With everyone waiting in suspense, Joyce decided a bit of subterfuge was required. He sent John out through another gate with his hat pulled well down over his eyes and accompanied by a plain clothes policeman. Sarah followed, escorted in the same way, while Joyce and the Makin girls slipped out through the front courtyard gate.

Joyce and the girls mingled with the crowd and were able to escape unnoticed. But when Sarah and John were sighted, they were surrounded and jostled by the crowd. Even though there was no hostility or violence, John turned 'deadly pale' while Sarah, appearing indifferent, walked quickly and firmly 'with her custodian' across Hyde Park with people rushing from all directions to see them. Without the reach of the telescopic lens of today's papparazzi, these crowds were eager to see and touch for themselves the most infamous couple in the Australian colonies.

The evidence builds

For the bored court reporters, the 'protracted' inquest into the death of Baby 4 continued for several more days.[7] They would have realised this inquest was unlike previous ones since Constable Joyce had gathered many more witnesses. As the case became more and more sensational, it appears more and more witnesses came forward. Since the babies' faces could not be identified, the whole case would turn on who had given the Makins particular clothing and what clothing the dead babies had been buried in.

Daisy Makin gave evidence on day four of the inquest. Her mother had been taken to Darlinghurst Gaol Hospital the previous day after her apparent collapse. While Sarah was able to walk into the courtroom on this Wednesday morning, 'her step was very feeble and during the whole of the day she sat with her head bowed and ... her face partly hidden by her hat'. Outside, crowds of people again 'thronged' the yard around the court, although this time constables were stationed at the door of the courtroom to prevent the curiosity-seekers from invading.

Little Daisy stood on her own in the witness box under the gaze of the whole court with her collapsed mother sitting nearby. In the temporary break that Sarah had orchestrated the day before, she, Florence and Blanche had probably tried to cajole Daisy into saying as little as possible. When asked to repeat the oath, Daisy said she did not understand it but 'she would promise to tell the truth'. She then 'commenced to sob, but by consoling terms of sympathy' from the Coroner, Daisy calmed herself. She gave her name and said she thought she was 11 years old. She told the court she lived with her married sister, Minnie, and remembered the night the family moved to Burren Street.

Although Daisy revealed little information, what she did say was incriminating. When the family moved to Burren Street, her mother had taken two baby girls with her, one in long clothes, the other in short clothes, indicating that one of them was less than two months old. She used to nurse the younger baby, who she identified as the child of Minnie Davies and Horace Bothamley. She also remembered the baby had worn pink and white bootees but when shown the bootees that had been found on Baby 4, Daisy said she had not seen those ones before.

She was also unsure about the other clothing found on Baby 4—after staring intently at a blue and white striped dress and a coloured shirt for a few seconds she said she did not recognise them. The Coroner was suspicious:

> Coroner: Has any one spoken to you about coming here and giving evidence?
>
> Daisy: No, sir.
>
> Coroner: Nobody has told you what to say?
>
> Daisy: No.

When asked what had happened to the child of Minnie and Horace, Daisy replied that the child died and was laid out in the house for its parents to see. Later, she was told by her mother that an undertaker had taken it away. Under further questioning, Daisy revealed that a white shawl had been accidentally burnt in Burren Street after being left to dry on the oven door, and that pieces of it had been found wrapped around two of the buried babies.

Mr Williamson objected to this evidence because it had nothing to do with the inquiry into the death of Baby 4. But the Coroner had lost his patience.

> Coroner: I have overruled that objection several times. I wish you would sit down and not interrupt me again …
>
> [Mr. Healy, representing the Crown, agreed.]
>
> Coroner: Are you satisfied Mr. Williamson?
>
> Mr. Williamson: Well, with all due respect to—
>
> Coroner: Oh, sit down, please, Mr. Williamson.

With that dismissal, the Coroner turned to Daisy and continued to ask questions about the burnt shawl. This shawl had belonged to Minnie

Davies, who had given it to the Makins. Daisy was then shown pieces of the burnt shawl that had been found on Babies 3 and 5. When asked whether she recognised them, she stared at them then replied, 'I think so.'

It was now the turn of Williamson to cross-examine Daisy, although as he got to his feet, the Coroner remarked, 'I hope you will be considerate, Mr. Williamson'. When Williamson replied that he thought 'it's a cruel thing to have the child brought here to give evidence against her parents', the Coroner told him off while Daisy burst out crying. Williamson retorted that 'the girl had not cried because of any remark [I have] made, but because of the suspense'. While Mr Williamson was allowed to ask Daisy a few questions, he failed to change any of her previous answers.

∂∕⊕

CHAPTER THIRTEEN

The mysterious Mr and Mrs Wilson give evidence
16–28 November 1892

The inquest into the death of Baby 4 was the first one to hear evidence from two people who might have been the parents of the child who was the subject of the inquest.

It was inevitable that Minnie's and Horace's baby daughter, the child who had kept John up 'all night', would not last long in the Makin household. Although they would lose the weekly nursing fee of ten shillings, the baby's death was the only way the Makins could extract Minnie and Horace from their lives as the Makins readied themselves for their next move, and, with money running out, their next batch of babies. By the time Mignonette died there were six other babies interred in the backyard of Burren Street, including those of two other mothers who were also keen on visiting the Makins.

After taking the oath, Minnie Davies told the inquest that she and Horace chose to call themselves Mr and Mrs Wilson to hide the fact they had an illegitimate child although they eventually registered their baby's birth in the name of Bothamley since Horace had wanted to ensure his daughter took his name. But Minnie was determined that her identity would remain secret and gave her surname as Wilson rather than Davies on her daughter's birth certificate.[1]

She also explained that she knew the Makins as Mr and Mrs Burt, who had given them their new address at 25 Burren Street after adopting Baby Mignonette in George Street. While this behaviour was unusual for the Makins, Mignonette was the Makins' nursing baby—the one they displayed to the world and who was to be kept clean, fed and healthy, at least initially, since she was bringing in a regular income.

Minnie and Horace made their weekly visits to the Makins until August. On their first visit to Burren Street, they delivered clothes for their daughter. Some of the clothing included a white shawl with a fringe. On their arrival, they were surprised to find their daughter was not dressed in any of the clothes they had previously given the Burts and that they were required to pay ten shillings for the short clothes Mrs Burt said she had purchased.

Minnie testified that on 4 November she and Horace had accompanied Constable Joyce to the South Sydney morgue where she identified two pieces of material which had been cut from the shawl she gave Mrs Burt. These wrappings had been found on Babies 3 and 5 and when she was shown them again in the courtroom Minnie was certain they had come from her shawl.

Minnie also identified two babies' gowns she had purchased at a draper's shop in Oxford Street, Paddington. Along with other clothing, these gowns had been found by Constable Joyce at Mr Burke's Pawnshop at 155 George Street, Redfern. One of the gowns recognised by Minnie had been worn by her dead daughter when she and Horace arrived with their bunch of flowers to see her one last time. Minnie told the court she had not authorised the Makins to sell or pawn this clothing.

When Mr Burke later gave evidence he stated that on 8 August 1892, ten babies' gowns had been pawned in the name of Mrs Makin, although he did not recognise Sarah in the courtroom. Instead, he had seen Blanche Makin in his shop several times. On 9 August more babies' clothing was pawned at his shop by someone who signed their name as Wilson of George Street West.

Minnie explained that, from the middle of July, her baby's health deteriorated until 11 August when Horace received a telegram from John telling him to 'Come at once'.[2] When she and Horace arrived at Burren Street with their bunch of flowers on the afternoon of 11 August, John brought the body of Mignonette, laid out on a board and dressed in a long white gown, into the sitting room.

He told them their baby had been diagnosed by Dr Agassiz as suffering from a wasting disease, 'to which all children are liable'. Although Horace offered to reimburse the Makins for the doctor's fee, uncharacteristically John said 'he would not ask him to refund him that'. When asked in court if there were any marks on the child's head, arms or legs, Minnie said her baby appeared to be well cared for, clean and well dressed.

Dr Agassiz's diagnosis suggests the Makins were deliberately starving Mignonette, which would explain why she cried such a lot. When asked about any substances given to her child, Minnie said she had seen either John or Sarah administer some medicine to Mignonette which 'seemed to give the child some relief' and could have been Godfrey's Cordial. It is likely that the more the baby cried, the more Godfrey's Cordial she was given and the less she was fed, eventually leading to her starvation. How Minnie and Horace failed to see that their baby was getting thinner on their weekly visits is a mystery, since an underfed baby loses the characteristic baby fat on her face, arms and legs.[3]

Although it was not possible for Baby 4 to be identified by Minnie and Horace due to the degree of decomposition of her body, upon being shown a lock of hair taken from Baby 4 Horace emphatically identified it as being 'exactly like the hair from our child', which was light brown, although Minnie was less sure. The Coroner directed the jury to compare the lock of hair with the hair colour of Minnie and Horace to draw their own conclusions. The couple were asked to stand with their backs to the jury, which created much laughter, although one journalist was not amused:

> the jury appeared to treat the matter as a joke. 'Don't pull any out,' said one of the jury while handling Miss Davi[e]s's hair. 'Have you a pair of scissors?' remarked another juror as he gazed at Bothamley's hair. 'No,' said the witness, jocularly, 'I only had it cut yesterday.' The scene altogether was a ridiculous one.

At the end of the day's hearings, Mr Williamson rose 'to draw the Coroner's attention to the sensational articles and cartoons referring to the inquest in which a section of the Sydney press was indulging'. He was concerned they would 'prejudice the interests of [my] clients'. But the Coroner was disinterested, informing Mr Williamson that although he could not prevent the jury from reading the newspapers, he had every confidence that the jurors, 'composed of intelligent gentlemen', would take no notice of anything they read or heard outside the court. When Williamson continued to protest, several jurors interrupted: 'That's alright your Worship. We won't allow anything like that to affect us'.

Mr Williamson and the Makins had to be satisfied with that, although another fracas at another inquest would show them exactly where the jurors' sympathies lay.

A crowd becomes agitated

Throughout the day of Minnie's and Horace's evidence large numbers of people attended with 'solicitors, barristers, members of Parliament, justices of the peace, clergymen, and people from all grades of society' coming and going to get a view of the Makins. When the court adjourned, a police van arrived at the court gates to collect the prisoners. With a huge crowd of about 1000 people congregating near the entrance, the van tried to drive directly into the courtyard but could not pass under the archway. As the horses were backed up, 'the crowd became very unruly, and the horses very restive'.

Instead, the van drove to the Equity Court gates to collect John, Sarah and their daughters. When the crowd caught sight of them, 'they flocked round the van, while others mounted the railings and gates'. Although some in the crowd began to hoot, the jeering failed to catch on. Nonetheless, it spooked Sarah, who 'exhibited signs of great fear when leaving the court, and pleaded with a constable: "Oh I'm so frightened; don't take me through the crowd"'.

The crowd was the culmination of a bad day with the graphic evidence given by Minnie and Horace confirming, if confirmation were needed, that the Makins were in the business of adopting children for a fee. It was also a bad day for Blanche since she had spent the day 'continually sobbing' because her sweetheart had called to visit her at the court but had not been allowed to see her.

No. 103 ~ Apprenticed &c.

This Indenture,

made the *Eighteenth* Day of *February* in the Year of Our Lord One thousand eight hundred and *Thirty* between the Trustees of the Clergy and School Lands in New South Wales, and *Francis O'Meara of Sydney*

WITNESSETH, that the said Trustees have placed *Sarah Bolton* aged *Nine* Years, or thereabouts, received into the *Female* Orphan School on the *10th* Day of *May 1825* with *him* to dwell and serve *6 years* from the Date of these Presents, until the *18th* day of *February 1836, or until her lawful marriage with consent of* During all which Term the said Apprentice *Sarah Bolton* faithfully shall serve, in *the Trustees* all lawful Business, according to *her* Power, and Ability ; and honestly, orderly, and obediently, in all Things, behave *her* self towards *her* said *Master* and towards all other Persons having lawful Charge of said Apprentice, during the said Term. And the said *Francis O'Meara* for *him* self doth covenant with the said Trustees, and their Successors for the Time-being, by these Presents, that *she* the said *Sarah Bolton* the said Apprentice, in the Art, Trade, and Mystery of *a Servant* shall and will teach, and cause to be taught in the best Way and Manner, and shall allow competent and sufficient Meat, Drink, Apparel, Lodging, Washing, and all other Things necessary and fit for an Apprentice, that *she* be not in any Way a Charge to the said Trustees, during the said Term, and that the said *Francis O'Meara* and all Persons who shall have lawful Charge of the said Apprentice, shall observe and conform to all such Rules, Orders, Bye Laws, and Regulations as the said Trustees shall make from Time to Time, pursuant to the Colonial Act, 4 Geo. IV.

In Witness whereof, these Presents have been duly executed by the said Parties, the Day and Year first above-written,

Signed, sealed, and delivered, by the said *Trustees &* the S. *Francis O'Mea* in the Presence of *me* *Charles Cowper*

The indenture which apprenticed nine-year-old Sarah Bolton, sister of Ellen Bolton, to her brother-in-law in 1831. The date on the indenture is incorrect. (State Records NSW)

Right: A sketch of the house at 25 Burren Street, Macdonaldtown, where seven dead babies were discovered in the backyard. (*The Evening News*, 10 November 1892, p. 4.)

Facing page, top: The gallows at Darlinghurst Gaol were located inside the gaol walls in the corner of the Y-shaped E Wing which faced the rising morning sun. (*The Bulletin*, 31 January 1880, p. 5)

Left: A treadmill operating in Brixton Prison, London, 1822, was similar to the ones used to punish convicts in Australia. (American Antiquarian Society)

THE HOUSE IN BURREN-STREET, MACDONALD-TOWN, WHERE THE MAKINS RESIDED.

A sketch of the backyard at 25 Burren Street. The crosses show where each of the seven babies was dug up by the two drainlayers (1A and 2A) and the police (1–5). (*The Evening News*, 10 November 1892, p. 4.)

An 1889 trade card promoting Mrs Winslow's Soothing Syrup, another name for Godfrey's Cordial. The syrup was advertised as a remedy for children's teething, wind, colic and diarrhoea. (Lithography by J Ottman. Scanned and digitised by the Miami University Libraries Digital Collection)

Sarah Makin.

Sketch of Sarah Makin. (Sketches from *The Evening News*, 10 November 1892, p. 4.)

James Joyce.

John Makin.

John Makin.

Sir Julian Salomons, the eminent barrister who appeared for the Makins at their first appeal. (Mitchell Library, State Library of NSW – GPO1 – 11619)

Police lined up outside the Newtown courthouse, circa 1912. (*The Jubilee Souvenir of the Municipality of Newtown, 1865–1912*, p. 53; scanned and digitised by the City of Sydney Archives, Newtown Project)

The imposing gates of the Darlinghurst Gaol, now the National Art School. (User: Sardaka, Wikimedia Commons, licensed under a Creative Commons Attribution 3.0 licence)

An aerial view of Darlinghurst Gaol, 1936. (National Art School Archives)

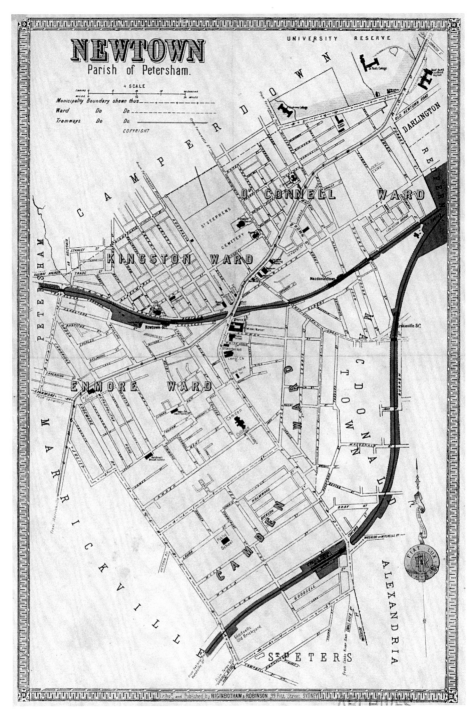

Map of Newtown, circa 1885 (City of Sydney Archives)

The Benevolent Asylum, corner of Pitt and Devonshire streets, Sydney, 1901. (State Records NSW: NRS 4481, Government Printing Office, Glass Negatives)

In the nurses' room, Alexandria baby clinic, c. 1914. By now the state was beginning to play a more active role in monitoring the health and welfare of infants. (Mitchell Library, State Library of NSW – GPO1 – 16188)

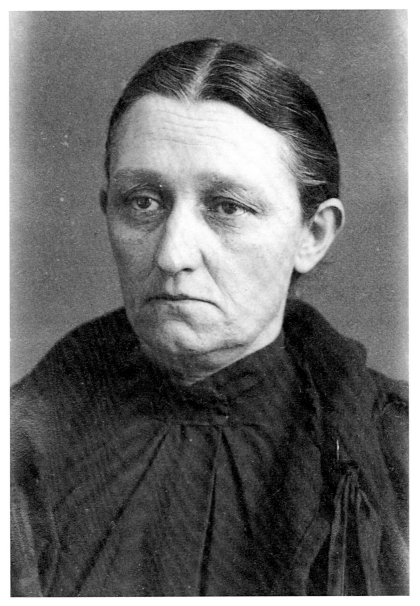

Sarah Makin, unknown photographer, taken in December 1892 in Darlinghurst Gaol. (State Records NSW: Gaol Description and Entrance Books, 1818–1930, Record for Sarah Makin, No. 5568)

John Makin, unknown photographer, taken in December 1892 in Darlinghurst
Gaol. (State Records NSW: Gaol Description and Entrance Books, 1818–1930,
Record for John Makin, No. 5567)

Wednesday 3.
1941.

Dear Matron
Just a few lines,
to express my very deep gratitude to
You, the Governor, + all the staff
connected, for the many kindness
I received, while with you, my life
being such a very sad one, you
did all you possibly could, to
brighten it. May God keep you,
+ every blessing that can be sent
to one, who always did her best
to brighten, the life of others.
Dear Miss Peraithwaithe I shall never
forget while it is God's will to
spare me, to be truly thankful, to
the Minister of Justice, also the
Controller General, + Deputy Controller, for all they have done
for me. I have not been very
well since, I came home, being very
nervous, But with the Lord's help
I will have strenght given me to
keep a brave heart.

Thanking you one + all.
Kindly remember me to all
the officers, + May the
good Lord send every
blessing to you all,
Yours sincerely
Sarah Makin

243. Abercrombie St
Redfern

Letter written by Sarah Makin after she was released from prison.
(State Records NSW: Letter 11/8853, filed in Register 10/11136)

Other rumours swirled around the Makins—including one exciting bit of gossip that John was so enraged by the hordes of people each day at court that he'd hatched a plan 'to run amok' in the crowd. This rumour took hold after John had been seen slipping an open pen-knife from his vest pocket to his boot. As one journalist reported, anything unusual on the part of the Makins was likely to lead to sensationalism and he suggested the truth was more mundane—that he had been hiding the pen-knife so he could cut up tobacco while in prison and feared it would be found on him.

A doctor's mysterious evidence

As the inquest entered its fifth day, matters became more and more mysterious when Dr Alfred Agassiz took the stand. He was a doctor who advertised in the local papers, telling prospective patients that he gave 'advice and Medicine' for two shillings and six pence and boasting he had practised at the Royal Infirmary, Edinburgh and the University College Hospital, London.[4]

Dr Agassiz testified that a Mrs Helbi attended his rooms at 603 George Street with a very sick female child about two months old sometime between the end of July and the middle of August.[5] The child was suffering from diarrhoea and marasmus. The surname Helbi was the name of Sarah's married daughter, Minnie. When Mrs Helbi was called into the courtroom, Dr Agassiz gave the contradictory evidence that 'he was almost certain that she had been to him for advice' although he could not swear it nor 'connect her with the child'. Even more strangely he did not recognise any of the Makins in court. When asked about the cause of marasmus, Dr Agassiz said starvation was the 'most potent agent' while 'the diarrhoea could be caused by improper food or by food that could not be assimilated'.

He testified that the child had suffered from marasmus for about two weeks when he first saw it on Monday 8 August. This suggests that the Makins had begun starving Baby Mignonette around the end of July, which coincides with the last date on which they saw another mother in Burren Street, Agnes Todd, on 31 July. As we will see below, by this date it was becoming apparent the Makins needed to cut their losses and run. Any excess babies would now need to be disposed of.

When Minnie Helbi was recalled to give evidence she testified she had never seen Dr Agassiz 'until to-day' and had not visited his rooms with a child. She had also never visited 25 Burren Street nor seen Minnie Davies' child. Despite her denials, Dr Agassiz's recognition of Minnie suggests she was involved in her mother's baby-farming business. Her home was a place of refuge when Sarah knew the police were waiting for her in Wells Street. She was also one of the people to whom Sarah turned when she wanted to get rid of babies' clothing. But without conclusive identification from Dr Agassiz that she had brought the starving baby to see him, her denials protected her.

The court then heard from the Registrar of Births, Deaths and Marriages for the district of Newtown. At Constable Joyce's request, Mr Newman had searched the register for the death of an infant by the surname of Makin, or from Burren Street, from 11 July 1892 onwards. No such record was found.

The Coroner informed the jury that seven bodies in total had been found in the backyard of 25 Burren Street. He decided to call all the witnesses who had given evidence in the first two inquests so that the jury could consider whether or not Babies A or B could be Miss Davies' child. The bored court reporters probably shuffled and rearranged themselves on the unforgiving wooden benches in the court before taking an afternoon nap as the inquest 'dragged wearily on' under the stewardship of the colony's thorough and obsessive Coroner.

When Edward Jordan, John Makin's former cell-mate at Newtown police station, returned to give evidence, he revealed a little more of John's confession, claiming John had told him:

> When my daughters made that statement at Newtown Station I
> knew I was gone—me and the old woman—they knew no better.
> They'll have me for perjury and illegally burying; but no doctor can
> say I poisoned them because I never went to a chemist for anything.

As Makin left the cell the next morning he apparently told Jordan, 'Don't say anything to anybody about what I have been speaking to you'. These admissions were particularly damaging because they revealed John's guilty knowledge and that, as a guilty man, he was weighing up his options. Although it appears he was responsible for burying the seven babies, had he actually murdered them?

Miss Todd and her 'painful position'

Agnes Todd was typical of the women who produced illegitimate children in the late 1800s, most of whom were unmarried domestic servants aged about 25 or younger.[6] Although Agnes had given evidence at the inquest into the death of Baby 1, she revealed much more about her relationship with the Makins at this inquest. She told the court she had nursed her baby, Elsie May, for three months but was eventually forced to hand her over to Mrs Sutherland, a midwife, who nursed her for another three months for a fee.

Agnes had employed Mrs Sutherland to look after Baby Elsie since she had to earn a living and her baby was 'in her road'.[7] Because payments to Mrs Sutherland had become a drain on Agnes' small income, she placed an advertisement in *The Evening News* on Friday, 25 June 1892 seeking someone to adopt her baby but using the name and address of an acquaintance rather than her own:

> Wanted, a kind lady to adopt a baby girl at once, small premium.
> Alice, 48 McCauley-street, Leichhardt.

Agnes received a reply on Monday 27 June from Mr J Leslie at 109 George Street, Redfern. She visited the same day and was shown into the house by Mr Leslie, who introduced his wife. Agnes identified Sarah and John Makin in the courtroom as the people she met that day, as well as Daisy.

John conducted the negotiations, suggesting his control over the baby-farming business. He told Agnes 'he was willing to take the baby and adopt it for life', assuring her he would be a good father, that her child would be well looked after and she could visit when she liked. Sarah played her part by telling Agnes she was very fond of children and was keen to be a mother to her child. Agnes must have felt relieved because here was a couple who said what she needed to hear.

When asked about the premium, Agnes offered £3, probably all that she could afford on an annual wage of less than £20, the typical income of a domestic servant in Sydney in the 1890s. But it was enough to satisfy the Makins. The terms of the deal were very clear, with John writing an agreement which Agnes signed immediately, taking no time to think it over.

When Agnes was not able to pay the full amount, the officious Mr Leslie noted on the bottom of the agreement: 'Received on account £2; in full, £1—all dues and demands £3—J.H.L.'. The next day, one day before the Makins moved to Burren Street, Clarice collected Elsie May from Mrs Sutherland's house in Phillip Street, Alexandria. Mrs Sutherland was later able to identify some of the clothing found on the Burren Street babies, including a binder that had been wrapped around Elsie May when she was adopted.

The Makins had organised their move to Burren Street before they collected Elsie May, since Agnes visited Burren Street four days later to pay £1 of the premium she still owed. She was directed to number 25 after asking a puzzled Mrs Hill where a man by the name of Leslie lived. At the time, Agnes thought that Elsie looked 'quite well' although she must have expressed some concern because John reassured her: 'You need not be afraid. I will look after the child and it will be well cared for'. When she heard the sound of another baby crying, John, the master of the ad-hoc explanation, told Agnes the baby belonged to his married daughter 'who had gone to the theatre'. When Minnie Helbi was recalled to give evidence, she told the court that although her youngest child was eighteen months old at that time, she had never left it at her mother's house.

Agnes made her second visit to Burren Street on 9 July to pay the remaining £1 she owed. Baby Elsie was still alive. But on her third visit on 31 July, John Makin told her 'they were all out', explaining that his wife and daughters had taken Elsie with them. By this time, Agnes' baby was probably dead. Under Agnes' inquiring gaze, John knew Agnes would return and there were only so many stories that could be invented on the doorstep of chance.

No doubt this is why the peripatetic Makins could not afford to settle in one place. The Makin household was plagued by the baby who cried too much, the weekly visits from her parents and the ongoing visits from Agnes. Other babies in the house had to be kept quiet but the Makins also ran the risk of a certain awkwardness if Agnes met up with Minnie and Horace. This shows how stressful the Makins' lives must have been— scouring the newspapers, writing letters, collecting babies, keeping them quiet, searching for cheap accommodation, evading landlords and mothers, killing, burying, packing and moving.

When Agnes did return, some time after 16 August, the Makins had disappeared. Although Agnes did not suspect anything at the time, it is almost certain that Elsie May was one of the four female babies dug up in the backyard of Burren Street. Elsie was six months old on 28 June when she was delivered into the callous care of the Makins. It is likely she died sometime between 9 and 31 July, before she was despatched to her backyard grave.

Although the Makins had disappeared, this was not the end of Agnes' contact with John. When the newspapers reported the Burren Street discoveries, Agnes wondered if Makin was the man she knew as Mr Leslie. Somehow she tracked him down to 6 Wells Street, Redfern. When John opened the door, he was face to face with the very problem he had always tried to avoid—a concerned mother.

Agnes demanded to know the whereabouts of her baby. Nonplussed, John told her, 'It is alive and well and ... staying with a friend until the case is over'. John's reference to 'alive and well' and 'the case' suggests that Agnes had asked whether Elsie was one of the dead babies discovered in Burren Street. John reassured her he would organise to make her baby available on Tuesday 1 November. But when she returned to Wells Street that day, the Makins had moved.

Coincidentally, when Agnes returned to Wells Street to visit her baby, John 'happened to pass by'. Agnes called out: 'Where is my child you promised to bring her, Mr Makin'. But John had another ready excuse. Mrs Makin was away in Kiama with Elsie but he would bring her for a visit next Saturday to Agnes' live-in situation in Chippendale. Not satis- fied by this third manufactured story, Agnes decided to report her missing baby to the police. Two days later, on 3 November, the Makins were arrested. Agnes must have realised she would never see her child again. Even when she confronted John at the inquest and asked where her child was, he replied he had never seen her before.

After Agnes finished giving her evidence, the Coroner observed that even though she had paid the premium for Elsie's adoption, Agnes continued to visit her baby:

> I think she deserves special consideration for the way she came forward in this case to give her evidence as her position is a very painful one.

The jury thanked the Coroner for mentioning Miss Todd. Hers was indeed a very painful position. She had lost her child and 'outed' herself as an unmarried mother—a brave step for a working-class woman in the 1890s and one that most of the mothers of the Burren Street babies did not take.

Over to the Makins

When all the witnesses for the police had been heard, the Coroner asked Mr Williamson whether his clients would be giving evidence. After a short adjournment, Williamson informed the court he would not be calling the Makins to the witness stand. He probably advised that giving evidence would have been a great risk, since, unlike in previous inquests, the evidence in this one was stacked against them. All they had left was silence to avoid the Coroner's curt and incisive questions. Or a confession that they were indeed baby farmers, an approach that would lead to awkward questions about how seven babies came to be buried in the Burren Street backyard.

The court adjourned until Monday morning to enable the Coroner to review the extensive evidence over the weekend before addressing the jury about their decisions.

The verdict

The Coroner had more than 300 foolscap pages of evidence that he was required to sum up to the jury before they could begin their deliberations about the two questions they had to decide—the identity and cause of death of Baby 4.[8]

The Coroner told the jury that, since the infant was six to eight weeks old at the time of her death and had been buried for 12 to 18 weeks, this evidence tallied with the age and date of death (10 August) of Minnie and Horace's child. Although Minnie had not been able to identify any of the clothing found on Baby 4, the Coroner did not think this was significant since, according to the evidence, 'the clothing was distributed among the children found buried ... at 25 Burren-street, regardless of ownership'.

He was also sure that none of the other six bodies found in Burren Street, because of their sex and ages, could have been the child of Miss Davies. The Coroner reminded the jury that hair from the head of Baby 4 had been identified by Minnie and Horace. If they believed the evidence given by these two witnesses, 'it would not require any strain of reasoning to arrive at the conclusion that No. 4 was identical with Minnie Davies' child'. However, the Coroner did not consider the fact that Baby 5 was the least decomposed of the Burren Street babies, which had led Dr Milford to surmise she was the last baby to be buried. If so, Baby 5, rather than Baby 4, was more likely to have been Mignonette, who was buried sometime between 11 and 16 August, the day the Makins left Burren Street. Miss Davies had also identified the clothing found on Baby 5 as some of the garments she had given to the Makins.

The Coroner thought that the estimated age of Baby 5, 6–14 days, meant she was too young to have been Mignonette. However, Dr Milford's age estimation of Baby 5 may have been inaccurate. He could not have known that some of the babies died from starvation when he examined them. Because she had 'wasted away', Mignonette would not have been the normal size of a two-month-old baby (in the 1890s) when she died.

The cause of death of Baby 4 was harder to ascertain and came down to whether the baby died from deliberate or accidental starvation—'through ignorance, or by wilful and foul means'. Both Dr Milford and Dr Agassiz had been asked about the likelihood of a very young child, separated from its mother, dying from starvation. Both considered it unlikely unless the baby was given unsuitable food by an inexperienced carer.

The Coroner reminded the jury that Mignonette had been strong at birth, thrived on infant formula and 'was by no means a peevish child'. Yet the neighbours in Burren Street heard the child crying constantly. John Makin had told Mr Hill the baby kept him awake all night, using such foul language that the newspapers could not print his words. So awful were his comments, the Coroner remarked, 'no man with a spark of manliness in him would use such language in reference to a little child. It indicated a brutal and cruel nature'.

The Coroner was satisfied that the baby seen by Dr Agassiz was the child of Minnie Davies and that she was suffering from dysenteric dia- rrhoea and marasmus. So severe was the malnutrition that Dr Agassiz had described the child as 'a mere bag of bones'. Dr Milford had said that if a child 'in the last stage of emaciation suffering from dysenteric diar- rhoea' subsequently died, he would conclude it died from starvation. If the jurymen believed this evidence, said the Coroner, they had to decide if the Makins had deliberately starved the child, particularly since they had brought up a family of their own and 'could not possibly be ignorant' about how to care for a young baby.

Suddenly, an unforeseen legal door opened—a possibility the Makins could not have imagined. If they had known about this law they would never have agreed to take in a baby to nurse for a weekly fee. Because the Makins had signed a contract with Minnie Davies to care for her child for ten shillings per week, the Coroner said they had a duty to protect the life imposed by the contract, according to the *Coroners Act*. Failure to do so amounted to either murder or manslaughter. Under such a contract, any person taking custody of someone who is helpless and who is not provided with food, or is provided with insufficient amounts of food, was guilty of murder.

The Coroner was also concerned by the number of lies told by the Makins: if they had not 'wilfully cause[d] the child's death, why did they tell so many lies about it, and cause their children … to lie about it?' The Coroner listed the Makins' many lies—they had acquired Baby Mignon- ette the day after they moved to Burren Street (rather than in George Street); the parents had collected the child before moving to Melbourne; the

Makins said they would register the death of Mignonette and pay for her burial; that an undertaker had taken the child away; and the Makins' use of false names when presenting themselves to Minnie and Horace. Added to this long list was the Makins' hurried departure from that residence, all of which combined to show they had something to hide, especially when an innocent person would not 'jeopardise their liberty ... by withholding evidence that would clear them'. Their motive for starving Baby Mignonette, said the Coroner, was to obtain the payment of ten shillings for long enough to concoct the child's illness and to acquire a sum of money for its burial with further monies obtained from pawning the baby's clothing.

The Coroner also wondered whether Baby Mignonette, kept clean and apparently cared for, was used to allay any suspicions the neighbours would have had from hearing babies cry or seeing baby clothes drying in the backyard—as if this baby had been used 'as a kind of stalking-horse' to hide the Makins' real business.

He reminded the jury that if they were satisfied the death of Baby 4 had been wilfully caused by Sarah and John, they could return a verdict of wilful murder. As to Florence and Blanche, the Coroner decided the case against them was different, '[p]ossibly [because] their mouths had been shut by their parents'.

Just before the jury retired, the Coroner's outrage increased as he announced that these inquests had revealed 'crimes of the deepest dye' which were 'a scandalous disgrace to a civilized community and would be an enduring blot on the fair fame of this city'. Pointedly, he told the jury that if there was a failure of justice in this case it 'would be a national calamity' but he 'trusted justice would be done'. He hoped this case 'would put a stop to the chances of any further ghastly discoveries, and that it would increase the vigilance of the police' as well as 'every man, woman and child in this country'.

With these final pleas, the Coroner had lost his impartiality. When Mr Williamson rose to make a request, the Coroner interrupted:

Mr Williamson: Well, your Worship, before the jury retires direct—

Coroner:	I will say no more.
Mr Williamson:	I was going to say—
Coroner:	Will you sit down, sir.
Mr Williamson:	Perhaps your Worship will listen to me first.
Coroner:	Sit down, sir! Sit down, sir!
Mr Williamson:	Surely your Worship will not manifest an autocratic position?
Coroner:	Will you sit down, sir?
Mr Williamson:	Oh well, if you will not listen to me, it can't be helped.

Armed with 333 foolscap pages of evidence and a book of Coroner's Instructions, the jury retired to consider their verdict at 10.41 a.m. on the morning of Monday 28 November 1892. Quick and efficient, 65 minutes later they sent word they had reached a verdict, an ominous sign. As the jurymen filed into the court, Sarah moaned, quite agitated. When the foreman stood, the Coroner asked:

Coroner:	Have the jury agreed upon a verdict, Mr Foreman?
Foreman:	Yes, Your Worship.
Coroner:	What is the verdict in inquest number 1252/92?
Foreman:	We find that the infant No 4 is identical with the child of Minnie Davies and Horace Bothamley; we further find John and Sarah Makin guilty of manslaughter. We find that there is not sufficient evidence before us to connect Blanche and Florence Makin with a guilty knowledge.

The Coroner had pushed for a verdict of murder. The jury had baulked. Manslaugher as a result of neglect was a more cautious verdict. Mr Williamson regained his feet and, like a bothersome child, pleaded with the Coroner about the jury's failure to refer to marasmus as the cause of death. But the Coroner, like a father pushed to his limits, shouted him down:

Coroner:	Will you sit down, sir?
Mr Williamson:	But, your Worship, I would like to point out to the jury—
Coroner:	Sit down, sir; will you sit down when I tell you.
Mr Williamson:	But, I am in duty bound—
Coroner:	You are not in duty bound at all.
Mr Williamson:	I am in duty bound—
Coroner:	Sit down, sir! Sit down!
Mr Williamson:	To point out that the jury never said anything about marasmus …
Coroner:	Will you sit down, sir, or will you drive me to extremes?

While Mr Williamson collected himself, humiliated but defiant, the Coroner asked the jury whether they wanted to have their verdict altered, to which the foreman replied no.[9] Satisfied that he had won the day, the Coroner ordered John and Sarah to rise as he committed them to stand trial at the Criminal Court in Darlinghurst for the manslaughter of Miss Davies' child.

Blanche and Florence were now free. Blanche cried out and hugged her sister, the emotion of it all overwhelming poor Florence, who fainted. Sarah slumped in her seat, raising her hands and announcing, 'Heaven forfend this day!' The constables rushed to assist Florence while Blanche moaned 'piteously'. As Blanche escorted Florence out of court, she cried out, 'God help my poor mother' but Sarah declared:

> Don't cry my child. There's a God in heaven and I will get justice in a higher court. I will get justice … Oh, why didn't they tell the truth? Oh, oh, God forgive them. God forgive them. Oh, they will kill me.

With outstretched arms, she stood and fell to the floor in a faint, although she was rapidly revived with a bit of sprinkled water. Was Sarah's statement the product of real distress or make-believe? Out of all the witnesses, who had not told the truth? Minnie or Horace? Clarice? Agnes Todd?

John was the only family member to remain unaffected by the verdict. He continued his 'air of nonchalance' and talked and joked with the police constables in court 'as if he had not the slightest trouble on his mind'. He may even have found it amusing when Mr Williamson attempted to enter the lion's den one more time:

Mr Williamson: At this stage, Mr. Coroner I will ask for bail.
Coroner: Certainly not ...
Mr Williamson: [T]hey are entitled—
Coroner: I have a discretion and I intend to use it. I distinctly refuse bail.

But there were more surprises in store. When the Makins were returned to Central police station, fresh charges were laid by Captain Fisher, who charged Sarah and John with having caused the death of the illegitimate child of a Miss Amber Murray on or about 27 June last. Even more surprisingly, Blanche and Florence, who thought they were free, were charged 'on suspicion with having been concerned in causing the death of' that child and rearrested.[10] Bail was not allowed and they returned, a distressed family, to Darlinghurst Gaol.

Constable Joyce's obsessions had more than paid off. But who was Miss Amber Murray?

❧

The obsessions of James Joyce: digging, redigging and more digging
9–14 November 1892

On Tuesday 9 November 1892 there 'were some fresh and sensational developments' in relation to the 'mysterious MacDonaldtown discoveries' when Senior Constable Joyce ordered his constables to take their picks and shovels to Redfern. He had continued his obsessive investigations during the Burren Street inquests, 'not sparing either time or labour' to gather more evidence to prosecute the Makins. As he began to realise that the Makins had been baby farming for much longer than he originally thought, he tracked down all the previous addresses of the Makins for the past two years. Because this particular Tuesday in November was a public holiday, it was 'considered a good day to re-commence digging operations' since the police hoped there would be enough locals 'holiday-making' so they could dig in peace. Joyce selected the two addresses that had been most recently occupied by the Makins.[1]

The house at 55 Botany Street was the first in a terrace of eight houses known as Smith's Terrace about two minutes' walk from Redfern police station. The Makins had relocated there on 16 August after their hurried departure from Burren Street. Oddly enough, they left about ten days later after the landlord gave the Makins notice to quit.

When Constables Brown and Griffin arrived at 55 Botany Street, they found the backyard had been recently bricked over and decided if there had been any buried babies, their remains would have been discovered by the workmen. Upon hearing this news, Joyce sent his men to the house the Makins had lived in just before moving to Burren Street. Number 109 George Street, Redfern was a roomy, 'pleasant-looking cottage of a kind suited for a workman in receipt of good wages'. Located next to the post office which backed onto Redfern Court, it was just one door up from the Redfern police station. At the time, the cottage was owned by Mr Jacob Fischer, although it no longer exists today.

Joyce and the Redfern police had previously inspected the backyard, with the permission of the new tenant, Mr Ralph, who, coincidentally, was the assistant stationmaster at Macdonaldtown. Mrs Ralph told the police that when she and her family moved in she had 'noticed almost immediately ... a most offensive odour proceeding from the back yard' which she put down to bad drainage.

The backyard was divided 'into two unequal parts by a substantial iron-railed fence'. As soon as Joyce entered the backyard he pointed to the section closest to the house, which had once been a garden enclosed by the wall of the kitchen, the fence of the next door neighbour and the iron-railed fence, and declared: 'If we find anything it will be there'. He reckoned that if there were any bodies they would be found here because it was the most concealed spot from the neighbours and the earth was soft enough for digging.

Not long after the digging started on this wet November day, the first body was found, a badly decomposed baby wrapped in a red and black shawl with a small slit on the side of its skull. Despite the public holiday, a crowd of about 200 people had gathered to see the baby extracted from a grave about eighteen inches deep. The clamour and chatter were deafening as more digging in a corner of the garden uncovered two more bodies, well wrapped together in a piece of black shawl with square patterns on it.

While these three bodies were transported to the South Sydney morgue, the police continued to dig in the heat and the 'indescribable' stench as they tried to keep the sightseers from overrunning the yard. They found nothing else in the enclosed garden. Perhaps it was the tenant of the house, Mrs Ralph, who then produced a bottle of disinfectant which was liberally splashed around to 'keep down the smell'. As the police paused, sweating in their heavy woollen uniforms, 'the idea occurred to ... Joyce to dig up the beaten path which ran along the side of the back kitchen', which was the most concealed spot from the neighbours. Without knowing it, Joyce had made a momentous decision that would cement the fate of the Makins and change the course of legal history.

It was just underneath the kitchen window that he found a fourth body wrapped in 'some gray stuff and white calico'. Although the digging continued until five o'clock no more bodies were found, while the Ralphs had to deal with the excited sightseers who did not disperse until well into the evening.

These discoveries meant that 11 dead babies had been found in the back-yards of two houses lived in by the Makins. Joyce was struck by the fact that the bodies found in Burren and George streets had all been wrapped 'in the same manner and buried at about the same depth, something under 2ft'. Although the backyard at 109 George Street had a rear entrance, Joyce supposed that 'if persons living elsewhere buried the infants ... they would not choose the spot nearest the house'.

The dig at George Street gave Joyce renewed impetus. On the morning of 10 November, Constables Brown and Griffin were ordered by Joyce to return to 55 Botany Street. Although they dug up the brick paving in that backyard for over an hour with a growing crowd pushing into the yard, no bodies were found. Joyce was undeterred. He ordered his constables to visit 2 Kettle Street, where the Makins had lived for about three months from January to May 1892. They found 'most of the yard had been asphalted' and was 'hard as adamant'. Instead, the constables dug up a piece of adjacent land where the Makins had been in the habit of depositing their rubbish. No bodies were found there or in a nearby house at 16 East Street.

Dissatisfied with his constables' work, Joyce decided to go over old ground. In East Street he 'turned out the contents of a woodshed and tore up the ground' and ordered his constables to drive 'their picks into nearly every inch of the hard footpaths'. When nothing was found, they trooped back to 55 Botany Street, under the obsessive eye of Joyce, who ordered them to search outside the backyard in a right of way and a deserted stable. Still there was no sign of dead babies.

Like a starving man, Joyce was unfulfilled but he had to call it quits. He was now required at the South Sydney morgue where the post-mortems on the George Street babies were about to be held. But the one place Joyce had not thought to dig was the nearby Redfern Park, an obvious place for late night burials.

Hunches and dividends: the excitement in Levey Street

Digging resumed the next morning, on Thursday 11 November, at 11 Alderson Street, a narrow thoroughfare off Kettle Street close to Redfern Park. The street consisted of a row of single-storey cottages, 'chiefly occupied by Assyrians and other coloured people'.[2] The Makins had lived in a three-roomed cottage at number 11 for less than two months from 7 December 1891 to 28 January 1892 according to Mr Illsley of 59 Alderson Street, who let the house to the Makins. Although the yard at number 11 'was almost completely open to the view' of neighbours, Constable Griffin discovered the body of an infant wrapped in a piece of black cloth at a depth of two or three feet. Joyce's hunches were paying dividends.

When the body was examined by Dr Milford, it was covered in adipocere which, mixed with soil, had the consistency of mortar. After an examination of the skeleton, Dr Milford estimated that the child, called Baby E, was between two and six weeks old when it died, but was unable to give a cause of death or determine its sex.[3] The presence of grave wax that is hard and crumbly indicates that Baby E had undergone rapid decomposition—something that is more likely to occur if it was buried in summer. This supposition coincides with the time the Makins were living in Alderson Street—the summer of 1891–92—and is supported by Dr Milford's estimation that the child had been dead 6–12 months.

Never before had the newspapers had so many gruesome details to report since '[a]lmost every day some new development of a horrifying character is brought to light by the efforts of the police in connection with the great baby-farming case'. The next new development was the dig at 28 Levey Street, Chippendale two days later, on 13 November.[4]

After re-examining the backyard of Burren Street, where they failed to find the eighth body John Makin had confessed to Edward Jordan,

Constables Joyce and Brown made their way to Levey Street, undeterred by the overcast and muggy weather. The Makins had lived in Levey Street for about six or seven weeks in the second half of 1891. The house was a two-storey terrace with about five rooms, standing in a row of other similar houses next door to the Appin Hotel. It still stands today. Like most of the streets in which the Makins lived, Levey Street was 'occupied by houses of an inferior class, which are let to persons of humble means'. Named 'Redfern' and 'Chippendale' after the original landholders,[5] these inner city suburbs had developed to provide housing for workers in the railway workshops and other local industries.[6] By 1858, the housing was described as 'a shocking sight', consisting of 'two long continuous rows of weatherboard cottages' which were 'filthy' and 'uniformly abominable throughout'.[7]

The street in which the Makins had lived was named after Solomon Levey, an ex-convict who had been transported to Sydney in 1815 to serve a seven year sentence as an accessory to the theft of 90 pounds of tea and a wooden chest. His transportation was the making of him, since Levey prospered as a storekeeper, shipbroker and agent so that by 1825 he claimed a turnover of £60,000 a year.[8] As one of Sydney's early and successful entrepreneurs with a shrewd economic mind, Levey would have understood the market economy the Makins were engaged in but possibly not the cruelty of the baby trade.

The new tenant of 28 Levey Street, Mr Rivers, had approached the police after reading about the 'Mysterious Discoveries' in Burren Street and because he had noticed unpleasant odours coming from his backyard for some time. This was something neighbours had also noticed when the Makins were in residence: 'horrible odors were always noticed about the place, and anyone who went into [the] house was in the habit of remarking on the disagreeable smell in the kitchen'.

Constables Joyce and Brown arrived in a police van from Burren Street shortly before four o'clock in light, drizzling rain. They found a backyard that was surrounded by 'an ordinary paling fence' and 'open to observation, except near the kitchen wall' where it was more concealed. Experience had shown Joyce that the best place to find a body was in an area of soft ground hidden from the view of neighbours.

Despite the rain, 'as soon as the news spread that the police were digging', a large crowd 'flocked to the scene', climbing fences and neighbours' vegetables gardens, 'determined to obtain a glimpse of what was going on':

> [t]he fences and outhouses were literally black with people, and
> many climbed on to the roofs of houses which overlooked the yard
> in their endeavours to see what was going on.

Supplied with the 'necessary implements' by the tenant of 28 Levey Street, the two constables 'set to work' in the midst of the chattering crowd as theories and opinions were swapped and crucial information, such as the fact that two babies had been in the care of the Makins during their stay in Levey Street, was shared.

At about 5 p.m. '[s]uddenly a halt was made'. The onlookers craned forward. After digging near the kitchen wall, Joyce removed something from the ground. When the crowd realised the police had unearthed the bones of an infant the excitement intensified with 'men and boys nearly tumbl[ing] off the roofs in their eagerness' to see. But 'hardly had the spade been put into the ground again when, at the same spot, immediately underneath, another parcel of bones was found'. By the time the bodies were discovered, the crowd had broken down the paling fence. As they surged through, the shouts of surprise and revenge probably drowned out the stentorian voices of the police, with the noise and the rain and the awful discoveries turning the afternoon into an unpleasant suburban rabble.

Both bodies had been buried together at a depth of two feet and were the most decomposed found so far, consisting of skeletal remains only, although one still had hair attached to the skull. While bodies buried at a depth of two feet or more generally decompose slowly because of low temperatures, lack of oxygen and insect activity, a burial during the summer of December 1891, when the Makins were in residence in Levey Street, would have speeded up the decomposition process. The bodies were wrapped in badly degraded cloth which 'fell to pieces when handled'. While the police went on to dig the whole of the backyard to a depth of two feet no other bodies were found. One newspaper reported that this depth was greater than any of the other burials found so far so that 'it is probable that had any of the infants been placed at that depth in the ground at [any] other house' they may have been missed by the police.[9]

When Dr Milford examined the remains at the morgue, he found a box containing 'greyish sandy soil, debris of wood, stone and glass, with bones' and a piece of rotting blanket. He separated out the bones of a sheep and pieced together 'portions of two skeletons' which were called G and H. Baby G had a clean cut fracture to one of the skull bones, although this could have been the result of the police digging.

The depth of burial and the fact that only skeletal remains were discovered fitted Dr Milford's estimated time of burial of 9–14 months. The femurs of Baby G were measured at 3⅛ of an inch while those of Baby H were three inches in length. These measurements allowed Dr Milford to estimate that Baby G was aged about six months and Baby H from three to ten weeks at the time of their deaths, although he could not determine their sex.[10]

After the constables had finished digging the backyard of 28 Levey Street, neighbours told them they were confident that 'if the floorboards were removed more bodies would be found'. They also revealed that the day after the Makins left 28 Levey Street, children broke in and wandered through the empty house. In an upstairs bedroom they found a little parcel. One of them took it home to her mother who unwrapped the bloodstained calico to find five long, very fine, rusty needles which were too long and fine for sewing. Because the neighbour saw nothing sinister in the package, she put the needles aside and they were eventually lost. This discovery would later form the basis of Joyce's theory about how the Makins murdered their baby-farmed children.

When Constable Joyce raised some of the floorboards of the kitchen of the Levey Street house, he found nothing but dead rats along with bones and rubbish collected by the rats, all of which accounted for the smell coming from the house. No more babies' bodies were found in Levey Street, or during another dig at 113 Bullanaming Street, Redfern where the Makins had lived for five or six weeks some time in 1889.[11] Although Constable Joyce also dug up the backyard of 6 Wells Street, where he had first interviewed the Makins, he made no additional discoveries.

An awkward number

At the end of Joyce's obsessive, six days of digging, including Burren Street, a total of 12 bodies had been discovered, although one body was later found to be sheep bones. Together with the two babies who had been dug up by the drain-layers in Burren Street, 13 dead babies had been discovered since that October day in Macdonaldtown when the Makins' lives began to unravel. All up, the discoveries represented 'the biggest system … of baby-murdering operations that had ever been carried on in the colony'.[12]

This total does not include another decomposed baby found by a passer-by in a vacant allotment in Zamia Street, Redfern. The male child, who was about two weeks old and had been dead for some days, was suspected to 'have been disinterred from the backyard of the Makins' house in Wells street'.[13] If this was the case, the disinterment occurred just after Joyce's first visit to the Makins on 12 October. Joyce had taken a look around 6 Wells Street the day he returned to interview Sarah and found a hole in the backyard. Although empty, he was struck by the smell of death emanating from it. The neighbours had seen him 'taking up handfuls of earth … and smelling the earth, and much amusement was created' at the sight of Joyce's strange behaviour. When questioned, Makin gave the excuse that he had buried something which 'the dogs must have uprooted'.[14]

Joyce was convinced the Zamia Street baby was associated with the Makins, since he had been 'wrapped up in a manner' similar to Babies A and B (of Burren Street). Agnes Todd and Mrs Sutherland were able to identify some of the clothing on the baby as that worn by Baby Elsie when she was adopted by the Makins.

It is a short walk from Wells Street to Zamia Street, Redfern. Shorter at night, when a person is in a hurry with a small bundle under his arm, carrying a shovel. Perhaps it was before Constable Joyce had interviewed her that Sarah, in a panic, had ordered John to get rid of the baby buried in the backyard. Sometime on the evening of 12 October 1892, John dug up the dead infant in the backyard of Wells Street, breathing through his mouth as the smell of death deepened. He was in a hurry, guilt-edged with Sarah's panic. Not thinking clearly, he forgot to fill in the burial hole as Sarah worried about where to hide the body.

John walked to the end of Wells Street with his smelly parcel, turned right into Chalmers then left into Redfern Street. With few gas lights, he was well camouflaged by the shadows. He stopped as he turned right into Zamia Street, where not even a rat hissed. He quickly scraped a shallow grave in a vacant lot with the shovel, unlike the deep graves he had previously dug. Close to the surface, the grave sent a strong, odorous invitation to local dogs, since the discovery was reported to the police the day after Joyce interviewed Sarah.[15]

It is very likely there were other babies who were never discovered by the police. Although Constable Joyce thought he knew the Makins' pattern of disposal, the Makins are likely to have used a variety of places. While Joyce had lifted floorboards in the Levey Street house, the canny Makins appear to have dug graves under other floorboards when they ran out of space in a particular backyard, as another inquest would later reveal.

Although Joyce told newspaper reporters he intended to visit all the Makins' former houses going back five or six years, no more digging took place because Joyce thought it was only in the last twelve months that they had engaged in 'suspicious operations'. What Joyce did not know was that the peripatetic Makins had relocated frequently between 1884 and 1888, suggesting a family who was either evading rent or anxious mothers.

Snapshot of a baby farmer

The bodies discovered in Burren and George streets provide a snapshot of the Makins' activities over a twelve week period. During this time they had at least ten babies in their care. If they were adopting about one baby per week this could mean they were adopting about 50 children per year. Some weeks may have been more lucrative than others. From 23 to 27 June they adopted four babies (for a total of £7 10s) which allowed them to pay four weeks' rent in advance when they leased 25 Burren Street.

The Makins had been baby farming since at least 1889. A former neighbour told police that when the Makins 'cleared out of a house in Redfern' in 1889, they left a baby behind whom the neighbour took to the Benevolent Asylum.[16] Because the Makins' house-moving increased in frequency from 1889 to 1892, it is likely they were constantly avoiding inquisitive mothers rather than avoiding the payment of rent. If so, they could have adopted at least 150 babies during this three year period. But how did the babies die?

Because Minnie Davies and Horace Bothamley reported no sounds of crying babies when they visited Burren Street, the Makins must have drugged their babies using Godfrey's Cordial. Miss Davies had testified that on one of her visits to Burren Street, the Makins had given her daughter a mixture which soothed and stopped her crying. The Makins would have been well aware of the effects of too much opium on babies and the varying concentrations of different chemists' mixtures.

We know from the outcome of the inquest into the death of Baby Mignonette that the Makins were found responsible for starving her. At the George Street inquests, we will hear from another mother who will give evidence that her baby was thin and hungry when she saw her child, suggesting that underfeeding, along with liberal doses of Godfrey's Cordial, was, as for most baby farmers, part of the Makins' repertoire. Yet Constable Joyce had a different theory which was based on the discovery of bloodstains on the wrappings of one of the infants found buried in George Street. These bloodstains were on the left hand side, near the armpit and the baby's heart. Similar stains had been found on the wrappings of Baby 2 (of Burren Street). These bloodstains and the discovery of a packet of long, fine needles in the Makins' empty house in Levey Street had confirmed for Joyce his 'theory that death was caused ... by a large needle being driven through the heart from the left side'.[17] A doctor had told a reporter that if such a long needle were to pierce the heart, death would not result immediately. The very small outside wound would probably close and the children would die a lingering death from a slow internal haemorrhage.[18] Perhaps this was the final act causing death when the Makins found it necessary to quickly dispose of their drugged, underfed babies as they prepared for another late night move.

❦

CHAPTER FIFTEEN

Mothers, mothers everywhere: the George Street inquests begin
12 November–16 December 1892

Sydneysiders were in for more excitement and intrigue with the beginning of yet another set of inquests after Constable Joyce's busy day of digging at 109 George Street. The Burren Street inquests had lasted 14 days with 26 witnesses and 453 sheets of evidence being faithfully written down by an exhausted clerk of the court.[1] If the government had been able to charge for seats in the Coroner's Court, they would have made a tidy sum.

At the George Street inquests, the public's fascination with the Makins turned to ridicule as they were escorted, handcuffed and herded between their police guards, from the Coroner's Court at Chancery Square across Hyde Park to Central police station at the end of each day, with crowds heckling, gawking and throwing bits of rotten food. Once so cavalier and untouchable, the Makins were now the subjects of a ditty that mocked them:

> *Big Constables James and Brown*
> *Went to Macdonaldtown*
> *Many babies there were found*
> *Buried underneath the ground.*
> *What will Mother Makin say*
> *On Resurrection day*
> *When those kids rise up and say*
> *Ta-ra-ra, ta-boom-dee-ay.*[2]

Before the George Street inquests commenced, Constables Joyce and Brown had been 'out all hours of the night hunting up witnesses'. Joyce took evidence from more than twenty, as well as five unmarried mothers who said they had given their children to the Makins. One of these babies was Horace Amber Murray, who was born on 30 May 1892 to 18-year-old Miss Amber Murray. When Miss Murray asked John about her baby in the courtroom, he shook his head and replied, 'I will let you know that when I get in the witness box'. Each unmarried mother would experience highs and lows during the inquests and some would learn what had happened to her child. For others, their only comfort was seeing the Makins trapped for all to see in the dock of the King Street court.

At the South Sydney morgue on Saturday, 13 November 1892, the Coroner opened the inquest into the deaths of the four babies found in the backyard of 109 George Street the previous Tuesday, who were called Babies A, B, C and D.[3] Two of the babies were male and one was female while the sex of the fourth was unknown. All were in a similar state of decomposition, which seemed to confirm that receiving babies for 'adoption' was a regular practice of the Makins.

The same 12 jurymen from the Burren Street inquests were sworn in. Sarah and John along with their two daughters were present at the morgue, all in police custody, for an unpleasant start to a third lot of inquests. The Makins knew the tightly spun ball of their secret lives had unravelled with babies, long dead, being dug up at an alarming rate. But they made no further statements to the police. Perhaps nearly two months in Darlinghurst Gaol had convinced them that silence was their only defence. Silence, hope and the vagaries of circumstantial evidence. They must have wondered whether it would be enough.

'A great sensation'

The first George Street inquest was quick and uncontroversial, if a little peculiar, since Dr Milford gave evidence that Baby A was actually a pile of sheep bones.[4]

The second George Street inquest was much more interesting for the hungry spectators in the court. This inquest concerned the death of Baby B, a female, whose body had been discovered on 9 November wrapped in a shawl along with the pile of sheep bones. According to Dr Milford, she had died between two and six weeks of age, discarded with the leftovers of the Makins' family meal.[5]

During this inquest, Clarice Makin made another star appearance as a witness for the police. Almost immediately, her mother began to moan 'and fell helpless on her husband's shoulder' while Constable Joyce gave her a glass of water to revive her. Sarah spent the rest of the morning with her face buried in her handkerchief, resting on John's shoulder.

Clarice identified the tweed material that had been found wrapped around Baby B as part of a shawl belonging to her mother. She had last seen it in George Street about a month before her parents moved to Burren Street. At the time she saw the shawl her mother was caring for four babies, two girls and two boys, although one of the female babies had disappeared before they left for Burren Street. Clarice did not know what became of it.

Under questioning by the Coroner, Clarice then revealed the sensational evidence, amid 'mutterings of surprise' in the courtroom, that there had been *six* babies in the house at George Street who were all alive when her parents left for 25 Burren Street.[6] Clarice recalled seeing Miss Amber Murray at the George Street house. Horace Amber Murray became the sixth child in the house. This evidence contradicted Clarice's previous statement at the inquest into the death of Baby 4 (of Burren Street) when she said only two babies had been taken by her parents to Macdonaldtown. Under cross-examination by Mr Williamson, she explained she had said two because Constable Joyce had only asked about two babies. Although Clarice denied the suggestion that she and Joyce had discussed the evidence she would give at *this* inquest, what encouragement had Joyce given her?

More cracks in the cone of silence

Even though she could only read 'a little', Clarice read over the handwritten transcript of her evidence, and left the court on the receiving end of the 'most insulting jeers' from her whole family. Panicked by Clarice's evidence, 'a violent scene' occurred between the Makin family 'who appear[ed] to be divided amongst themselves'. As the court adjourned for lunch, Makin joked with the constables 'about some wax figures that he heard were being exhibited as the Makin family', ignoring Sarah, who was crying to herself, muttering, 'Oh let me die, let me die'. Blanche began to abuse her father, at first inaudibly, then 'with great vehemence she accused him of being the cause of all the trouble that they were in'. She rose to her feet and exclaimed:

Why don't you look after mother. You take it very cool, you do.

She then let fly about all the injustices she felt:

we have been here six weeks for nothing. They charged us with killing Murray's child, and I told them I did not know anything about it. And yet Florrie and I have to sit here and listen to the lies told by that girl who has just been in the box. I was taken away from my work, and have got no decent clothes. I have to come here in these rags, all through you. Why should they keep us here. We have told enough lies to screen you ... and it's through telling these lies that we are here. You ought to be ashamed of yourself. You're no father.

Blanche then 'completely broke down'. John's reaction was a revelation. Rather than the jocular story-teller, the reassuring adoptive father or the impassive, silent figure in court, his face, 'as he listened to the violent denunciation of his daughter, was the picture of rage' and it even appeared at one stage as if he would strike Blanche as he met her accusations 'with defiant jeers': 'Shut your mouth, girl, shut your mouth!'.

But Blanche was not finished as she accused her father, 'This is all through Mother Robinson putting you up to it. If you had not known her we would not have been put to all this trouble and wouldn't be here'. With a few more jibes she gradually calmed down as the constables intervened. Sarah 'cried and groaned in a dreadful fashion', appealing to heaven to witness the lies told by Clarice, while Florence 'buried her face in her pocket-handkerchief'. Mrs Makin, who had grown much thinner during her time in gaol and was very weak, had to be assisted out of the courtroom by her daughters.

Blanche's denunciations suggest that John was the ringleader of the baby-farming business, exploiting and relying on Sarah's mothering skills as well as those of his daughters to give the appearance of a suitable home for unwanted babies. But who Mother Robinson was and why she would put John 'up to it' is an intriguing mystery. Did he owe her money? Another newspaper reported that Blanche accused *Clarice* of 'having been "put up to this by Mother Robinson"'. Had Mother Robinson persuaded Clarice to give evidence as a form of payback? For some reason, John did not want this information revealed in public. Perhaps he was involved in other shady activities which he did not want his Wollongong family to know about.

The landlord and the rent collector

After lunch, Mr Jacob Fischer, the landlord of 109 George Street, told the court the Makins had leased his house on 21 May in the name of Mason and paid two weeks' rent. When the Makins moved into 109 George Street on the night of 23 May, they did not have far to go, since they were living at 16 East Street, Redfern, one block away, where they had resided for only three weeks. Mysteriously, they were on the move again.

Jacob Fischer testified that by 15 June the Makins were already in arrears with the rent so he sent his son to collect the outstanding amount. When that was unsuccessful, he visited the premises himself. Mr Fischer claimed there was no answer when he knocked on the door. It is easy to imagine the Makins waiting, still and silent, for the rap, rap, rap on the front door to cease before they could creep out of hiding. But they had not been quiet enough. When he heard whispering inside, Mr Fischer walked in through the open door. It was then that John Makin appeared and asked him out onto the verandah, perhaps concocting the first excuse that came into his head with his crafty, story-telling ways.

The landlord's son, Herman Fischer, was the rent collector who testified that five weeks after the Makins moved in, he arrived to collect the rent but found the house open and empty. His evidence supported the Makins' story that they had left George Street because of unpaid rent. What Herman did not know were the other, more urgent reasons for the Makins' sudden departure which had been planned some days before. Paying Mr Fischer his unpaid rent would have been a waste of the Makins' tight resources.

Clara Risby's 'delicate' child

The first mother to give evidence in the George Street inquests was Miss Clara Risby, an 18-year-old domestic servant living in Woolloomooloo who had given birth to a baby girl, Elizabeth May, on 16 April 1892 at the Benevolent Asylum.[7] While she was recovering in the Asylum, her step-sisters placed an advertisement in *The Evening News* on 4 May which offered a generous premium for her 'delicate' baby:

> Will kind person adopt baby girl for life; premium £5. A.B., Macdonaldtown Post Office.

Miss Risby told the court she had received a reply from a Mrs S J McLoughlin of 16 East Street, Redfern, who wrote a reassuring letter the same day:

> Dear Madam,
> In reply to your advertisement in the EVENING NEWS of this date ... it is my husband's wish that I should apply for it, as we have no small children of our own. I should give it all a mother's love and care. It is not for the premium we write for, as the £5 we should spend [o]n an outfit for the baby. As we are going to live out of town we should very much like to take a baby with us, so you can be sure it will have a good home and attention and care. If this will suit you I can give you any references you require. I can call on you if you send your address, and any instructions you send will be attended to. This is genuine—no baby farm. I can explain matters to you personally better than in writing.
> I remain yours faithfully,
> S. J. McLoughlin.

Clara's two step-sisters, Mrs Adams and Mrs Sargent, travelled to 16 East Street to see 'what sort of people' the McLoughlins were. Even then, a little subterfuge was evident upon their arrival. When Mrs Sargent asked a girl inside the house at 16 East Street whether Mrs McLoughlin lived there, the girl replied, 'No'. But John quickly appeared, reassuring his daughter, Daisy, and spoke to Mrs Sargent about Clara's three-week-old baby.

The final arrangements for the adoption were made by Clara and Mrs Sargent on 16 May when they arrived in East Street with the one-month-old baby. John met them at the corner of the street and escorted them into number 16, where they met Sarah, Blanche and Clarice. Mrs Makin 'promised she would look after the child' after Mrs Sargent said she hoped they would care for it since she did not 'want to give it to anyone who will put it on the doorstep'. John reassured her that his daughters were very fond of children. After handing over her baby and various babies' clothes, Clara paid the £5 premium and was given a receipt signed by John McLoughlin.

True to form, John spun Clara a marvellous tale about how he had inherited a fortune and bought a poultry farm at Rockdale. Clara was told she could visit the child anytime and he would send the Rockdale address to her soon, reassuring her that her child 'would be comfortable'.

However, Clara was still very attached to her child. She visited East Street on 18 May and was told by Sarah that her daughter 'had been very cross'. A few days later, on 22 May, she visited again, although this time John looked over the fence and told her that Mrs McLoughlin 'was out with the child'. By this date, it is more than likely that Clara's baby had been disposed of. The Makins had their £5. There was no point in keeping Clara's baby alive, especially since they had signed an agreement the day before with Mr Fischer for the lease of 109 George Street. On 24 May, Clara visited 16 East Street one more time but the house was empty. She did not suspect anything because she thought John was 'a respectable man'. So she waited for a letter with his Rockdale address and his arrival in a cart, since he had promised to drive down to collect her for a visit. When asked to identify some babies' clothing, Clara recognised the garments that had been worn by her child when the Makins adopted her.

Clara Risby's ongoing interest in her child explains why the Makins only stayed in East Street for three short weeks. Not only did they have to deal with Clara, but they were also visited by Clara's step-sister, Mrs Adams, the day after the baby was adopted, because she was suspicious of the Makins' motives. Sooner or later they would run out of stories.

At the end of day one, Sarah and John were taken to the Central Criminal Court where they appeared at their first hearing into the charge of manslaughter of the child of Minnie Davies. They both pleaded not guilty, although a journalist reported they were 'impressed with the gravity of their position'. How many more charges would they face?

Day two of a 'very trying ordeal'

On day two, Sarah turned up to court 'deeply veiled ... very much distressed and ... suffering a very trying ordeal', although for the first time she held her head up and watched from behind her veil as the witnesses gave evidence.[8] With the courtroom crowded with 'sightseers', Sarah had gone into the only form of hiding available to her.

Clara Risby's step-sister, Mrs Adams, gave evidence on day two. She confirmed that Clara's baby was 'delicate' but not ill. About three or four weeks after the adoption, John had called at Mrs Adams' house in Buckland Street, Waterloo. He had been to his farm, he said, and dropped by with the baby, obviously to reassure her. She noticed it was 'not so stout' as when she had last seen it.

Makin told her he was very fond of the child and 'would not give it up for fifty pounds' although the pragmatic Mrs Adams replied that she 'wouldn't give 50 pence for it'. When she asked John for his new address, he put her off with various excuses. Mrs Adams ran into John again a few months later in Botany Street when he was coming out of a grocer's store. She was unsure of the date. Most likely it was the end of August 1892 when the Makins had relocated to Botany Street after leaving Burren Street. Mrs Adams tried to overtake John to find out 'how the child was getting on', but the artful dodger was too quick for her. He sped up and she was unable to catch him. She saw him enter a house but when she visited a day or so later, the house was empty. This event would explain the short stay of the Makins in 55 Botany Street, since they only spent ten days there before moving to 6 Wells Street where Constable Joyce found them.

The final piece of evidence implicating the Makins in the disappearance of Clara's baby was given by a local pawnbroker, Joseph Lopez, who had received a parcel of babies' clothes from Daisy Makin on 8 August. Clara's step-sister, Mrs Sargent, later testified that some of the clothing pawned by Daisy in the name of Mrs Wilson had been worn by Clara's baby.

Was Clara's one-month-old baby one of the infants found buried in George Street? Because of the evidence discussed below, it is unlikely she was. Where her child was buried, Clara would never know.

Miss Stacey's fretful search for Mr and Mrs Ray

The next witness at the inquest was Miss Mary Stacey, a domestic servant living in Petersham who had given birth to a girl, Daisy Pearl, on 17 April 1892 at the home of Mrs Bentley, a midwife in Neville Street, Marrickville. After 'lying-in' for nine weeks, Mary advertised on page one of *The Evening News* on 18–21 June for a kind lady to adopt her baby using an unusual alias:

> WANTED, Kind Lady to adopt little girl 2 months' old, or to care
> for. Iran, Petersham post office.

The Makins would have been busy writing during the week of 18–24 June, with *The Evening News* giving us a picture of what a Sydney baby farmer could expect each week.[9] Many enterprising baby farmers also advertised that week, showing us that the Makins were in competition with other 'kind motherly' persons for the children on offer:

> WANTED, by kind Motherly Person, Baby to Care.
> 7 Little Cleveland-st, off Chelsea-st, Moore Park.
> WANTED, kind Person to Adopt Baby Boy few days
> Old, £10 premium. Elsie, G.P.O.
> WANTED, Lady Adopt at once Baby Girl, 10 days old
> Premium £3. Mrs. Williams, G.P.O. Sydney.
> WANTED, a person to Adopt Boy, 3 years old, allow-
> ance for clothes. X.I., General Post Office.

WANTED, Adopt baby Boy, at once, small pre. re-
quired. 5 Victoria-st, Paddington.
RESPECTABLE Married Couple would Adopt healthy
Baby; premium required; reference. M.C., 140 George-st,
Waterloo.
WANTED, by kind motherly person, Baby to care,
good refs, terms mod. 20 Regent-st, Paddington.
WANTED, kind Person to Adopt Baby Boy, 9 days
Old, must be Catholic, no premium given. B.C.,
Post Office, Surry Hills.
WANTED, kind motherly person adopt fair Baby Boy,
3 weeks, small premium. A.L., Oxford-st P.O.

Miss Stacey received a number of replies to her advertisement, including a quick response from Mr Ray who lived at 109 George Street:

Dear Iran,
I will take your little baby for life at a small sum of £3 or £3 10s,
or whatever terms we may come to. It is not just for the sake of the
money, but just to give the child an outfit. You need never trouble
about your baby's welfare. She will have every attention and the
love of a kind mother. We are on the eve of going to the suburbs on
a poultry farm to a fine healthy part, so if you will come down we
will explain things and make arrangements.
Yours faithfully,
Mr Ray
109 George-street, Redfern, up the steps.

Perhaps attracted by Mr Ray's tidbit that his family was moving to a farm in a healthy suburb, Mary considered his letter 'the best' and took her baby girl to George Street on 21 June. When Clarice answered the door, Mary asked for Mrs Ray. Unfazed, Clarice went to fetch her.

In the front room, Mary Stacey met the Makins. The family certainly had some winning ways, with Sarah taking the baby in her arms straight away. A little bargaining took place because Miss Stacey said she could only afford £2, to which Sarah agreed. But Mary was not in a hurry, since she refused to make a decision there and then, saying she would write and let them know if she would place her child in their care. She was reassured by the family's bona fides when Sarah and Clarice 'professed to take a great fancy to the baby, and kissed it affectionately' as she was leaving, with Sarah remarking, 'Oh, it might be ours yet'.

Miss Stacey later wrote to inform the Makins she had chosen them to take her child, and would deliver her in a few days. But the Makins were in a hurry to collect Baby Daisy. Sarah sent Clarice and Blanche to Marrickville on Thursday 23 June to collect the baby with a letter:

> Dear Miss Stacey,
> We will be so busy packing and cleaning out on Friday and Saturday, and my girls are over anxious for the child, so they have come out to-day for her. I hope you will let them have it.
> Yours faithfully
> Mrs Ray
> Received the sum of £2 for adoption of baby girl for life.

With the money, the baby and a promise to return for a visit, the girls left with some extra clothing which Miss Stacey was able to identify in the courtroom. This clothing, all handmade by Miss Stacey, had been discovered by Constable Joyce at Mrs Leonard's pawnshop in Botany Road, Redfern. Joyce produced a number of pawn tickets as well as the receipt for the clothes of Miss Stacey's child that he had found at the home of Minnie Helbi, Sarah's eldest daughter, suggesting that Minnie was also involved in her parents' baby-farming business.

It seems things then followed a bit of a pattern. John and Blanche visited Miss Stacey on Monday 27 June with the baby to reassure her, although she testified that her child, strong and healthy when she was adopted, 'looked very bad and was very restless', 'crying and twisting as though something was the matter with it'. When Mary changed her, 'she seemed quite hollow and empty and thin ... as if [no] food had been given to the child'. The

Makins had only had Baby Daisy for four short days, yet Mary's account, along with the evidence about how Baby Mignonette Davies died, shows us how the Makins were 'caring' for the babies they adopted.

When Miss Stacey went to warm a cold bottle of milk John had brought for her child, she found 'it was nothing but milk and water, or "slops"'. As she told her heartrending tale, she 'was completely overcome with emotion' and had to sit in the witness box until she calmed down.

John told Mary he and his family were moving to Hurstville but he would call again when he came to town to buy a cow. When Makin did not keep his promise to return, Mary 'began to fret for her baby'. After she discovered an empty house at 109 George Street, she and her midwife, Mrs Bentley, spent two days searching Hurstville for a family called Ray. Although Miss Stacey made a report to the police that a couple had disappeared with her child, the Makins' alias protected them. Miss Stacey never saw her baby again.

But for the chance discoveries in Burren Street, Mary would have been left confused and grieving. Mary's story also suggests she was one of the reasons for the Makins' hasty exit from 109 George Street, a young woman who had a deep attachment to her baby. The Makins would have known the signs.

An 'enraged' John Makin, Constable Joyce and the juryman

After the damaging evidence from Mary Stacey, Clarice was recalled to explain her involvement in the adoption of Mary's baby.[10] She admitted that she and Blanche had travelled to Marrickville to collect Baby Daisy and had given a false surname under instructions from her father. Clarice sometimes nursed and fed Baby Daisy, although the last time she saw her was in George Street, lying on the sofa. She did not know what became of her but Clarice was positive that Daisy was not taken to Burren Street when the Makins moved on the rainy night of 29 June.

Daisy could not have been Baby C or Baby D discovered during the George Street digs since both were male, but Baby B was female and when Dr Milford told the court about his examination of the female child, Baby B, he produced the thigh bones in court. Their length of 3¼ inches indicated that Baby B was less than a year old, although the most precise he could be was to say that she was two to ten weeks of age when she died. Miss Stacey's baby was nine weeks old when adopted by the Makins.

Just after Clarice finished giving her evidence, one of the jurymen complained to the Coroner that Makin 'had been in conversation with a spectator all day'. When Constable Joyce escorted the man from the courtroom, Mr Williamson objected, telling Joyce he had 'no right to turn that man out'. In the alarming scene to follow, John Makin let slip the mask behind which he hid his emotions, becoming enraged and accusing the juryman of telling lies:

> Don't tell lies. You look after the evidence and never mind me. You have been continually throwing it up at me. Remember I have not been found guilty yet although some of you have found me guilty. You attend to the evidence, that's what you are paid for.[11]

The Coroner then ordered John:

> Will you be kind enough not to address the jury. Please sit down.

When the court adjourned for lunch, John complained to the Coroner:

> He said the jury were condemning him unfairly, and they had continually been passing insulting remarks at adjournments, which were quite unjustifiable. He ... did not hear the stranger speak to him, and the juryman ... was very smart in drawing the coroner's attention to it. 'Why, the —— jurymen are sleeping half their time,' said Makin, 'instead of attending to the evidence'.

Constable Joyce then gave Makin a piece of his mind:

Joyce:	You know, Makin, you have no right to speak to anybody in court.
Makin:	I'll speak to whom I like.
Joyce:	No, you won't.

Makin (enraged):   You won't stop me.

Joyce: Yes, I will.

Makin: Then you will have to cut my tongue out.

When it was announced that lunch was ready, Blanche and Florence refused to leave the court and, in tears, complained that Clarice had been telling a lot of lies 'and she should have been in their place'. Sarah tried to reassure them, 'Come on, my children ... they can't hang your mother; they can only put her in gaol'. With a hint of triumph, Makin had the final say, 'That's where it pinches them. They can't say we murdered them'.

Before they left the courtroom, Constable Joyce brought in one of the afternoon's witnesses, who recognised Sarah straight away. Sarah replied, 'Well, I'm blowed. I never saw the woman in my life' while Blanche observed, 'Oh, I suppose they will bring Paddy the blackfellow next to see if he knows you'. Not only was the morning's evidence against them, the afternoon seemed to be promising more of the same.

The smelly bedrooms and Sarah's spying skills

Things did not improve for the Makins after lunch when three more women gave damaging evidence. The first two, Miss Wells of 111 George Street and Mrs Fitzpatrick of 107 George Street, testified that they had seen three babies when the Makins lived at number 109 and frequently heard babies crying.[12]

The new resident of 109 George Street, Mrs Ralph, told the court she had noticed a very unpleasant smell from the first night she spent in the house. It was worse in the bedrooms and so bad that her family could not sleep 'on close nights'. Her family eventually got used to the smell but were relieved that it disappeared once the bodies had been unearthed by the police. Constables Joyce and Brown had also examined the floorboards throughout the house but decided that none had been removed. Joyce even climbed through the manhole in the ceiling of the back bedroom but 'emerged covered with cobwebs [and] with empty hands'.

Mrs Ralph then revealed that Sarah Makin had called at her house on a Sunday night about eight weeks earlier, during the very first inquests but before the police had dug up the backyard. On the doorstep, Sarah asked about the previous tenants and wanted to know whether 'the floor of her house had been taken up by the [Redfern] police'. When Mrs Ralph replied no, Sarah sympathised in relation to the inconvenience of having the police around and revealed that the previous tenants 'were great friends of hers and nice people'. Mrs Ralph retorted that they could not be that nice since they left 'without paying the landlord his rent'. Sarah then inquired whether or not the Redfern police had found a baby in the backyard and left, rather pleased, when she was told they had not.

The verdict

Mary Stacey and Clara Risby had given evidence in the second George Street inquest in the hope they would find out what had happened to their babies. Despite their evidence, it was unclear who the mother of Baby B was. Clara's baby girl would have been nearly six weeks old, if, when the Makins moved to George Street, she was still alive. This age fits within Dr Milford's estimated age range of two to ten weeks for Baby B. But it is equally likely the Makins disposed of Clara's baby while they were in East Street and before their sudden move to George Street. John Makin had told Clara that his wife was 'out with the child' the last time Clara visited East Street, his usual excuse when a baby had met its end.

We know from Clarice Makin's evidence, however, that Mary Stacey's child had lived with the Makins in George Street and was not one of the six babies taken to Burren Street, making it highly likely that Baby B was Mary's baby. Despite this evidence, the Coroner was unconvinced.

During his summing up to the jury, the Coroner told the jurymen that although the case was 'one of very strong suspicion', with no cause of death and no identifying features on Baby B, 'it was impossible for them to bring in any other verdict but an open one'. The jury retired. After an hour they returned to inform the Coroner they disagreed with him. The Coroner was not happy. Three jurors were holding out for a guilty finding against the Makins. The foreman asked if it were absolutely necessary to prove identification. If not, it would be much easier to incriminate the Makins. The Coroner instructed them it was essential to identify Baby B. He would give them another fifteen minutes. When they returned, the jury had fallen into line by deciding there was insufficient evidence 'to determine how, when, where, or by what means the infant came by its death', despite the gravest suspicion against all of the Makins. There would be no answers for either Mary or Clara as a result of this inquest.

John Makin's prediction, that 'they can't say we murdered them', was right. This time. But John had forgotten that just after they disappeared from George Street, two mothers in particular were keen to find out what had happened to their babies. It was perhaps inevitable that one of them would, unknowingly, orchestrate the downfall of Australia's most notorious baby farmers.

❧

CHAPTER SIXTEEN

The day Miss Amber Murray visited the Makins
20–21 December 1892

The inquest into the death of Baby D opened on 20 December 1892.[1] The Coroner, the jury and the packed public gallery were in for another nail-biting journey into the gloomy underworld of baby farming.

This inquest commenced after the jury had decided not to deliver a verdict in relation to the death of Baby C until they had heard the evidence concerning the death of Baby D. This decision was made in order to see if either Baby C or Baby D could be the child of the star witness for the day—Miss Amber Murray.

After the discovery of the George Street babies, Amber had made her way to Newtown police station from her home in Paddington. She gave Constable Joyce the letter she had received on 24 June in response to her advertisement in *The Evening News*, the day that Miss Stacey had advertised in the same newspaper:

> WANTED, kindly, motherly person, to adopt fair baby boy, 3 weeks, small premium. A. L., Oxford-street P.O.

The long, sympathetic letter had been signed by a woman calling herself E. Hill, who knew how to reassure a concerned mother:

> In reply to your advertisement in EVENING NEWS to-day for a kind person to adopt baby boy 3 weeks old, small premium, having

no small children, only three grown daughters, I have great pleasure
in applying to you for it. I will give it a mother's love, and attention—
in fact all that a mother can give to it—if it was her own. I will take
it for—say £2 10s—or £3, just to get it a small outfit. ... It is our
intention of going to live in the suburbs, where we will keep a cow, so
you will have no fear for your baby, as it will get plenty of outing and
fresh air from the girls, as we are very fond of children. I may also
tell you we are comfortable, and have an income. If this should suit
you you can call on me on Saturday (to-morrow) evening or any time
through the day. I can explain more to you if you can, if possible, call
on Saturday as we may be out of town early on Monday morning. If
you give us the child you can see it every week ...

I remain, yours faithfully,

E. Hill, 109 George-street, Redfern, near post office, tram to
George-street.

You need not fear about your baby, as you will find it will be taken
as much care of or more so than yourself would care for it.

Amber had given birth to a strong, healthy son on 30 May 1892 at the
home of Mrs Patrick, a midwife in Brisbane Street, Paddington. Like
all the other unmarried mothers who had testified, she was a domestic
servant who was vulnerable to unwanted pregnancies and perhaps the
sexual attentions of gentlemen staying at the Royal Hotel in Glenmore
Road, Paddington where she lived-in. One newspaper described her as
'a young barmaid'.

The day after her advertisement, Amber received three replies, although
the reassuring letter from E. Hill saw her take the tram to George Street
the next evening at about eight o'clock. Amber said she was taken into the
house by Daisy and met Mr and Mrs Hill in the front room. The Hills
began their usual tale with a few extra embellishments. Mrs Hill was keen
to bring up Amber's baby because she had lost a child who was two years
old and wanted another boy to take his place, even though her two-year-
old son, Tommy, was probably in the house.

Mr Hill concentrated on the money side of things. Like a good salesman, John had some winning arguments, since Amber agreed she did not mind paying £3 'as long as he took care of the child'. John assured her that he would 'bring it up as one of [our] own' and give it a good education. On cue, Sarah told her she had nothing to fear. Then came the Makins' code, the meaning of which was unknown to an adopting mother. John announced the family would very soon be moving to a much healthier place to live, in Hurstville. She was reassured when John promised she could visit her child once a week and Sarah chimed in, 'Oh yes you can. I am a mother myself and I know what a mother's love is'.

When Amber visited Newtown police station, she also gave Constable Joyce the agreement for her son's adoption, dated 27 June. Amber said she had got it from 'a gentleman friend', George Anderson, who 'travels on boats'. Possibly Mr Anderson, a sailor, had previous experience in dealing with the inconvenience of an illegitimate child, since the agreement was 'drawn up in exaggerated legal phraseology'. Extremely precise in its terms, it reads like a standard form contract of the type we have today for commercial transactions and provides more evidence that the sale of children in the colony had developed its own market with its very own standard legal approach to adoption. The adopter agreed to adopt 'the child' for a premium of £3, while Amber agreed not to interfere with the child without the consent of the adopter. If she did she was liable to pay a penalty of £500 Sterling. The agreement was signed by Amber and John Hill. On the day he was adopted, Horace was three weeks old.

Before Amber left George Street, the Hills said they would call at the home of her midwife to pick up her baby. Between 6.30 and 7 p.m. on 27 June, John arrived with his daughter Florence. John was full of praise as Florence took the baby in her arms, saying, 'It's just the kind of child we want'. For some reason Amber did not have the £3 premium but promised that 'as she had to go out' she would deliver both the money and the child at 8 p.m., her words suggesting she had to collect the premium from someone. Perhaps her mysterious friend George had agreed to pay the fee and had not turned up. But John was in a hurry, insisting that he take the child there and then, perhaps afraid that Amber would change her mind. John told her not to be later than eight o'clock as he had some friends coming.

When Amber arrived, she sensed the Makins were keen to get rid of her. They had been watching for her arrival since, as Amber walked past number 109 by mistake, John called out to her. As he showed her into the front room he explained, 'I have not long to spare' because he was expecting friends, and 'you might meet someone here you would not care to meet'. In reality, the Makins were expecting a visit from another mother, someone the Makins themselves would not want Amber to meet.

Amber was asked by a juryman what the inside of the house at 109 George Street was like. She replied it was clean and comfortable but 'poorly furnished' although Mr Hill had told her he would be buying 'fresh furniture' with a fortune he had just inherited.

Sarah brought Amber's son into the front room and handed him to Clarice, who fed him from a bottle while Florence and Blanche looked on. In fact, '[t]hey all seemed confused, and appeared anxious that [Amber] should go away quickly'. But she was not put off so easily. Unusually for the unmarried mothers they dealt with, Amber was unwilling to hand over the £3 premium until the legal agreement was signed. When she 'laid the agreement on the table', John said, 'What's this? I don't understand it'. Amber told him to read it. John replied, 'I have no time to waste any longer' and sent Florence outside to watch for the friends he was expecting.

But the Makins were in a corner. John signed the agreement in the name of John Leslie, perhaps betraying his subconscious thoughts about the arrival of the mother to whom he was known as Mr Leslie. In the complicated life of the Makins, 27 June was the day they also adopted Agnes Todd's baby. As soon as John realised he had signed the wrong name, he wrote his other alias, 'Hill', over the word 'Leslie'. Amber signed the agreement as the parent and filled in some of the blank sections. John knew enough about the requirements of a legally binding contract to say that 'he would call for the agreement, put stamps on it, and sign it properly, as he had signed it before the blanks were filled in'.

Satisfied, Amber paid her £3 and gave Sarah some clothes for her baby son. John agreed to register the birth of her child and to give him a name while Sarah announced, 'I have thought of a pretty name for your child. We will call it Horace Amber Murray as it is so near your own name'. When she kissed her son goodbye, Amber did not know it would be the last time she would see him. John reassured her he would visit on Saturday or Tuesday next when he planned to come in to town to buy a cow and would give Amber the family's new address. Sarah crooned, 'You have nothing to fear. You have given your child into good hands'.

In the witness box, Amber identified the long white gown and the shirt that Baby D had been wearing when he was dug up. She recognised the gown because she had made it herself, while the shirt had been given to her by Mrs Patrick, her midwife. She also identified four other long gowns she had given to Sarah Makin on 27 June, telling the court that all the garments had been made by her 'and she could identify' her own sewing, including one item with one sleeve 'shorter than the other'. Constable Joyce had recovered this clothing from a pawnshop in Waterloo where Daisy Makin had pawned it in the name of Mrs Wilson for 13 shillings.

After her baby was adopted, the next time Amber saw John was on Thursday 30 June, the day after the Makins had moved into Burren Street. He called at 58 Brisbane Street, the home of Amber's midwife, to announce that his family had moved to Hurstville. When Amber asked how her child was, John replied, 'Oh, quite well … but it's not your child now'. John promised to visit with the child on Saturday. Mrs Patrick suggested that she and Amber could visit them instead but John excused his family as being so upset by the move they would not be settled for six weeks.

Mrs Patrick was the next witness called to give evidence. She recognised the babies' clothing Amber had given the Makins, including a shirt she had made as a gift. Mrs Patrick then described the meeting between Amber and John on 30 June.

But why did John not just disappear quietly from Amber Murray's life after his move to Burren Street? It seems he was creating a bit of a charade, although the next stage of his performance would contain an unexpected change in the script. A lot of convincing improvisation would be required.

John had announced he had only come to sign the agreement. When Amber said she had given the papers back to her gentleman friend, he replied, 'Oh, they are no use to you, my girl or to me either. The chap simply gave them to you so that you and the child would have no more claim on him'. Amber agreed with this astute assessment of her situation but she replied that her child 'is not going to be slighted for all that'.

John informed Amber that her baby was not well. He began by asking whether her son had had a rash before the Makins adopted him. Amber admitted he had suffered from thrush but was quite recovered by the time she handed him over. John then dropped his bombshell: 'a rash came out on its face' which made him think the child was suffering from 'some disease from either the father or mother'. Mrs Patrick and Amber were quite shocked since John was referring to syphilis. Mrs Patrick hotly denied this could be the case, describing the baby 'as clean at birth as a child could be' when he was born. Amber offered to take her son to a doctor herself but John demurred: 'My wife is a midwife and had fifteen children of her own ... She knows all about children'. Unfortunately for John, Mrs Patrick was a bothersome woman with her own views. She put John on notice:

> I don't hold with people adopting children, it is only a money
> making game and fancy for £3. I would not take the best child to
> adopt for £300. Had [my] husband been home from sea he would
> not have allowed it.

John hung his head and confided his own little boy had died and he merely wanted Amber's child to replace him and 'keep his daughters in at night'. But his contrition did not convince Mrs Patrick, who recognised a shyster when she saw one. As John left, she said if anything happened to the child she would report it to the Coroner if Amber did not. She offered to take the baby back if his circumstances changed and asked for his address. But he refused to give it, saying he had forgotten. Although John promised to call every week to let Mrs Patrick see the child, a week later Mrs Patrick saw him in Oxford Street posting three letters 'but he would not face her'.

Mrs Patrick's threat to report him to the authorities would explain why John created the next part of his charade. On Tuesday, 5 July, he called at her house along with his daughter Blanche, who was carrying a baby. The door was answered by Mrs King, the next witness at the inquest, who was a widow lodging with Mrs Patrick. Neither Amber nor Mrs Patrick was at home.

When she invited John and Blanche inside, Mrs King did not recognise the baby because 'it was so altered' with 'bad sores all over its face'. She must have been quite taken aback, since she told Makin, 'I would not know the child as Amber Murray's child if you had not brought it, it is so changed'. She told John the baby seemed to have 'the thrush' but John informed her he thought it was something else. Although John and Blanche waited for two hours, Amber did not return so they said they would bring the child another time. As they left, Mrs King 'kissed the child but had a sore mouth and a sore tongue for about a fortnight afterwards', symptoms which indicate the baby was suffering from a severe case of thrush.

When asked if she thought it was Amber's child, Mrs King told the court she only thought it was because Mr Hill had brought it. She was quite certain that when the baby was adopted on 27 June his thrush had cleared up and he only had 'some spots on his face and bottom [but] was in good health and taking [his] food well'. In the space of seven days, Baby Horace had not only become reinfected with thrush but had come down with something more serious. Mrs King's description of a baby with 'bad sores' all over its face suggests he was suffering from the weeping sores associated with congenital syphilis, which seep fluid then form a crust. This matches Mrs King's observation that the baby's face was so altered she no longer recognised him.

But was this baby Amber's child? Had John planted the idea five days before that Baby Horace was suffering from some disease from either the father or mother and then, like a magician, presented a sick child as proof that he was not long for this world? John certainly had several other babies to choose from at 25 Burren Street. Because of the prevalence of syphilis in the colony, it is no surprise that one or more of the babies they adopted would have been suffering from congenital syphilis.

Despite his promise that he would visit again, perhaps John thought he had stepped too close to the fire. If Mrs King did not recognise the child, he could expect a more marked reaction from Mrs Patrick and Amber if he were to try this trick again. By 5 July, it is likely that Baby Horace was dead. Whether he was one of the babies buried in George Street was something the jury had to decide.

Amber waited, day in, day out, for Mr Hill to return with news of her son. After waiting two weeks, Amber travelled to Hurstville where she made inquiries about Mr and Mrs Hill. Like Mary Stacey before her, who had searched for a family called Ray, Amber's search was fruitless.

Clarice's selective memory

The next witness at the inquest into the death of Baby D was Clarice Makin, whose dislike of her family must have run deep. In a poor family of four daughters and one favourite son, resentments were inevitable. As the third daughter, Clarice may have been caught in the middle of a family hierarchy, bossed around by Blanche, Florence and her mother. As the only daughter who had left home, she may have been 'farmed' out to work, since she told police she had been 'out at service' for nearly two years.[2] While the Makins needed Blanche and Florence to look after their baby-farmed children, Clarice was able to earn a small income for the impoverished Makin family, who always seemed to be short of money. Although she had turned informer, questions hovered over her—was Clarice's evidence really the truth and nothing but the truth?

Clarice told the court she remembered Amber Murray and her parents talking about adopting a baby a few days before the family moved to Burren Street. Unbeknown to Amber, when she first visited the Makins on 27 June, there were five babies in the George Street house. When Florence and John returned with Amber's baby, 'it made the sixth in the house', according to Clarice, who did not remember any other children being adopted before the family moved on 29 June.

Although some newspapers reported that Clarice was unsure whether Baby Horace accompanied the family to Burren Street, Clarice's signed deposition is clear that she said all six babies left with the family on 29 June for Burren Street. Horace looked well the last time she saw him and she could not remember 'any sores or marks on its face'. While Clarice only stayed in Burren Street from 29 June to the following Wednesday when she 'went into service', all six babies were in the Burren Street house when she left, although she also gave the contradictory evidence that she did not see Baby Horace after the move to Burren Street.

At this point, Sarah 'gave vent to loud sobbing' and moans and called out, 'Oh, God bless her for the lies she has told. Oh, her poor mother'. When she looked as if she would faint, the gaol warders in the courtroom gave her a glass of water which she drank unsteadily, but water would not save her: 'immediately afterward Mrs. Makin was seized with a faint and fell back helpless'. Blanche and Florence burst into tears and 'another painful scene followed'. While it was some minutes before Sarah recovered, she had cleverly diverted the court's attention once again from the damaging evidence given against her. But was Clarice lying as Sarah had declared?

When questioned by Mr Williamson, Clarice was a little uncertain about which babies were in the Burren Street house, answering that 'she did not look into the faces of the children while living at Burren-street, and would not swear that Miss Murray's child was not amongst them, but she never saw it'. Crucially, this evidence supported the police case that Amber's baby was killed and buried in George Street.

As Clarice signed her depositions and left the courtroom, Sarah Makin moaned again, 'God forgive you for telling lies', leaving more questions for the jury and the public to ponder.

From all the evidence given in the inquests, the move to Burren Street would have been a secretive and silent process so as not to alert the neighbours. One set of neighbours, in particular, must have been quite put out that the city's most notorious baby farm had operated right under their noses. At about 7.30 p.m., John parked a hired, horse-drawn van in the narrow rear lane behind 109 George Street which was directly opposite Redfern police station. Because the owner of the van was 'under the influence of drink', John was forced to drive it himself. Nonetheless, the migratory Makins may not have wanted to employ a driver. Much safer for John to do the moving himself.

John carried out their few bits of furniture—mattresses, a table, some chairs. With Clarice and Blanche, he drove to Burren Street. When they returned to George Street for the second and final load, a couch, a cane pram and a cradle were loaded. Two babies were in the pram and two in the cradle while Sarah carried one and Daisy held another, according to

Clarice. But who were the six babies they took with them that night? We know two of them were Elsie May Todd and Mignonette Davies. Another, it appears, was Horace Amber Murray. But who were the other three?

Because most of these six babies had only been in the George Street house for about a week, they were the new batch of babies that had been collected after the last batch had apparently been killed. Clarice said in her first police interview that just before the family moved out of George Street, she saw three babies in a bed. Later, Clarice was told by her mother that 'the parents of the children ... took them away'.[3] It likely that the babies in the bed became the one female and two males, known as Babies B, C and D, discovered in the George Street backyard.

Clarice's see no evil, hear no evil, do no evil

Clarice was probably downplaying her role in the family's baby-farming business, since she was selective in her memories, failing to remember things she might have been involved in but remembering those that incriminated her parents. She could not remember whether Amber Murray's baby was in the Burren Street house and failed to see the contradictions in her evidence when she told the inquest:

> I saw all the six babies in the [Burren Street] house on the morning
> after we moved and all the six babies were in the house when I left
> on the Wednesday but I did not see Amber Murray's child.

Despite her uncertainty, Clarice had a remarkably good memory for other events. She remembered Agnes Todd's baby was received on 27 June, the same day as Amber's child. She also remembered seeing Miss Todd's baby in Burren Street two days later. Perhaps the final part of her testimony is the most telling, since it ensured her 'innocence' and damned her parents:

> I did not look at the faces of the babies when they were being put
> in the van ... I did not look at their faces on the morning after we
> got to Burren Street ... [nor] at any time ... before I left home on
> Wednesday. I said I did not see Amber Murray's baby in Burren

> Street because I did not hear it cry … I knew its cry. It had a
> squeaky voice … I never saw Miss Murray's child in Burren Street,
> nor did I ever see my mother dressing it there. I did not help to put
> any of the children … in the van. I rode in the van with them, but
> I never looked at any of them.

Clarice was covering her tracks by denying all the normal things the daughters of a baby-farming family would have been doing—dressing, changing, feeding and drugging six helpless babies. Her inconsistent evidence suggests she knew that Baby Horace had been taken to Burren Street. For some reason, Clarice decided to contradict herself to make the jury think that Baby D could have been Amber's baby. Since this incriminated her parents in the death of Baby D, it is possible that Clarice had been influenced to change her evidence by the obsessive Constable Joyce—the man who had worked so hard to gather evidence in the hope of convicting the Makins of murder.

When Daisy Makin testified, she also told the inquest that six babies were taken to Burren Street. Unlike Clarice, Daisy remembered a baby called 'Brisbane Street' in the Burren Street house, a piece of evidence that reveals the cold world of baby farming where a street name was identification enough for a pair of busy baby farmers. 'Brisbane Street' must have been a reference to Amber's son since he had been collected from the home of Mrs Patrick, who lived at 58 Brisbane Street.

Miss Murray revisits the witness box

After Daisy finished giving evidence, Dr Milford was called to testify about the autopsy he had conducted on the body of Baby D. He estimated the child had been two to nine weeks old when he died and had been buried from three to five months. The autopsy found that Baby D 'bore no marks of violence to [his] head, and no trace of poison was found in [his] stomach, but decomposition was so far advanced that it would be impossible to detect many vegetable poisons, and no cause of death was shewn'.

When Miss Murray was recalled to the witness box, counsel for the Coroner, Mr Healy, handed Amber a small, buff-coloured envelope with spidery black handwriting on the outside that read:

Exhibit
Hair of D
Series of 4 Infants found George
St Redfern on the 9th Nov. 92.

He asked her to open it. Inside was a lock of hair from Baby D. Perhaps Mr Healy had become too used to death as a result of his work for the Coroner's Court to understand the impact of what he had just done.

As Amber took out the lock of light coloured hair, she 'broke down in tears' as her fingers held this missive from the grave. Mr Healy inquired whether she wanted a short adjournment. She decided to press on, revealing that the lock of hair was 'the same colour as my baby's'. Questioned further, she said: 'Yes I am sure. The colour and the texture are the same'. She held the lock to her lips, perhaps remembering the smell of her child, and asked whether, when 'all this business is over', she could have the lock of hair 'as that is the only thing I have to remember my baby by'. The Coroner asked Constable Joyce to arrange for that to be done at the end of the inquest.

The verdict

On Wednesday 21 December, the Coroner summed up all the evidence in the inquest. He was certain about the identity of Baby D because:

> the evidence was conclusive that the hair was similar to that on the head of Amber Murray's child, and the clothing found on the remains was positively identified as having been handed over with the child.

Ignoring the contradictory parts of Clarice's evidence and all of Daisy's evidence, the Coroner decided there was no evidence to show that Baby Horace had been taken to Burren Street. Mr Williamson objected and asked Mr Woore to direct the jury that there was no evidence that Miss Murray's child had *not* been taken to Macdonaldtown. The Coroner refused, informing Williamson he would say nothing more on that matter.

Although it is more likely that Amber's baby was taken to Burren Street, the jury was pushed in the other direction by the Coroner's persuasive instructions, a result of his being utterly persuaded by Amber's shocked reaction to Baby D's lock of hair as well as her and Mrs Patrick's identification of the clothing in which Baby D had been found. The medical evidence that Baby D was from two to nine weeks old when he died coincided with the age of Horace, who was four weeks old when adopted by the Makins. While there was no evidence about the cause of death, 'there was the gravest suspicion against the Makins'.

At 4.45 p.m. the jury retired to consider its verdict for both Baby D and Baby C, as the jurors had hoped that the evidence into the death of Baby D would help them make a finding about the death of Baby C. When they returned just over an hour later this proved not to be the case, with insufficient evidence to identify Baby C or determine his cause of death. They returned an open verdict, which meant the Makins could not be implicated in the death of Baby C. But their lucky streak had just run out. The foreman of the jury announced sombrely:

Foreman: We find a verdict of wilful murder against John and
           Sarah Makin.
Coroner: Did you identify body 'D'?
Foreman: Yes, as Amber Murray's child.
Coroner: Did you find how the child was murdered? ...
Foreman: We came to the conclusion that it came to its death by
           some foul means.

Satisfied, the Coroner announced he would formally commit John and Sarah to stand trial for murder at the next sitting of the Criminal Court.

The end of Act I—the final court drama

When the verdict was announced, Sarah 'moaned piteously', like someone in physical pain, while Blanche and Florence 'repeatedly kissed her'. Another newspaper reported that it was the girls who 'wept hysterically and the mother kissed them repeatedly'.[4] John remained impassive and emotionless in the dock.

When Sarah was pulled out of her daughters' arms by a policeman, she 'became slightly hysterical, screaming, "Amber Murray's child was taken to MacDonald Town. Wilful murder, the liars!"', and repeating the word 'liars' over and over. She was defiant as she stepped into the police van, calling out to her children, 'Be good, my darlings. Good-bye. You all know that Amber Murray's child was taken to Macdonaldtown'.

In the shock of the moment, Sarah had finally admitted she was a baby farmer by confirming Amber's evidence that the Makins had taken her child. But had Baby Horace been taken to Macdonaldtown? Was he one of the seven babies found in Burren Street? Although it is easy to discount Sarah's denial as the panicked lie of someone committed to stand trial for murder, I think Sarah blurted out the truth. While Baby D's estimated age matched the age of Horace when he was adopted (four weeks) and the clothing in which he was found matched that of Amber's baby, it is hard to dismiss the evidence of Clarice and Daisy, both of whom had said that Baby Horace was the sixth child in the George Street house and that six babies were taken to Burren Street.

Because the Makins swapped clothes between their adopted babies, the use of babies' clothing was an unreliable method of identification. Along with the fact that hair colour can lighten as a result of decomposition during burial, it is possible that Baby D was not Amber's child. Out of the three male babies found in Burren Street, Baby 3, who was 6–12 weeks when he died, was close enough in age to Horace for Sarah's dramatic declaration to have been true, especially if he had been kept alive for another couple of weeks in Burren Street.

After the verdict, the jury wished to 'record their appreciation of the services of Senior-Constable Joyce and Constable Brown, and consider some recognition should be made ... for the able manner in which those officers have prepared the case'. It had been Joyce's obsession with digging that resulted in his decision to dig underneath the kitchen window of 109 George Street. There he found the grave of Baby D. With the outcome of this inquest, Joyce finally had the Makins for murder. Although they would still have to stand trial on a charge of murdering Baby Horace, the case against them was strong—so strong that this case would change the course of legal history.

Outside the court, the Makins were led to the black police van. Although John appeared completely indifferent when the verdict was announced, he betrayed his feelings when, climbing into the back of the van, he 'used a disgusting phrase' and gave 'a half smile and scowl to the bystanders'.

At the end of Act I, the crowds inside the court had witnessed the long arm of justice along with the excitement of the Makins' court dramatics. They would have to wait a few months for Act II to begin on the first day of the Makins' trial.

Age estimations of infants: an inexact science

Dr Milford frequently used the length of a baby's thigh bone (femur), and sometimes its spine, to estimate the ages of the infants discovered in George and Burren streets. He may also have made age estimations based on his examination of the skull bones. But in the 1890s, as well as today, these estimations were an inexact science.

The length of a baby will vary based on its birth weight and nutritional intake after birth. In the 1890s, disease played a major part in a child's growth after birth, indicating that the skeletal development of Sydney's baby-farmed infants would have varied widely. The femur is considered to be the most reliable of the human long bones for age estimation in children even though its length at birth can vary from 69 to 78.7 mm. Like adults, a baby might be short or long depending on the length of its femur.[5]

Age estimations based on skeletal development may also be unreliable since a well-fed baby will increase the lengths of its long bones significantly more compared to an underfed or starved baby. This is why dental age estimation is more reliable than use of the long bones. This type of age estimation is possible even for babies whose teeth have not yet erupted, since unerupted teeth are discernible in the upper and lower jaws with the use of x-rays. But without this tool in 1892, Dr Milford would have only used dental eruption occasionally, since he was frequently required to estimate the ages of babies under the age of six months.

Without the use of modern methods, there was a degree of inaccuracy in Dr Milford's age estimations. Today forensic scientists know that it is important to use a number of indicators to estimate the age of human remains, including the degree of closure of the cranial sutures in the skull, the appearance of the ossification centres (the sites where bone forms), radiographic measurement of the length and width of the wrist bones, microscopic analysis of bone remodelling, dental eruption and attrition, closure of the ephiphyses (the ends of the long bones), the length and diameter of the long bones, and the length of the vertebral column.

The six bones of the skull can also be used for the age estimation of very young babies, as well as the dense connective tissue, called 'fontanels', which separates the skull bones. The extent of fusion of a baby's skull varies from child to child so that it is possible for an age estimation to be out by several weeks or months.[6] Dr Milford's estimations would also have been hampered when a baby's remains were so badly decomposed that the skull bones had no connective tissue keeping them together.

But Dr Milford did not know that, in some cases, he was estimating the ages of babies who had been underfed or starved. In such situations, age estimations based on dental development are considered to be more reliable because tooth eruption is less affected by malnutrition than skeletal development.[7] But Dr Milford was required to estimate the ages of children who may have had no erupted teeth, and who had suffered malnutrition which, if severe enough, can delay tooth eruption. These factors may account for some of his divergent age estimations such as two to nine weeks for Baby D.

Because of the limitations in Dr Milford's age estimations, the age he estimated for Baby D was probably not accurate enough to support the jury's finding that he was the son of Amber Murray. In reality, Baby D's identity was impossible to determine, something the judge in the Makins' trial would come to realise.

The Makins would never know that confusion about the identity of Baby D would seal their fate, leaving nothing but bewilderment for the jury in their extraordinary trial, for the appeal judges in both appeals and for anyone looking back from the twenty-first century. Because of this confusion, it is possible the Makins were wrongly convicted of the murder of Amber Murray's baby.

PART III

TRIALS, APPEALS AND VARIOUS PETITIONS

CHAPTER SEVENTEEN

The trial of the century: a judge out of his depth
6–10 March 1893

On 6 March 1893, the trial of John and Sarah Makin began in the New South Wales Supreme Court for the murder of Horace Amber Murray. Although charges had been laid against the Makins for the manslaughter of Mignonette Davies, this trial did not go ahead as a result of the outcome of the trial concerning Baby Horace.

On 7 January 1893 John pleaded to the Sheriff of the Supreme Court that he was 'entirely without means' for his defence in an attempt to gain access to all the depositions (or testimony) that had been given by witnesses in the various inquests:[1]

> I do myself the honor to make application herewith for copies of
> the depositions in the several cases taken at the Coroner's Court ...
> Being entirely without means I am reluctantly compelled to adopt
> this course, and would respectfully ask that they may be furnished
> me at your earliest possible convenience.

After this letter was received, Constable Joyce made inquiries with the Wollongong police about whether or not further funds were available for John's defence. Sergeant Grieve replied on 28 January that George Makin, John's younger brother and the trustee of his mother's will, had already arranged for £61 to be advanced to Mr Williamson for John's defence.[2] John had also agreed to assign his rights to his monthly payments to the tune of £70 to pay Mr Williamson at his forthcoming trial.

Perhaps seeking some control over his defence John wrote two more pleading letters requesting that the depositions be sent 'at once as I have only two weeks to prepare my defence'. He received a curt reply from the Sheriff of the Supreme Court:

> Be so good as to inform Mr. Makin that his <u>brother Mr George Makin</u> has reported that Mr T. M. Williamson has received two sums viz.- <u>£21 and £40</u> for his defence, that a further sum of <u>£70</u> is to be paid to Mr Williamson to defray the expense of the trial ...
>
> Under the circumstances the Crown Solicitor does <u>not</u> supply copy depositions gratuitously.[3]

The trial of the century begins

On the Monday morning of day one of the trial, twelve men were sworn in as the jury although, for the sake of justice, we hope they were not the same jurors who had sat during the many inquests. When the jurymen took their seats in the jury box of the cedar-lined courtroom, waistcoated in their Sunday best, they joined the talkative curiosity-seekers who packed the public gallery while a crowd at the door tried to cram inside. Sydney had never seen anything like it. Not so much the trial of the decade, it would become the trial of the century, the outcome of which would inform the common law in both England and Australia for more than a hundred years because of the controversial evidence that was allowed to go to the jury.[4]

As the Makins were brought up from the cells below the courtroom they saw some familiar faces. Mr Healy, who had been counsel assisting the Coroner, was seated at the Bar table as the Crown prosecutor while Mr Williamson, on his left, appeared for the Makins. John made himself comfortable in the dock, crossing his arms and legs. Right to the end, he manifested an air of bravado, his body language announcing he would not be cowed, unlike Sarah, who hid her face with a handkerchief throughout the day.[5] Perhaps Blanche and Florence had managed to find a seat in the public gallery along with their uncles, John's brothers, who keenly felt the shame that John had brought upon their family.

As Justice Stephen entered in a peacock display of horsehair wig and red and purple robes, the courtroom clattered to its collective feet. The customary bowing between judge and lawyers took place. Before the proceedings could begin, the charges against the prisoners were read out by the Sheriff:

> John and Sarah Makin, you have been charged with having on 29 June 1892 at 109 George Street, Redfern feloniously and maliciously murdered Horace Amber Murray. You have further been charged with having … feloniously and maliciously murdered a certain male infant, whose name to the Attorney-General was unknown.

The second, alternative charge was included in the indictment because Amber Murray's child had never been baptised or registered in the name of Horace Amber Murray. Officially, Amber's child was 'unknown' to the law, being known only as Baby D.[6]

The Makins were asked to reply to the charges. Standing like cattle on display, would they have a quick change of heart? Or would the experience of Darlinghurst Gaol make them hold out for the slimmest chance of acquittal? The Sheriff eyed John and asked:

Sheriff:	John Makin, how do you plead to the first charge against you, guilty or not guilty?
John Makin:	Not guilty.
Sheriff:	How do you plead to the second charge, guilty or not guilty?
John Makin:	Not guilty.

John's clear answers resonated around the courtroom. Many were probably more interested to hear from Sarah. Just who was this woman who had betrayed her sex by killing children?

Sheriff:	Mrs Sarah Makin, how do you plead to the first charge, guilty or not guilty?

Sarah Makin:	Not guilty.
Sheriff:	How do you plead to the second charge, guilty or not guilty?
Sarah Makin:	Not guilty.

Her voice from behind her handkerchief may have trembled but she was still defiant. Right to the end, Sarah considered she was not guilty. Was she deluding herself or was she really innocent of the charges against her?

Mr Healy's opening address to the jury recounted the story that had been revealed at the inquest in December about the birth of Amber Murray's 'fine, strong, healthy' boy on 30 May 1892 and her advertisement in *The Evening News* for 'a kind, motherly person' to adopt her son. But this trial was not just about the death of Baby Horace. Mr Healy told the jury about all the other police discoveries in the backyards of Burren, George, Levey and Alderson Streets, as well as the many aliases the Makins were known to have used.

At the time when the police made their gruesome discoveries in the various backyards, *The Sydney Morning Herald* published an interesting observation—because none of the autopsies on the bodies of the 13 babies had found a cause of death, 'a most important link in the chain of evidence is missing'.[7] The absence of this link provided a weak foundation for the trial. Mr Healy probably suspected he would not get a conviction unless the evidence of the other babies was admitted in the trial.

He told the jury it was their job to determine whether Baby D was the child of Amber Murray as he described the uniqueness of the clothing worn by the child—made by Miss Murray's own hand and recognisable because she 'was not an expert needlewoman'.

Although Mr Healy informed the jurymen they were to decide the case solely on the evidence and not to consider anything they may have heard, the question to this day is whether or not the Makins received a fair trial and were convicted of the death of the wrong child. To answer that question I will take you into the heart of the trial proceedings and compare them with the way a murder trial would be conducted today.

How to prove a murder has happened when there's no evidence

In 1892, forensic science was in its infancy. There was no DNA testing that could positively identify Baby D as the child of Amber Murray. It was also not possible for the Crown to prove how the baby had died because of the degree of decomposition of the body.

The fact that a dead baby was found in the backyard of a house where the Makins had lived does not mean they killed him, even if they had buried him. He could have died from natural causes or an accidental overdose of Godfrey's Cordial. But the Crown did not have to prove *how* Baby D had died, just the fact that he had been murdered by Sarah or John or both. Was there enough evidence to prove this?

There was sufficient evidence—from Amber Murray, four other unmarried mothers, Amber's midwife and the prison informant, Jordan—to show that the Makins were baby farmers. This evidence also showed that the Makins were only receiving £2 to £5 in return for adopting babies 'for life'. Because these premiums were so small, the Makins could not afford to feed and clothe their baby-farmed children for any length of time, giving the Makins 'an interest in their death'[8] and the motive for murder.

The secret burial of Baby D's body, the initial lies told to Amber and Mrs Patrick that her child was doing well, the lies about the Makins' move to Hurstville, and the apparent substitution of another baby covered with sores to show Amber how sick her son was, all pointed to the Makins' concealment of the unnatural death of Baby Horace. This evidence was, however, circumstantial. There were no eyewitnesses—or at least none willing to talk—to describe if, when and how the Makins had killed Amber's baby. Yet Mr Healy guessed if he was allowed to call Constable Joyce to give evidence that another 12 dead babies had been found in four backyards of houses previously occupied by the Makins, the jury would conclude the Makins were a pair of baby murderers. Whether Justice Stephen would allow this evidence was the key question in the trial. The Crown case depended on it. The Makins' fate would be decided by it. Without it, Mr Williamson could more easily defend them by arguing that Amber's baby had contracted a disfiguring rash and within a week had died and been buried in Burren Street. Although the Makins failed to register his death and give him a proper burial, they were not murderers.

But first there had to be some evidence that Horace died an unnatural death, said Justice Stephen. For example, if Horace had died in a foundling hospital and there was evidence that 12 other babies had also died in that hospital, without more evidence, it would not be possible to conclude that Horace had been murdered. But in this case there was more, said Mr Healy. He argued that Horace's death was unnatural because Amber Murray's baby had been healthy when she handed him to the Makins while John had admitted to Edward Jordan that he had buried the Burren Street babies. This was sufficient for Justice Stephen to reason that Joyce's evidence about the discovery of 12 other babies should be heard by the jury because it showed that 'the prisoners carried on a regular system of getting rid of these unfortunate babies, and to shew that the death of [Horace] was not accidental'.[9] But was his reasoning based on too many assumptions?

Constable Joyce is called

There were more than a dozen witnesses who would give evidence in the trial because of the investigations of Constable Joyce,[10] so it was fitting that he was the first, a man whose obsessions had paid off as he described how the remains of 13 infants had been discovered in the Makins' backyards. Joyce's authority would have added weight to his evidence as the jurymen recognised him as 'one of them', a hard-working man compared with the shabbily dressed Makins in their prison garb, the couple who had tried every rat-trick in the book to evade the torch-light of the law on their penny-pinching lives. The Makins carried an aura of guilt about them, with every literate man in the colony having read about their nefarious, baby-farming ways. For a man to stoop to this level to earn a living, and for a woman to abandon her 'natural' instincts, was a national shame. The problem faced by the Makins' lawyer was how to overcome this prejudice.

Mr Williamson objected to Joyce's evidence, arguing that it would adversely affect the minds of the jury. He reminded Stephen that the

Makins had only been charged with the murder of one child (Baby D) while the Crown was presenting evidence about the death of several other children, 'leaving the jury to draw their own conclusions'. Although Stephen conceded the Makins might be prejudiced, he believed the jury had a right to hear that a short time before the discovery of Baby D, other bodies were found in other yards in similar circumstances.

Because there were conflicting opinions from other cases on this particular legal point, Stephen decided to follow the example of an English judge, Justice Butt, who said that 'the safest rule to be guided by is one's common sense'. Today a trial judge is required to weigh the strength of this type of evidence against its prejudicial effect, exactly the thing that Williamson was at pains to point out.[11] But he had lost round one in a very long legal battle about Joyce's evidence.

When Amber Murray was called to the witness box, the jurymen must have wondered why a young unmarried woman would publicly reveal her shameful secret if there was no truth to her story that she had advertised for someone to adopt her illegitimate child and received a reply from Mr and Mrs Hill at 109 George Street. When Williamson pressed her about the health of her child she admitted he had suffered from thrush but 'was perfectly cured' when adopted by the Makins. Amber's midwife, Mrs Patrick, also gave evidence that Amber's son was 'a very healthy little chap'. In reply to Williamson's probing questions, she admitted he had suffered from thrush but other than that '[n]othing ailed it'.

Williamson was trying to establish that there was something not quite right about Baby Horace when he was adopted. While Amber and Mrs Patrick were keen to stress the baby's thrush had cleared up by this time, Williamson did not think to press the issue further. Perhaps he was ignorant about the significance of a child who suffers from thrush in the first weeks of life even though he knew that John Makin had apparently taken Baby Horace, covered in bad sores and suffering from a severe case of thrush, to Mrs Patrick's house on 5 July 1892.

If a baby has a weakened immune system or an inability to fight infection because of a chronic disease, it has an increased risk of developing thrush (or candidiasis). A baby may suffer some or all of the common symptoms, which include white patches on the tongue and inside of the baby's mouth and red lesions on its bottom and genitals which may spread to its thighs and abdomen.[12] The presence of thrush on Baby Horace indicates that although he appeared healthy he had a weakened immune system, probably as the result of a disease such as congenital syphilis. Williamson had missed something vital to the Makins' defence—he had failed to emphasise that Baby Horace had suffered from thrush *before* he was adopted and that the baby taken to Mrs Patrick's (and seen by Mrs King) by John on 5 July had a very bad case of thrush. All of this suggested that Baby Horace had been taken to Burren Street as Clarice and Daisy had testified at the December inquest so that he could not have been Baby D. In a trial today, the defence would call a doctor to give their opinion about the significance of recurring thrush for a child's immune system and whether the symptoms described by Mrs King were consistent with that of a syphilitic baby. In an era when syphilis was rife and infant mortality was remarkably high,[13] death by natural causes could not be discounted.

Clarice's loss of memory

The public gallery must have whispered expectantly as Clarice was called to the witness box, the only child of the Makins to give evidence at their trial. She readily informed the court that there had been five or six babies in the George Street house before the move to Burren Street. But instead of repeating what she had said at the inquest in December—that *six* babies were taken to Burren Street when the family moved—she swore that her father and mother only took five babies and that Baby Horace was not one of them. Questioned closely by Williamson about her previous evidence, she denied giving it even though it had been recorded in her signed deposition.

This was a surprising turnaround. Clarice's evidence now unequivocally supported the Crown case that Baby Horace had been murdered and buried at 109 George Street. Had someone asked Clarice to change her evidence? Why else would she deny giving her clear and detailed evidence from three months earlier? Despite his efforts with Clarice, Williamson did not make a dent in the wall of evidence that Mr Healy had skilfully built on the first day of the trial.

Day two of 'a most extraordinary case'

Agnes Ward, the first witness on day two, had advertised in *The Evening News* on 27 April 1892 for a 'kind person' to adopt her baby son who was 'very delicate' and unable to keep his food down, vomiting soon after feeding. He suffered from a hard, swollen stomach and a red rash from the middle of his stomach to his hips, all of which were symptoms of congenital syphilis. His worsening health meant she could no longer look after him.

Sarah Makin had called at the home of Agnes' midwife in Summer Hill on the evening the advertisement appeared, although Agnes was out. She returned the following morning with reinforcements—John and Daisy—to reassure Mrs Terry, who had become suspicious when Sarah mentioned the family was moving to a farm. Going by the name of Wilkinson, the Makins must have been desperate for money because they waited all day until 5 p.m. for Agnes to return home.

The Makins agreed to adopt her baby for £5, although John explained they were not taking him for the money but to fill the gap caused by the death of their own son. They would put most of the £5 in the bank for him for when he grew up. John wrote out an agreement to complete the bargain under the keen eyes of Mrs Terry.

Although they were living in Kettle Street, Redfern, John said he had an inheritance and was planning to buy a piggery in Balmain or the North Shore. He promised to send the address so Agnes could visit. When, in tears, Agnes handed over her ten-week-old baby, Sarah also cried, explaining, 'I am very soft. As soon as I see anybody crying I must cry too'. That day was the last time Agnes saw her delicate baby, since she heard nothing more from the Makins.

Mr Williamson decided to object to this type of evidence being given one more time. But on day two Justice Stephen decided a speech was needed, pointing out to Mr Williamson that:

> this was a most extraordinary case. In fact, there had been no case like it ... [Agnes'] child ... had been received by the accused ... and nothing further had been heard of it, and other children had been received in a similar manner and nothing further had been heard

> of them ... [I]t seemed ... that the matter must be decided ... from
> the common sense standpoint. If the law subsequently decided
> that ... [the evidence] was ... wrongly admitted ... the prisoners
> were perfectly safe, for, if found guilty, they would be subsequently
> discharged [after an appeal]. If ... he rejected the evidence, he
> might possibly be interfering with the fair and equitable adminis-
> tration of justice.

Stephen seemed to be admitting that he was out of his depth so he would use his commonsense. If he were wrong in doing so, the appeal court would have the final say. To him, this was better than risking an acquittal because he had excluded what surely was quite powerful evidence.

The Makins had to watch a parade of mothers give evidence about their baby-farming activities even though none of them was connected with the other 12 babies discovered by the police. Next into the witness box was Clara Risby, who had relinquished her child to the Makins when they lived at 16 East Street, then Mary Stacey, who had given her baby daughter to the Makins when they were in George Street. Finally, the evidence of Agnes Todd served to complete the picture that the Makins had had a very busy month in June 1892 as they collected babies and premiums, squeezing more and more children into the house in George Street.

Then came Mrs Hill with her suspicious evidence about picks and shovels, followed by Mr Jordan, who recounted John's confession and the juicy tidbit that John had confessed to burying the children in Burren Street. By the time the present tenant of 109 George Street, Mrs Ralph, gave her evidence—that Mrs Makin had called to make inquiries about whether the police had found any bodies *before* three dead babies were discovered in the backyard—some of the jurors must already have made up their minds.

The Crown's case had now closed. Mr Healy could be well pleased by how each of the Crown's witnesses had come up to proof, especially Clarice. The judge was on his side and he must have thought if he were a betting man, the odds of losing were very low indeed.

Mr Williamson addresses the jury

On day three of the trial, the Makins offered no defence and called no witnesses. As at the inquests, Sarah and John had decided not to give their own version of events. This meant the trial proceeded to hear the closing addresses of the prosecutor and defence counsel. On the morning of Thursday 9 March, Mr Williamson stood to address the jury. It was a fine speech. He must have been up most of the night preparing it. He began by stating the obvious—that the baby-farming activities of the Makins had been publicised widely during the many coronial inquiries. He urged the jury, as men who would perform 'their duty honourably', to put out of their minds anything they had heard outside the court, including any articles and reports that may have influenced them.

Williamson reminded them that Mr Healy had said during his opening address that the Makins had taken six children to Burren Street on 29 June. At no stage during the trial had Healy sought to withdraw this statement. But Healy 'could not blow hot and cold' because the witnesses did not support his assertion. Clarice had denied saying that six children had accompanied her family on the fateful night they moved to Burren Street. It is unclear from the court report what Williamson then said. Presumably he stressed that if Baby Horace had been the sixth baby in 109 George Street and six babies were taken to Burren Street, then Amber Murray's baby could not have been one of the three babies discovered in the backyard of George Street.

Williamson informed the jury of the 'two features' in the case that 'required their special attention':

1. Did Horace Amber Murray die, and, if he had died, had the remains been identified?
2. If [there was identification] had he died from natural causes or had he been murdered?

He told the jury that the Crown had 'attempted to build a house without a foundation' because it had not produced any evidence to prove the cause of death of Baby D: 'was it not an insult to [your] intelligence that [you] should be asked to think that because certain children had been found dead', Miss Murray's baby had been murdered?

Williamson was stressing that in a murder trial the Crown has to prove that the defendant committed the act causing death. This had not been done by Mr Healy because he was hoping the jury would make a leap of logic from the existence of dead babies in the backyards of Burren and George streets to the assumption that the Makins had murdered Baby Horace. It was a very tempting leap to make. But people ought not to be convicted of murder based on leaps of logic. The missing stepping stone was a cause of death. How did Baby Horace die?

When Mr Healy addressed the jury after Mr Williamson he focused on the question the jurors would have been asking themselves—why didn't the Makins give evidence? Although this type of comment by a prosecutor is not allowed in criminal trials these days, it was permissible in 1893. Healy also pointed out that the defence had not called any member of the Makin family to give evidence about what happened to Baby Horace. Again this failure pointed to the fact that the Makins had something to hide.

When Justice Stephen turned to the jury to begin his summing-up of the trial he made a startling admission—he 'now had to undertake the most arduous task that had ever fallen to his lot … in dealing with criminal cases'. He told the jury that the Makins' failure to give evidence should not be used against them because the law allowed them their right to silence. But he also revealed that other judges thought the opposite.

To find the Makins guilty, said Stephen, the jurymen had to be satisfied that 'the child murdered' was the son of Amber Murray. This was a very unfortunate phrase. He was assuming that Baby D had died as a result of murder, the very question the jury had to decide. He had probably made the same leap of logic Healy was hoping the jury would make.

Stephen reminded the jury that in '99 cases out of 100' the cause of death was known in murder cases. Even though it was not known in this case, he urged the jurymen:

> but in the administration of justice [you] must not be daunted at the outset for that reason, because in certain cases, if that happened, convictions would not be obtained where they ought to be.

Justice Stephen was hinting that this case might be one where a conviction 'ought to be' obtained. He reminded them that Amber Murray's child had been at the Makins' house in George Street on 27 June, which meant the child:

> had been in the vicinity of the place where its body had been found—it had not been 100 miles away. Bodies of infants had been subsequently dug up in the yard. What did that secret burial … point to? Who buried the bodies? If the prisoners did not do it … who had done it?

But Justice Stephen was making too many assumptions. What he should have said is that Amber's son had been in a house where *a* body, not *his* body, had been found since whether Baby D *was* Baby Horace was a fact the jury had to decide, based on all the evidence in the trial. Although it was tempting to think otherwise, the Makins were only on trial for the murder of *one* baby, not the deaths of the other unfortunate babies.

More confusion was to follow. Stephen said Constable Joyce's evidence of the 12 other babies had been given to demonstrate that other children adopted by the prisoners had also died, just in case the Makins had decided to argue that Baby D had died of neglect. But Mr Williamson had not mounted any such defence. Justice Stephen, out of his depth, was muddying the waters with too many assumptions.

Certainly, most people would agree that the Makins had buried the babies found in George and Burren streets, given their guilty knowledge about the burials. But illegal burial and killing are two different things. Mr Healy had not presented any evidence about how any of the babies, including Baby D, had died. The jury needed clarification about the cause of death but it was not forthcoming. Maybe this case had tested the limits of the legal minds in the courtroom. As Justice Stephen had said, it was an extraordinary and unique case for which his legal experience had not prepared him.

The verdict

With all of this information and misinformation, the jury retired at 5 p.m. While Stephen had been addressing the jury, Williamson had been busy scribbling away at the Bar table. He handed Stephen a memo containing the points he asked the judge to reserve for an appeal:

1. His Honor was wrong in admitting evidence of the finding of the bodies other than that of Horace Amber Murray;
2. His Honor was wrong in admitting the evidence of [Clara] Risby, Mary Stacey, Agnes Ward, Agnes Todd and [her midwife];
3. there was no evidence to identify the body as that of Horace Amber Murray;
4. there was no evidence of the death or the cause of death of Horace Amber Murray.

The memo reflected what Williamson expected—guilty verdicts.

When the jury filed out of the courtroom to consider its verdict, Sarah and John were taken to a room with their police guards to sit through the same anxious, gnawing wait of the guilty and the innocent alike. By six o'clock the jury had not agreed on a decision. Stephen announced he would return to the courtroom at nine o'clock. At 9.10 p.m., the foreman announced the jury had still not reached a verdict. There was some confusion, since the foreman asked Stephen to 'repeat the authority … as to the establishing of the cause of death'. This was clearly the issue that the lay jurors ought to have wrestled with. Stephen reminded the foreman that 'he had told them that he did not consider it absolutely necessary that the cause of death should be established in making out a case'. They must be satisfied that the child had 'met its death, not by a natural means, but some unlawful act'.

This was exactly what the jury wanted to know, said the foreman, but he warned there would be no verdict tonight, suggesting there was dissension in the jury room. The jury was locked up for the night while the Makins returned to their cells via the tunnel that connected the Darlinghurst Courthouse to Darlinghurst Gaol[14]—all for a restless night.

When the court resumed the next morning, everyone in the public gallery would have watched the jurymen file in with their eyes averted from the Makins, a bad sign which Mr Williamson would have clocked. The tipstaff asked the foreman of the jury:

Tipstaff:	Have you agreed on a verdict?
Foreman:	Yes.
Tipstaff:	How do you find the prisoners, guilty or not guilty?
Foreman:	We find the prisoners guilty of the murder of Horace Amber Murray but we strongly recommend the female prisoner to mercy.

The verdict hit the court like a bomb. Sarah 'threw herself backwards' in a 'fainting fit', 'sobbing most piteously', almost falling out of her chair. Two constables rushed to grab her. But John remained impassive: 'on hearing the decision, [he] manifested no concern', maintaining 'stolid indifference'. He did not even assist his wife. While Joyce and his constables may have cheered, perhaps the unmarried mothers, the two Agneses, Amber, Clara and Mary, hugged each other and cried. In the mayhem, Justice Stephen tried to bring everyone to order, banging his gavel.

He announced he would not sentence the Makins until their appeal was heard, since he wished to 'be spared the painful reflection' of passing a sentence should the appeal succeed. Finally, he thanked the jury and discharged them. When he ordered the constables to remove the prisoners from the court, Sarah had the last word as she wailed: 'It's Clarie, it's Clarie, it's Clarie that did it'. Sobbing bitterly and crying out 'Oh! Clarie, Clarie, Clarie' she was assisted down the stairs into the basement of the court by John and a constable, 'her sorrowful and reproachful cries … gradually fading away in the distance'.

Sometimes in the heat of emotion the truth is blurted out. While Sarah's final attempt to cast blame elsewhere was a habit of hers, she knew that all of her daughters were involved in the family's baby-farming business, even Clarice, which may have been one of the reasons Clarice decided to give evidence against her parents—to downplay her role in the deaths and to save her own neck.

Surprisingly, there was sympathy for Sarah, who some people thought had acted:

> under the domination of her strong-willed husband, of whom
> she may have stood in fear. Whatever her crimes, the wretched

woman's sufferings since the beginning of this terrible business have evidently been of the most poignant character. Her strongly emotional temperament ... has supplied one of the most painfully sensational elements in the many dramatic scenes which have characterized the legal revelations of the misdeeds of the inhuman husband and his weak and wicked wife.[15]

Did the Makins receive a fair trial?

It was not only the jury who had given their verdict. Newspaper editors, the public and even Justice Stephen thought the Makins were guilty because of the evidence about the 12 other babies. But the lengthy jury deliberation shows how difficult it was to convict baby farmers based on circumstantial evidence, even if this had been the most compelling case of the murderous practices of baby farmers that had ever been heard in the Australian colonies.

Compared to the conduct of criminal trials today, the Makins did not receive a fair trial for many reasons. The first glaring problem was that the prosecutor addressed the jury *after* Mr Williamson. This meant Williamson was unable to counteract any of the issues brought up in Mr Healy's closing address, in particular, Healy's focus on the Makins' decision to remain silent. Today the right to silence is jealously protected by our evidence laws.[16] Prosecutors are prohibited from referring to an accused's decision to remain silent to stop them from indulging in idle speculation as Mr Healy did, including the assumption that many people make—that a silent accused is a guilty accused. Although Justice Stephen had told the jury that the Makins' failure to give evidence should not be used against them, he also hinted that other judges thought the opposite, giving the jury a green light that they could do so as well.

Because the Makins decided not to give evidence, they were able to avoid a probing cross-examination by Mr Healy. While John may have withstood his incisive questions, Sarah's emotional volatility may have led to dramatic declarations, dangerous slips of the tongue and fainting fits.

In his closing address, clever Mr Healy had stressed that the Makins had not called any member of their family to explain what happened to

Baby Horace, implying they had something to hide. Today, the obligation to call a key witness is on the prosecution rather than the defence because defendants do not have to prove their innocence by calling witnesses.[17] Healy could easily have called Florence or Blanche Makin to give evidence but Williamson was not given the chance to retort that Healy should have done so and Justice Stephen did not recognise the problem.

More unfairness to the Makins arose because Stephen decided to allow the evidence from Constable Joyce and the unmarried mothers to be heard by the jury. He justified his decision by saying that if he were wrong in doing so and the Makins were convicted, the appeal court could have the final say. Stephen had gambled with his overriding duty to ensure the Makins received a fair trial by tossing a coin, thus creating a risk that the Makins might be convicted as a result of wrongly admitted evidence.

Stephen knew Constable Joyce's evidence was likely to produce an emotional reaction and could be misused by the jurymen. For this reason, he should have emphasised that they had to be satisfied, beyond reasonable doubt, that the Makins had committed the 'guilty act' causing the baby's death. He ought to have cautioned the jury that Sarah and John were not on trial for the deaths of the other 12 babies.

Stephen also made a mistake when he assumed that Baby D had been murdered even though it was the jury's job to make that decision. By using the words 'the child murdered', Stephen gave the jury a wink and a nudge that *he* thought the child had been murdered. He reinforced his hint when he said that, even without a cause of death, convictions can still be obtained 'where they ought to be'.

But it was at the end of his summing-up that Stephen confused the jury even more. He told them that there was insufficient evidence to prove that Baby D was Horace Amber Murray: 'I do not see any satisfactory evidence that this child was Horace Amber Murray, and you must take the case on the second count', the second count being the one charging John and Sarah Makin with the murder of an infant whose name was unknown.[18] This meant the jury had to ignore the evidence from Amber Murray and her midwife which had identified the clothing on Baby D as belonging to Horace. Instead, they had to decide whether or not the Makins had killed an unknown baby called Baby D. Did they wonder why Miss Murray's and Mrs Patrick's evidence had been given in the first place? If they did, they decided to ignore the problem. Because the jurors were confused, they assumed that Baby D was Horace Amber Murray. When the foreman of the jury read out the verdict, Sarah and John had been found guilty of the murder of Horace Amber Murray, not of Baby D.[19]

Without any evidence about how the baby died, it is possible the jury made the leap of logic Mr Healy hoped they would make—that the presence of 12 other babies in the backyards of four houses lived in by the Makins' was too suspicious and too much of a coincidence. Murder was the only explanation. And if the Makins murdered twelve they must have murdered Baby Horace. It seems as if the presumption of innocence got lost in the compelling and gruesome evidence given by Constable Joyce.

As it was, most of the problems identified above were not raised in the Makins' appeal. After all, this was 1893 when the laws of evidence and trial procedure were still in their infancy.

❦

CHAPTER EIGHTEEN

The first appeal: the Makins' struggle against the hand of fate
23–30 March 1893

The Makins had not received a fair trial but no-one, except Sarah, John and their lawyer, seemed to be too bothered that justice had been trounced. It was a common view that '[t]he Makin case is probably the worst which has ever disfigured the criminal records of Australia'. To anyone following the grisly details of the lives, deaths and discoveries of the unknown babies it was 'a crime which involve[d] the utmost meanness and callousness and cold-blooded brutality ... Such an act is a disgrace to civilization'.[1]

While one newspaper acknowledged that '[n]o one is so eager for convictions as to desire to see them based on evidence improperly admitted', the number of buried babies found in the former houses of the Makins was enough to satisfy all and sundry that John and Sarah were serial murderers:

> had the Judge excluded the evidence, that would have been a mistake without a cure. They could not have been tried again, had they been acquitted ... [a]nd the public, aware of the facts connected with the other bodies, and with the cases of the other women ... would have felt that justice had ... been administered in the dark.[2]

Other newspapers in the colonies also found comfort in the jury's decision:

> The old saying may be right, and hanging may be the worst use to which a human being can be put: but ... if ever a man specially

deserved to be asphyxiated by the hangman's rope it is the head of
the notorious baby-farming Makin family.[3]

Even before the jury returned its verdict, Mr Williamson had put Justice
Stephen on notice that he would appeal against Stephen's decision to allow
the jury to hear Constable Joyce's evidence of the discovery of the 12 other
babies. This particular question had apparently never been examined by
a court of appeal in 'the mother country'.[4] Were the three colonial appeal
judges up to the task?

A Rolls Royce defence

While the Makins slummed it in cold, dank and dark Darlinghurst Gaol,
the appeal against their convictions would be an expensive enterprise.
The couple who had haunted the inner city slums with little furniture
(auctioned by John's brothers for a mere 12 shillings), living hand to mouth
by apparently killing babies so they themselves could live, were represented
by Rolls Royce legal counsel. Faced with John's death, the Makin family
hired the services of one of the most eminent Queen's Counsels of the time,
Sir Julian Salomons. Had the family been willing to help feed John, Sarah
and their children at a fraction of the cost of all the legal fees, the family's
name would not now be synonymous with murder.

Salomons was the only son of a merchant in Birmingham. He had
arrived in Sydney at the young age of 17, starting his working life as
a lowly stockbroker's clerk and then as an assistant in a bookshop. But
Sydney was good to this young migrant, holding out opportunities that
may not have been available in crusty old England. Four years after his
arrival, Salomons had passed the examinations of the Barristers' Admission Board.[5]

A photograph of Salomons, later in life, depicts a thin-lipped man with
a fleshy face and determined chin. Though not particularly attractive and
considered to be short, his picture gives the impression of a man of authority. Described as having a 'certain emotional brashness and vanity … a
caustic tongue and a mordant wit', he was a workaholic run by unknown
demons. This resulted in a breakdown and admission to Bay View House,

a private 'lunatic' asylum at Tempe some distance from the city, for four months in 1866.[6]

Despite this setback, Salomons went on to become Solicitor-General for the government and was later appointed to the Legislative Council in 1870, although he resigned a few months later. Despite or because of these appointments, his recurring mental problems saw him take several trips to Europe for his 'health', perhaps persuaded by his wife that seclusion in Europe would attract less attention than a 'lunatic' asylum in Tempe.

Seven years before he represented the Makins, Salomons was a short man with a big reputation. When the Chief Justice of the Supreme Court died in 1886, Salomons was offered the post after two other eminent barristers turned it down. Reluctantly, he accepted. But Salomons was not popular amongst his fellow judges. In a class-ridden, small-town, colonial world, Salomons lacked '"artistocratic position", judicial balance and dignity'.[7] Perhaps his lack of these qualities was due to bipolar disorder, since he appeared to suffer from some of its symptoms—unbounded energy, high intellect and addictive work habits with periods of depression.

A well-respected judge, Sir William Windeyer, in front of whom Salomons would argue the appeal for the Makins, told him he was unacceptable as Chief Justice, accusing him of 'always breaking down mentally'.[8] Perhaps Windeyer instinctively knew that the pressures of the job of Chief Justice would combine like oil and water with Salomons' mental fragility. Windeyer's opinions were so harsh that Salomons remarked they would 'make any intercourse in the future between him and me quite impossible'.[9] They obviously bit deeply since Salomons was the only Chief Justice in New South Wales to resign before he took his oath of office, doing so 12 days after his appointment on 19 November 1886.

Nonetheless, he continued to seek and was rewarded with high office— he served as a member of the New South Wales Legislative Council for 12 years between 1887 and 1899 and was Vice-President of the Executive Council for two different periods.[10] Knighted in 1891, two years before Salomons represented the Makins, Sir Julian's eminence must have burned bright for John Makin's family, who hoped that his legal and oratory skills would be enough to turn the Makins' fate the other way.

The appeal begins

In the Supreme Court of New South Wales on 23 March 1893, Sir Julian appeared before the three Court of Appeal judges who would decide the case: Justices Windeyer, Innes and Foster. Although some may think the law works in mysterious yet just ways, these judges were men of their times, each carrying their own baggage of beliefs and sympathies, who lived a world away from the working-class streets inhabited by baby farmers. The appeal was dominated by Sir William Windeyer, who was known for his concerns about the social disadvantages experienced by women. Because of this:

> [he] proved controversial in criminal cases. With a rigorous and unrelenting sense of the retribution that he believed criminal justice demanded, he had a sympathy verging on the emotional for the victims of crime, especially women.[11]

His 'crusading impulse' to protect women from oppression had been instilled in him by his mother and his wife, Mary.[12] Controversially for the times, both Windeyer and Mary believed that 'contraception and family planning were fundamental to the removal of disadvantage' for women.[13] The Makins' case represented a collision between Windeyer's beliefs and the day to day realities for working-class women like Miss Amber Murray, whose social disadvantage had led her to the baby-farmer's door. For Windeyer, the link between lack of contraception, social disadvantage and the parasitical baby farmer could not have been clearer.

Windeyer has also been described as 'a forceful man, if not a judicial bully, who brooked little dissent in his courtroom'.[14] Even worse for the Makins, he had no respect for their colourful lawyer, Sir Julian Salomons. As Sir Julian pushed back his chair at the Bar table, he began his arguments for the sake of saving the necks of John and Sarah. But in case he should be misinterpreted, he announced he was only concerned with the legal arguments in the case, not 'with the moral culpability of either of these two prisoners'.

The court report of the long discussions between Sir Julian and the appeal judges shows that they were confused about how the trial had been conducted, as well as the grounds of appeal.[15] Sir Julian pointed out that Justice Stephen had decided there was insufficient evidence to identify Baby D as Baby Horace. He had instructed the jury to make a finding only on the second count—that is, whether or not the Makins had murdered an unknown child called Baby D. As stated in the previous chapter, the confused jury ignored this instruction.

The three appeal judges were also confused, so much so that Sir Julian had to point out, six times, that the question of identity had been withdrawn from the jury. The temperature was rising in the courtroom, judicial tempers were already fraying and voices were getting louder—at one point Sir Julian asked Justice Foster, 'Does not your Honor see that the body may be that of a child murdered by the accused, but ... that it is [not] the child of Miss Murray?'

Finally, the penny dropped for the judges and Sir Julian moved onto his next argument—if the jury only had to decide whether or not the Makins had murdered an unknown child called Baby D, why was the evidence from Miss Murray and Mrs Patrick about the disappearance of Baby Horace allowed to be admitted? Sir Julian then launched his main attack—the evidence regarding the other 12 bodies should not have been admitted as evidence of the murder of Baby D. Why? Because there was no independent evidence of the murder of these other children and none to show how Baby D died. To draw any similarities with the cause of death of the other 12 babies, 'there must first be evidence of [other] killing, and ... there must be evidence that the prisoner did the killing'. With no causes of death, the only similarities were similar burials.

Sir Julian argued there was nothing in the evidence that was 'inconsistent with the fact that they all died perfectly natural deaths'. The strongest case that could be made against the Makins was that Baby D had died from neglect. This meant the Makins could only have been guilty of manslaughter.

But Windeyer was unconvinced and made an extraordinary statement which revealed his views at the beginning of the appeal:

> [w]hen once an unlawful killing is established, the presumption is
> that it is murder, and it is for the prisoner to rebut that presumption.

Justice Innes interrupted to say that this was no longer the law because of recent legislation that had been passed in Parliament.[16] Windeyer was not persuaded and disagreed with his fellow judge. Nowadays we know that Windeyer's view is contrary to the presumption of innocence and the obligation on the Crown to prove its case beyond reasonable doubt.

Windeyer posed question after question as he ferreted around for some reason—any reason—to explain why the evidence of the 12 babies was correctly admitted. But Sir Julian would not budge. Furthermore, the evidence could not be used against the female prisoner since there was no other evidence implicating her in the murder of Baby D. Because the court could not say who was guilty out of the two prisoners, both should be acquitted. With that final statement, Sir Julian announced he had finished his submissions. As he made himself comfortable on the brown leather seat behind him, he probably guessed he had already lost even before counsel for the Crown opened his mouth. Justices Innes and Foster had both said very little beside their dominant brother judge.

Justice Windeyer's presumptions

It took the appeal judges a week to consider their decision, which they delivered on 30 March 1893. Sir Julian's clever arguments had not been enough. The gallows were looming closer for John and Sarah. The main judgment was written by Justice Windeyer, with whom Justice Foster agreed. It went on for 27 pages, full of awkward language and long, convoluted sentences snaking down the pages. Justice Innes went out on a limb and disagreed with Windeyer's reasons as to why Constable Joyce's evidence about the 12 babies had been correctly admitted. In the end, he agreed the Makins' conviction should stand but for different reasons.

Who was right? Quite clearly the Makins *were* baby farmers and were guilty of something—unlawful burials, failure to register at least 13 deaths, most likely neglect in the case of some of the babies and murder in relation to others. But those presumptions should have been put to one side because the question at their trial had been whether they had murdered *one* particular child, an unknown baby called Baby D. Nonetheless, these and other presumptions were allowed to sprout.

Windeyer's first presumption was that Baby D had been identified as Baby Horace. Sir Julian had argued otherwise but then abandoned all such arguments. The Makins were left in a very peculiar position— their jury had been instructed it could not decide if Baby D was Horace Amber Murray (due to lack of evidence), the jury had ignored the instruction, the appeal judges ignored the jury's mistake and Windeyer decided that Baby D was Horace Amber Murray even though this was a decision he could not lawfully make. On any view, the Makins should have been acquitted because the jury's verdict was unsafe and unsatisfactory.[17]

Windeyer said there was no authority to say that in every case of murder 'the exact mode of killing must be proved'. To raise the bar that high would mean many murderers would literally get away with murder if they were clever enough to destroy all traces of how the killing occurred. But how can a jury decide if a baby has been murdered if there is no evidence about how it died, such as starvation, poisoning or smothering? There was a gap and the gap was filled with assumptions.

Windeyer focused on the fact that the baby-farming Makins were only receiving 'small sums'—ranging from £2 to £5—that were 'obviously inadequate for [the babies'] support [for life]', which meant they 'had an interest in their death [and] supplied the motive for murder'. But here is where assumptions creep in like ants rushing to feed. Windeyer conceded that:

> [i]t is true that the conclusion of murder, which the jury were asked to draw from the evidence, was merely a presumption; but, in the absence of eye-witnesses of a crime, presumptions must often be acted upon in the administration of justice, if wrongdoers are not to enjoy immunity from prosecution.

Windeyer was acknowledging that legal decision-making is imperfect—it may appear to be based on reason but sometimes that reasoning will be flawed because of gaps in the evidence. One may as well toss a coin— heads, murder; tails, death by natural causes. The problem is that juries have to decide one way or the other. When there are gaps in the evidence, their own assumptions, like liquid silicone, will effectively seal them in the same way that Windeyer was using his.

Windeyer justified his reasons in ways that lawyers would not condone today. With a greater emphasis on the need for the prosecution to prove its case beyond reasonable doubt, no judge today would get away with saying: '[i]f no attempt is made to rebut a strong presumption, it is not surprising that, to the mind of a jury, such presumption becomes conclusive proof of guilt'. Windeyer was referring to the Makins' failure to give evidence. He went to great lengths to find support for this approach from other judges. But it was a fine line. When did 'mere loose conjecture', as one judge said, cross the line to become a presumption that was fair and just? Windeyer thought that presumptions arising from 'crimes of the highest nature', such as murder, were stronger or weaker according to the power of the defendant to produce other evidence to rebut them. But what about the presumption of innocence? Windeyer's reasoning had consigned it to the garbage bin.

In his separate judgment, Justice Innes was at pains to point out that he did not agree with Windeyer:

> I must not ... be taken in any way to assent to the proposition that the fact that the accused did not go into the witness-box to give evidence can be regarded, however slightly, as a circumstance to be taken into consideration by the jury as making against the accused.

What did Sir Julian think when he read Windeyer's judgment? He had argued that the prosecution had failed to produce sufficient evidence to show that an unlawful killing had occurred but Windeyer had turned the tables on him by arguing that the Makins had failed to produce sufficient evidence to rebut a presumption of murder.[18] No matter. This was a mere trifle of logic, light and fluffy like well-beaten cream. Windeyer had great faith in juries, quoting another judge who believed in:

> the unanimous judgment and conscience of 12 men conversant with the affairs and business of life.

The problem was that few men in 1893 had much knowledge about baby farming, disease and infant mortality.

Having dealt with the cause of death problem, Windeyer had to consider the main and sticky issue. Should the discovery of 12 other babies in the former houses of the Makins, as well as the evidence from the unmarried mothers who had relinquished their children to the Makins, have gone to the jury? Sir Julian had argued that this evidence could only be admitted if there was prior evidence of the killing of these babies by the Makins. Windeyer's reasons for concluding this evidence had been correctly admitted rested on flimsy foundations. Even though past criminal conduct by an accused was not normally admitted, he said, an exception arose when '*common sense and our experience of life* compel us to introduce' such evidence.

The problem with using commonsense and life experience is the huge variability in both. Windeyer thought that evidence of a defendant's past criminal conduct could be given when it was 'so connected with the prisoner as to explain his conduct or motives in the transaction which is the subject of the trial'. But therein lay the problem—the connection had to be woven out of the commonsense and life experience of ordinary human beings. Sometimes this link would be a tight weave, at other times, loose. Windeyer revealed that he was not particularly good at this type of legal weaving since he had woven a very loose thread between Baby Horace's death and the other dead babies by tying in the assumption that the mere existence of dead babies in the Makins' former backyards meant there was no other explanation for their deaths but murder. The danger was that juries might assume guilt based solely on a defendant's past criminal conduct. With no cause of death, this is what the jury must have done in the Makins' trial when they considered Constable Joyce's evidence of the 12 other dead babies.

Justice Innes disagreed with Windeyer's approach. He believed that evidence of previous crimes by a defendant should *not* be admitted in a criminal trial because he feared that:

> if you introduce any loose application of what untrained minds
> may call "a common-sense view" with reference to the reception of

evidence, there may be great danger of the wholesome safeguards
which surround the liberty of an accused person ... being broken
in upon and destroyed.

Unlike Windeyer, who thought that failing to admit such evidence would
allow a guilty person to go free, Innes believed that the shock is greater
and the threat to the justice system more profound 'when an innocent man
is convicted than when a guilty man escapes'.

With no cause of death for Baby D (who was assumed to be Horace),
what was the connection between the Makins and the 12 other babies in
their previous backyards? Innes recognised that the *degree* of connection
was the problem with Windeyer's reasoning. Commonsense says that the
Makins were connected to the bodies of all 13 infants found in their former
backyards, especially since most of the dead babies' clothes and wrappings
had been in the Makins' possession. Twelve people, using their experience
of life, might consider the Makins' connection to be none other than foul
play. But without a cause of death, commonsense also says that more is
required before you can say the connection arises out of murder, especially
in a society with a high infant mortality rate.[19] Another 12 people, looking
at the prevalence of congenital syphilis and other childhood diseases at the
time, will realise that Constable Joyce's evidence leads them no closer to a
cause of death. Although it shows that the Makins were baby farmers who
hid the deaths of their adopted babies by unlawful burial, the evidence
points just as easily to death by neglect or disease as it does to death
by murder.

Windeyer mistakenly thought that the evidence of the 12 other babies
showed similarities with the unlawful death of Baby Horace, but there
were no similar acts of killing, just similar burials. Although the Makins'
sudden disappearances from the houses in which the babies were found
looked terribly suspicious, as unregistered baby farmers Sarah and John
had good reasons for avoiding the law's scrutiny.

Justice Innes was an astute judge who realised that the admissibility of
Constable Joyce's evidence was dependent on proof of the act causing death
and proof of who committed it, John or Sarah. Answers to these questions

were necessary, otherwise the problem as to what evidence is enough to prove a connection would be left to:

> the varying views and turns of mind of different individual Judges—some, possibly, of an unreasonably convicting turn of mind, others, possibly, of a weak-kneed ... turn of mind ... It would introduce ... an irresponsible discretion in individual Judges which might be disastrous to the due administration of justice.

Innes had Windeyer in mind as 'an unreasonably convicting' type of judge when he wrote this, since he made even more pointed comments about his brother judge:

> if the loose practice which I understand my brother Windeyer to approve is to obtain, the day will not be far distant when an accused person will be tried and convicted of an offence, not upon evidence connected with that offence, but upon evidence that he has committed similar offences on other occasions.

But there was another assumption buried within Windeyer's reasoning: 'people are not in the habit of concealing the death of infants dying naturally by burying them in back yards'. Ordinary people might not, but baby farmers would. Why draw attention to themselves and their business practices by reporting any death, natural or unnatural?

Aftermath, after comments

The morning after the decision, the editor of *The Sydney Morning Herald* was satisfied with the outcome of the Makins' appeal:

> [t]he unanimity of the decision of the Supreme Court ... will be accepted by the public with that kind of satisfaction which is naturally felt when the common opinion of the community ... is ... upheld ... [by the law] ... If ... it had happened that ... the conviction had been set aside, the result would have been a shock to the

mind of the public and a weakening of confidence in the efficiency of our law.[20]

Another newspaper editor, also certain of the Makins' 'slaughter' of all the infants discovered, was more philosophical in his reflections as he predicted dangerous outcomes:

> Nemesis sometimes seems to dawdle but she almost inevitably overtakes her prey ... The notorious Makin couple ... have been the latest to discover that the purposes of fate, if slow sometimes, are relentless in their certainty ... If ... the Makins had been allowed to escape punishment through some purely technical flaw [that] fact would have been as strong an argument for Lynch law ... as their atrocious crimes are for the retention of capital punishment.[21]

To the public and newspaper editors, the Makins' guilt was obvious. The controversial evidence should have been admitted. This appeal and its outcome might have been the end of story. But there were to be several postscripts—the sentence, another appeal and a final desperate petition to the Governor.

❦

CHAPTER NINETEEN

The law passes sentence
30 March 1893

On the day they lost their appeal, Sarah and John made their final appearance in the Darlinghurst Supreme Court. Sarah had to be assisted into the dock, whereupon she 'hid her face in a pocket handkerchief', not removing it the whole time she was in court. Justice Stephen asked 'if they had anything to say why sentence should not be passed upon them'.[1] John stood 'in that semi-defiant attitude' which now characterised him, uncowed and without remorse, and simply stated: 'We are innocent'.

It may have been true they were, in a purely technical sense, innocent of the murder of Horace Amber Murray, since they knew that he had been buried in Burren Street. But likely as not, they were guilty of the manslaughter of Baby Mignonette Davies and other charges never to be laid.

Mr Williamson clambered to his feet and thanked Stephen for his 'impartiality and fairness shown throughout the trial', oblivious to the partiality the judge had actually shown. Williamson announced there might be an appeal to the Privy Council in England. But Stephen was not dissuaded from his task. He turned to the Makins and reminded them '[you have been] asked why judgment should not be passed upon you, and you have said nothing'.

John declared, still defiant, 'I have only got to say that we are innocent; for the sake of our children'. Perhaps he was conscious of the shame enveloping his family, although his daughters knew only too well what he and Sarah had been involved in.

Justice Stephen's stern voice reverberated around the courtroom as he announced, 'I have one duty to perform. I am simply the mouthpiece of the law'. Sarah leaned against John, alternately sobbing and moaning throughout Stephen's long speech. While there was no pleasure for Stephen in sentencing the contrasting pair before him, he was satisfied the jury's verdict was correct, since he was sentencing them not only for murder but also for 'wickedness':

> You stand before me ... convicted of the crime of murder ... [which was] accompanied by almost every incident that could possibly add to its wickedness. You took money from the mother of [Horace]; you beguiled her with promises which you never meant to perform, having already determined on the death of the child; you misled her by false statements as to your name; you deceived her as to your address ... Finally, in order to render detection impossible ... you buried the child in the yard ... as you would the carcase [*sic*] of a dog.

Having begun to catalogue their wicked ways, Stephen's emotions got the better of him. Before him stood the epitome of the underground trade in the lives and deaths of children in the city of Sydney, two people he believed were guilty of the deaths of every baby discovered by the police:

> you were engaged in baby-farming in its ... most hideous and revolting aspect. Three yards of houses in which you lived testified with that ghastly evidence that you were carrying on this nefarious and hellish trade, destroying the lives of those infants for the sake of gain.

It could not be expected that Stephen would inquire into the reasons why John and Sarah trod the degrading baby-farmer path to a conviction for murder, nor into a society that turned a blind eye to mother and child poverty while condemning unmarried mothers, their offspring and the supportive hand of baby farmers. But Stephen had more to say, this time not as the 'mouthpiece of the law' but as an ordinary citizen, distressed by everything he had seen and heard:

> [t]hese young women [who] testified against you ... called upon you, each of them with a cry, 'Where is my child?' To that cry ... you ... have never given an answer ... and do not even now. Who, then, can doubt that the children met with their deaths in one way or other by criminal conduct on your part? And what for? What for? For a paltry sum of £5, or £3, or £2 ... sums which you count as nothing against the lives and sufferings, and God knows the sufferings, of these poor babies.

Today, a judge would not make these types of comments, however heart-felt and morally correct, for the obvious reason that Sarah and John had not been found guilty of the murder of the babies of the other unmarried mothers. Then came the blackest moral judgement of all:

> Surely two people stand before me whose hearts must be as hard as adamant; utterly indifferent to human suffering, and in whom conscience must be utterly dead. I only hope that in the time that may remain to you your hearts will be softened, and that you will endeavour to find mercy at the hands of Him who gave the lives you have taken away. I do trust you will remember these 13 children—I am not unjust in referring to them—I only hope and trust ... that though you have given no account of them, the community calls upon you, and you must account to God.

Justice Stephen then placed a black cap on his head, which signified the transformation of judge into executioner:

> Nothing remains for me but to pass the sentence of death upon you. The sentence of the Court upon you, John Makin, is that you be taken to ... the place of execution ... and that there you be hanged by the neck until your body be dead.

The same sentence was pronounced upon Sarah but in her case Stephen had found some mercy in his heart:

> In your case, of course, I shall forward to the Executive the recommendation to mercy, where it will receive consideration, but the effect of that consideration I am not able to say. And may God have mercy on your souls.

As the sentence of death was pronounced Sarah collapsed altogether. She was 'carried bodily out of the court by two constables' down the steps into the tunnel below the court, sobbing loudly and wailing, 'Oh! my babies; oh! my babies'. Exactly which babies she was referring to is hard to guess.

The next day, the newspapers confirmed the views of Justice Stephen: 'from the popular point of view the conviction in one case stands for a conviction in all'.[2] Editors and letter writers were not interested in whether or not the Makins had received a fair trial. The horror and shame from having the underbelly of Sydney's baby market exposed was too great a burden to bear. The Makins had got their just desserts.

❦

CHAPTER TWENTY

Last stop, London
11 April–21 July 1893

The fact that the Makins had decided to appeal to the Privy Council in Britain—the highest court of appeal in the Australian colonies at the time—was a desperate move. But it was their only hope of putting off the gallows now being erected in their minds, if not within the grounds of Darlinghurst Gaol itself.

It was a complicated process with no guaranteed outcome. At stake was a legal principle that had not been acknowledged before—one that had ensured the Makins' conviction but, with a different set of legal minds, might ensure their acquittal. In order to appeal, however, the Makins would need the consent of the government. The 'Humble Petition of John Makin and Sarah Makin', signed by John and Sarah, was sent to the Executive Council on 11 April 1893.[1] On the same day, the Council decided to commute Sarah's death sentence to life imprisonment. It was one small mercy in an otherwise bleak year for the Makins.

Before the Council would consider the Makins' petition, the Minister of Justice wanted to ensure that if leave to appeal was granted it would be prosecuted straight away. Mr Williamson obtained a statutory declaration from John's brother, George, verifying that the leave to appeal was 'bona fide and not for the purposes of delay' and that he and his other brothers were 'in a position to pay the costs of such an appeal'. With that assurance, the Makins were in luck. On 21 April 1893, the Council delayed John's execution for three months to enable him and Sarah to petition the Privy Council for an appeal.[2] However, John was informed that if his appeal failed his sentence of death would be carried out, no matter how long the whole process took.

The Executive Council's decision was controversial. There was disquiet about the 'indefinite amount of delay' because no-one knew how long it would take the Privy Council to hear the appeal. Newspaper editors did not like matters to be 'practically shelved'[3] and harked back to a previous case in which an appeal to the Privy Council had taken such a long time, the death sentence was commuted to life imprisonment.[4] For the Makins, it was the torture of time, squashed as they were onto the back shelf of life, not knowing when, or if, they would ever taste freedom again. But the Attorney-General, Edmund Barton, who would later become Australia's first prime minister, decided there was an important legal question to be decided. With a difference of opinion between Justices Windeyer and Innes, Barton recognised this difference was 'likely to arise frequently in criminal trials [and] there was a need to have the matter settled'.[5]

The Judicial Committee of the Privy Council was an ancient institution comprised of judicial members of the House of Lords who sat as a court to hear appeals from the British colonies on behalf of the Sovereign, Queen Victoria. As expected, the petition to appeal had captured their legal interest, with the seven Law Lords deciding to review the case of two infamous baby farmers from a far-flung colony.

The Lord High Chancellor, Lord Herschell, announced their verdict in a cable message sent to the New South Wales Government on Friday, 21 July stating 'the appeal was dismissed, but the Privy Council will give their reasons in November'.[6] These reasons did not become available until 12 December 1893. When the New South Wales Attorney-General received the cable, there was nothing left to do but inform the prisoners and fix the date for John's execution. Although John died without knowing why his appeal to the Privy Council had been dismissed, ironically, his name lives on in the common law every time his case is cited as precedent, as it has been throughout the last 120 years. It was small comfort to the Makin family that the Privy Council's decision contained the first statement of principle or legal rule as to when a defendant's prior criminal conduct could be admitted in a trial.

Short and to the point: the Law Lords have their say

The New South Wales Government had hired an arsenal of barristers to oppose the Makins' appeal. If Sarah and John could have been colonial flies on the oak-panelled walls of the courtroom they would have dropped to the floor in shock to see the four English barristers who had been hired to oppose their own lawyer's arguments.[7]

As it turned out, four brains were better than one since, in their very short judgment, the Privy Council agreed with the four lawyers for the New South Wales Government that the evidence of Constable Joyce and the unmarried mothers was rightly admitted to rebut a suggestion that death was accidental, or to disprove any other defence raised by the defendants. The problem was no such defences had been raised by the Makins because they had denied being baby farmers and denied knowledge of the child. The essence of the Privy Council's judgment is encapsulated in the statement that '[t]heir Lordships do not think it necessary to enter upon a detailed examination of the evidence in the present case'. If they had done so, their reasons would not have withstood closer scrutiny.

The Privy Council's judgment and infant mortality rates

The Makin case has been described as 'perhaps the most important and most frequently cited case in the history of New South Wales criminal law'[8] because of the Privy Council's statement of principle. Unfortunately, that has been for all the wrong reasons.

The starting point for the Privy Council's decision was the Makins' statements to Constable Joyce that they were not baby farmers and had only ever adopted one child for a fee. The Privy Council decided that the evidence of all the unmarried mothers who had paid to have their children adopted by the Makins was correctly admitted to rebut this claim and to provide evidence of a motive for the Crown's case of murder.

The evidence of the discovery of the 12 other babies cannot be justified since the Makins offered no defence of neglect or accidental death. If the Makin case was tried according to the rules of evidence that apply today, Constable Joyce's account of the 12 other babies would be treated as highly prejudicial. Because of this expected prejudice, a judge today would need to investigate whether the evidence of the Makins' prior criminal misconduct had one or more alternative, rational explanations.[9]

One rational explanation arises because of the high infant mortality rate in the 1890s as a result of disease and/or undernourishment. Up until 1900, the infant mortality rate in the Australian colonies fluctuated between 101 and 130 per 1000 live births,[10] compared to an average infant mortality rate of 11 in the 1980s and 4.6 in 2012. In 1892, the likelihood of a baby dying in its first year of life was 26 times greater than in 2012 and similar to the infant mortality rates in Afghanistan and Somalia today.[11] Another rational explanation comes from the evidence of Daisy and Clarice Makin, who both said that Amber Murray's baby had been taken to Burren Street. Clarice's later retraction of her evidence is a strong hint she had been telling the truth originally. Baby Horace could not have been buried in George Street as assumed by the police, the lawyers and all the judges involved in the appeals.

Knowing very little about the mortality rates of infants, the incidence of syphilis in the maternal population and the living conditions in Sydney, the Privy Council made a legal decision based on no scientific or medical knowledge. As Justice Windeyer had said in a child death case four years before the Makins' trial:

> You might just as well try to prove that because the child died in the hospital and 50 other children died there, that the first child was murdered. You must raise some evidence that the child died an unnatural death, that there had been foul play, and that the person accused was guilty of it.[12]

In the 1890s, baby farmers were in a position similar to the diseased and unhygienic hospitals of the time. Diseases unknown in developed countries today were common and included cholera, diphtheria, smallpox and scarlet fever. The poorer baby farmers like the Makins accepted babies destined for the grave, while death came often to the homes of many legitimate midwives as well.[13] Some baby farmers underfed their babies by watering down the Nestlé's baby formula when money was short. While some of the

Makins' babies would have died from disease, others died from starvation or overdoses of Godfrey's Cordial. But without evidence of 'foul play' in relation to Baby Horace, and with the rational explanation that he had thrush before and after he was adopted, Constable Joyce's evidence ought not to have been admitted in the Makins' trial.

At the end of this strange, convoluted journey into the minds of the trial and appeal judges, it is possible that logic and reason were supplanted by an emotional desire to find any excuse for admitting evidence of the 12 other babies. To many people, this may not matter since the totality of the Makins' behaviour suggests they were baby farmers who had killed most of their adopted babies.

The morality of the Makins' profession was on trial, since Justices Stephen and Windeyer were concerned that baby farmers would literally get away with murder because their victims were small enough to be easily concealed by burial. But the greater moral question in 1892 was the lack of interest in the lives of illegitimate children before they were baby farmed. No-one explained why the lives of illegitimate children mattered more when they were dead than when they were alive. The decision in the Makin case did nothing to change the short lives and quick deaths of countless babies in the city of Sydney in the 1890s and beyond. Baby farming was the inevitable outcome of the clash between poverty, morality and women's place in Victorian society.

☙❧

CHAPTER TWENTY-ONE

Makin's last chance: an 'innocent' man under the thumb of a 'fiendish' woman
11–14 August 1893

After the final appeal, John Makin was placed in one of the six 'gloomy and dismal' condemned cells of E Wing in Darlinghurst Gaol which were located close to the gallows. Resigned to his fate, he was heavily ironed while his cell had 'an open iron grille ... so that the warder could keep continuous watch'.[1]

John's siblings were terribly distressed by the impending execution of their brother. After paying a small fortune for his legal representation, they marched down their very last avenue of appeal by petitioning the Colonial Secretary, Sir George Dibbs. Although John himself had sought a reprieve from Sir Henry Parkes, the Premier of New South Wales, his letter, which pointed out the weaknesses in the evidence against him, met with a cold response.[2]

On the morning of Friday 11 August 1893, Sir George received the deputation that had travelled from Wollongong to see him—George and Daniel Makin, John's sister-in-law, Mrs Joseph Makin, as well as Mr Campbell, a member of Parliament. Perhaps they thought they would obtain a fair hearing from a man with his own colourful past. Sir George had spent 12 months in prison from May 1880 to April 1881 in the debtors' wing of Darlinghurst Gaol for failure to pay damages of £2000 when a lawsuit for slander was brought against him by his sister-in-law's lover. Nonetheless, Dibbs adjusted to prison life well, restoring his health through his love of woodwork, '[i]n this "cheery, pleasant retreat where one can do martyrdom for principle's sake with every comfort"'.[3]

In presenting their petition, the Makin family deputation stressed that it had been signed by many Wollongong citizens, including mayors, aldermen, clergymen and Justices of the Peace. They did not attempt to re-argue the merits of the case against John:

> [t]hey simply asked ... for the sake of his brothers and their families, and his own family, that the extreme penalty of the law should not be carried out, and that his punishment should be made the same as that inflicted on his wife.[4]

But there was more. This last desperate attempt was to be an assassination of Sarah's character and a whitewashing of John's—a good man who had fallen in with a bad woman because it was 'the woman and not the man [who] was responsible'. Socially acceptable misogyny provided the Makin family with the tools to try to save their brother from the gallows.

Mr Campbell said he had known John since 'he was a lad growing up at Wollongong'. While he had a reputation for 'being a foolish young man' he was not known to have a 'disposition for cruelty or anything in that direction' and 'no one would ever have associate[d] him with murderers or brutal crimes'. These 'brutal crimes' were a shock to the Makin family who, Mr Campbell reassured Sir George, were 'most respectable people, and his father was for 30 years agent for the Illawarra S.S. Company at Wollongong'—so respectable that 'the surroundings of the condemned man were in every way of a creditable character while he was young'.

The problem for poor John was that he had been 'led to whatever he did by his wife' who was 'the arch-aggressor, the arch-fiend in the matter'. Mr Campbell appealed to Sir George's knowledge of the way of the world since he would know 'that the whole business was a woman's matter, as no man would ever start a baby farming business'. The problem was Sarah. Not only was she 'a strong-minded woman ... possessed of an almost fiendish disposition', she 'would not be wound round the fingers of any man'. John had been 'made use of by the woman whose neck had escaped' and if he had not known her, he would never have been convicted. Proof of this was to be seen in the lives of John's brothers, George, Joseph and Daniel, since no better fathers or men existed in New South Wales.

With this homily to John and his 'respectable' family, was Mr Campbell trying to save John's neck or was there more at stake? He let slip the truth when he revealed the family's expectations—'[t]o prevent the stigma resting on them and their children for generations, the relatives hoped that the sentence on the condemned man would be commuted'. George Makin then asked Sir George 'to have mercy on his poor wife and family' while Daniel Makin 'begged for mercy on account of the family, so that in time to come people would not be able to point the finger of scorn at them' as he tried to rescue some of the 'respectable' family reputation.

Mrs Joseph Makin enlarged on the theme of Sarah's badness. She had, she confided, seen Sarah 'knock her own blind mother down with a chair, and she had struck her mother-in-law in the face'. By contrast, 'a better-hearted young man' than John had never lived. John was like a piece of putty, it seemed, since 'his wife could turn him round her fingers' because he 'was easily led—in fact he was a fool'. At the time that John married her, Sarah was a barmaid with 'a temper more like a fiend than a woman'. She was, confided Mrs Joseph Makin, 'a terrible woman' and 'the whole cause of the trouble'.

George Makin then admitted that his family 'had had a good deal of trouble with John Makin, but it was all the fault of his wife, who used to drink, and spend all the money he earned'. Yet the family well knew that John, with an irregular employment history, had failed to hold down a steady job to feed his large family. They knew he had previous convictions, had accrued debts and been declared a bankrupt before he married Sarah. They could not have forgotten that John's mother had ensured that John would not be able to waste his inheritance by providing him with a monthly payment rather than a lump sum when she died. Out of John and Sarah, who had twisted whose arm to enter the land of murder?

George Makin's admission suggests that John had a habit of bothering his family for money, using the excuse that Sarah was drinking away his hard-earned income. Conveniently, John did not tell his family the truth about his role in the baby-farming business—how he conducted the monetary negotiations with unmarried mothers, signed the contracts, made up the many excuses as to why the mothers could no longer see their babies, buried the babies and used such language to describe the baby who cried too much that his words were unprintable. He may have been a foolish young man who was easily led but he had turned into a cunning adult with a gift for story-telling and deception. John's family would have been embarrassed by him long before his conviction for murder. They may have muttered to themselves that John would one day end up in a lot of trouble, just not the type of trouble to bring the family's name into such disrepute.

Sir George reminded the family that John had been found guilty and it was not the role of the Executive Government to overturn a jury's decision. A case could only be reopened if further facts were brought forward. While he would call a special meeting of the Executive Council on Monday morning and put before them all the matters raised by the family, he warned the deputation that they had not given him any facts to 'show that the verdict of the jury is not a just one'.

As expected, the Executive Council was unconvinced by the petition that begged mercy for John's life and 'decided the law should take its course'.[5] When the final decision was relayed to John he received it calmly 'without the least sign of emotion', merely saying: 'I am quite prepared'. After farewelling his daughters and son-in-law, 'the doomed man seemed to contemplate his fate with composure' and remarkable tranquillity. Perhaps this was the reaction not of a man coerced by his wife into being her partner in crime, but of a man who knew he was guilty of something. As the editor of *The Sydney Morning Herald* suggested, Makin's reaction 'may be accepted as his acknowledgement of its perfect justice'.[6]

Letters fly while editorials rant

At the same time as the Makin family tried to persuade the government to commute John's death sentence, a letter appeared in *The Sydney Morning Herald* about the unfairness of the penalty against him:

> I [would] have hoped that the ... almost intolerable apathy that so
> generally exists in our midst would not have been exhibited when

the sacredness of human life was at stake. "Yes," some of your readers may say; "Sacredness of human life? The very reason why the man must die." But ... as the life of the female prisoner, considered the most guilty of the two, is to be spared, so also should be that of the male prisoner.[7]

Up until this time, there had been few opinions in the newspapers about who, out of John and Sarah, was the 'most guilty'. The law had treated Sarah as acting under the influence of her husband but the letter writer, Charles Counsell, was convinced that Sarah was the culprit:

Stress is laid on the fact of John Makin receiving money on the infants being given up? Granted. Was this so heinous as the crime of the woman, whose natural instincts should have made her revolt from the diabolical horror of administering ... so little nourishment to the infants ... as would sooner or later bring about their death? ... Have not Governments and society at large too long "winked at" and given the "go-by" to it?

Mr Counsell also recognised what the courts and editors of newspapers had refused to—that the government and the public had tacitly condoned baby farming.

The similarity between the themes in Counsell's letter and the Makin family's pleas to Sir George Dibbs suggests the family tried to elicit public condemnation of John's execution. They were in for a shock. The next day, *The Sydney Morning Herald* printed a reply from a Mr Chamberlain, who growled at the suggestion that John should be reprieved:

I read the letter signed 'Charles Counsell' ... with mixed feelings of surprise and disgust ... To those people who think children's lives as of far less importance than those of adults, this sophistry may be plausible; but to those who think, with me, that the more helpless the victims the greater should be the protection of the law, the whole of Mr. Counsell's ideas will be repulsive ... Considering that

infants are slaughtered almost daily ... it seems ... that an example
should be made of the first really bad case sheeted home, and a
worse case than Makin's is hard to conceive.[8]

Mr Chamberlain was unconcerned that John's execution would not solve
the problem of illegitimacy because other mysterious influences were at
work to which justice must not succumb:

> If Makin is reprieved it will be ... ascribed to 'influence,' and his
> alleged threats of exposing people well to do in this city.

It is unknown what the alleged threats were but I am reminded here
of Blanche's allegation that Mother Robinson had 'put' John 'up' to
baby farming, which suggested John may have been involved in various
illegal activities.

Overwhelmingly, retribution was the preferred response in the colony.
Newspaper editors gloated about the decision to execute John, confident
that it 'will have the full concurrence of the general community', particularly since John was 'the prime mover and chief actor in the crimes'. Unlike
John's relatives, one editor believed there was:

> a strong and not discreditable aversion to the spectacle of the
> hanging of any woman; and ... there is much to be said ... for
> giving a certain amount of application to the old presumption of
> coercion, which held the husband primarily responsible for both.[9]

Others also had sympathy for Sarah, who was thought to have been a weak-
willed woman held by John 'in a sort of magnetic thrall' which, out of
fear, turned her into 'the instrument of a stronger nature than a voluntary
criminal'.[10] This was sexism operating in the opposite direction. But another
editor let fly with his outrage that Sarah had been recommended to mercy:

> Mercy! If either deserve it, it is Makin the man, in whom the
> brute might reasonably be expected to be more strong. But mercy

to a woman who had borne and suckled children, and in whom maternal and womanly love was dead that she could deliberately assist to slay eighteen [*sic*] tiny creatures whose helplessness a savage had spared, aye, possibly a wolf or a tiger ... Mercy! ... Rather the rope, for if ever the woman Collins deserved death, the far more barbarous woman Makin deserves it twice over.[11]

According to John's relatives, Sarah was the chief fiend while the prevalent legal view was that she was pliable putty in her husband's hands. But no-one seems to have considered their equal participation as a matter of survival. Only one editor recognised that baby farming is different from other types of murder:

[i]t was committed systematically, and as a matter of business. It was committed from the basest and most sordid of motives, the desire to make money by murder ... to make infant murder their daily bread.[12]

However, the real reason for John's execution was to remove:

[a] terrible stain [which] would lie upon this great city and upon our whole administration of law if the blood of these unhappy infants were to remain unavenged.[13]

John's final letter

John wrote an intriguing letter to his brothers on 14 August 1893, the night before he was executed:

I, John Makin ... to be executed on the morrow for the murder of Horace Amber Murray, sincerely and solemnly declare that the body of the infant found in the yard of the house at Redfern, and on which the charge of murder against me was based, and for which I am now to be executed, was not the body of ... the child of Amber Murray. Nor was the clothing found on the body, supposed to be that of Horace Amber Murray—and which Amber Murray and Mrs. Patrick swore to … —ever worn by the child. The clothing was never in their possession, nor had they ever seen it before it was produced for their identification … They have, I solemnly state, sworn falsely, and their false swearing is the cause of my life being taken away. My wife, Sarah Makin, did not murder the child supposed to be Horace Amber Murray; the body found was buried in the yard weeks before we got her child. And I also solemnly declare that the child myself and my daughter Blanche took to the residence of Mrs. Patrick … in the month of July, 1892, was the child of Amber Murray and no other.[14]

For me, this is the final piece of evidence that confirms the Makins were convicted of the death of the wrong child. Twice, once during the inquest into the death of Baby D and once during her trial, Sarah 'swore' that this child was not Amber Murray's and that Baby Horace had been taken to Macdonaldtown. The evidence given by Clarice and Daisy at the inquest into Baby D's death—that Baby Horace had been one of the six babies taken to Burren Street—corroborates what appeared to be, at the time, Sarah's dramatic but empty denials. Clarice's later retraction of this statement and her remarkable denial that she gave such evidence points to where the truth really lay.

Some will argue that all this evidence comes as it does from a family keen to protect itself. But Clarice's original evidence exposed her parents to, rather than protected them from, more criminal charges. What are we to make of John's letter when on previous occasions he had been ready to take the gallows? Perhaps he wrote the letter to reassure his family who were left to carry the shame of his actions. Yet the letter is not a complete exoneration—John's admission that 'the body found was buried in the yard weeks before we got her child' indicates he was the one who buried Baby D. If he was trying to salve his conscience, protect his wife and reassure his family, this admission was an odd way to do it.

If John's assertions were true, it is ironic that he died because he had been convicted of the murder of the wrong baby. Does it matter? Presumably, the administration of justice works best if defendants are convicted of deaths they have actually caused. But most people will be satisfied with this outcome of rough justice. The Makins may not have murdered Baby Horace but they were clearly in the business of burying an awful lot of children.

What is easy to forget is the charge that was never prosecuted against the Makins—the manslaughter of Baby Mignonette, the daughter of Minnie Davies and Horace Bothamley. The evidence that proved she had died as a result of starvation, even though the Makins had been paid ten shillings a week to nurse her, was irrefutable. Her starvation was probably deliberate since she had been a healthy baby when her devoted parents handed her to the Makins but ended her life as 'a mere bag of bones'.

It is no wonder that John accepted his fate with composure. But Sarah's was to be a long and drawn out struggle for survival in the notorious Darlinghurst Gaol and the more distant Bathurst Gaol. On the day John died, Sarah's journey as one of the longest serving prisoners in New South Wales had barely begun.

PART IV

❧

SARAH MAKIN,
REFORMED WOMAN

CHAPTER TWENTY-TWO

From convict daughter to convict
30 March 1893–29 April 1911

The construction of Darlinghurst Gaol began 23 years before Sarah Makin was born, while New South Wales was in its convict heyday—in the midst of a construction boom and buoyed by the slave labour of newly arriving convicts. A four acre site on the elevated land of Darlinghurst 'was chosen so that its imposing walls would be a constant reminder to the residents of Sydney that it was a Penal Colony'.[1] What had been a significant cultural site for the original Cadigal tribe before white settlement[2] was turned into a sinister cultural site for the new British colony, with many of the local Aboriginal population being later imprisoned in the gaol.

Although construction began in 1822 under the authority of Governor Brisbane, the labour of convicts was slow and money throughout Sydney's colonial history waxed and waned as governors balanced precarious budgets. Funds for the construction of two of the cell-blocks (A and D Wings) were not available until 12 years later and it was another four years before they were completed. So it was not until 7 June 1841 that the prisoners housed in Sydney Gaol occupied Sydney's brand new and comparatively luxurious gaol.[3]

Darlinghurst Gaol was a world away from the inhumane conditions of Sydney Gaol, which was so crowded that up to 300 prisoners were housed in two small dormitories, 32 by 22 feet each. Not all the prisoners could sleep on the floors at any one time so that 'many were obliged either to take their turn of standing during the night, or to be on top of others'.[4] During a Royal Commission into the administration of the colony in 1820,[5] Commissioner Bigge recommended the building of a new gaol to address the lack of space in existing gaols and the hulks anchored in the harbour which arose from the colony's obsession with imprisoning children, the mentally ill, drunks, vagrants, debt defaulters, the sick and the aged.

One wonders what the 119 male prisoners of the old Sydney Gaol thought as they were marched from Lower George Street, 'manacled and chained', along Macquarie Street under the eyes of their 50 police guards to the imposing sandstone structure that greeted them in Darlinghurst.[6] They were followed by 50 female prisoners dressed in shapeless black dresses who were 'jeered and pelted ... with fruit' by the crowd that followed the prisoners' procession.[7]

When Darlinghurst Gaol was finally completed in 1885, seven years before the Makins were driven through its grand gates in a black police van, it was an architectural masterpiece based on a radial design.[8] Inside, a circular chapel stood in the middle, an obvious visual and symbolic focal point for the prisoners. Six rectangular cell-blocks and an observation wing radiate out from the chapel, like spokes on a wheel, with all eyes on the house of God and final retribution, or the pathway to redemption. The open plan design of the gaol was broken up by high stone walls separating each cell-block, dividing the wheel into segments, with the yard of each cell-block surveyed by warders in watchboxes.

When the Makins were first imprisoned in November 1892, they would have been 'taken straight down the stairs to the basement of the governor's quarters' then marched through an underground tunnel to the basement of the chapel and the bathing house where they were stripped, bathed, fumigated and examined by the gaol doctor. Deprived of their clothing and possessions, they were dressed in prison garb before John was taken to A Wing for men and Sarah to D Wing for women, the two windowless cell-blocks on either side of the governor's elegant sandstone residence.[9]

Housed in separate wings, Sarah and John would have had no contact, other than perhaps glimpsing each other on Sundays in the chapel where the women were segregated from the men in a gallery on the top level. When the guards were not looking, men and women threw notes in calico-wrapped parcels to each other during church services, or over the walls that separated the women's wing from the men's.[10]

Sarah served her time in three different gaols, Darlinghurst, Bathurst and Long Bay, with her health worsening over time. She was unlike other female prisoners, since most were incarcerated for short periods of time for petty crimes such as drunkenness, vagrancy, petty theft, 'riotous behaviour, indecent language or for having no visible means of support', a euphemism for prostitution.[11] With the New South Wales colony just a couple of generations from the end of transportation, which officially ceased in 1849, Sarah, a convict daughter, spent her years living in spartan conditions that surely reminded her of where her father had come from.

Life in gaol

When Sarah began her life as a convict, gaols were, at least, no longer houses of death because of reform in the years since transportation had ended which saw improvements to health, hygiene, sewerage, food and exercise, so much so that the death rate in Darlinghurst Gaol had dropped to less than the death rate for the general population from 1889 onwards.[12] For many prisoners who had been pickled in poverty, it was the first time they had proper clothing and three meals a day.[13]

In 1905, a new system of rations was introduced based on the industriousness of prisoners. This system 'had a marked effect on the industry of prisoners. Now that the ration is regulated by amount of work done, instead of time served, even the loafer finds that he must work'.[14] A daily hard labour ration consisted of bread (24 ounces), maize meal (6 ounces), meat (16 ounces) vegetables (16 ounces), salt, sugar (1 ounce), soap (½ ounce) and rice or barley (¼ ounce).[15]

All of this stands in contrast to Henry Lawson's description of the gaol as 'Starvinghurst Gaol' in his poem *One Hundred and Three*.[16] Lawson was first gaoled in 1905 for his failure to pay alimony to his estranged wife, who had sought a legal separation from him[17], while his second sojourn in Darlinghurst Gaol was for child desertion in 1908. Suffering from manic depression (now known as bipolar disorder), he spent time in the Darlinghurst Mental Hospital for drunkenness and depression.[18] Perhaps his bleak tag of 'Starvinghurst Gaol' was merely the pessimistic view of a depressed man with his stark confession that:

> They take the spoon from the cell at night—and a stranger might
>   think it odd;
> But a man might sharpen it on the floor, and go to his own Great
>   God

While Lawson may have been describing the sheer blandness of a diet of 'bread and water and hominy, and a scag of meat and a spud' or exaggerating the conditions in gaol ('Tis slow starvation in separate cells') as suggested by medical historian Philip Norrie,[19] some of the events he describes in the gaol hold a grain of truth since all prisoners sentenced to three years or more spent the first nine months in solitary confinement on a diet of bread and water, with only an hour a day for exercise:[20]

> In all the creeds there is hope and doubt, but of this there is no
>   doubt;
> That starving prisoners faint in church, and the warders carry
>   them out.
> ...
> The press is printing its smug, smug lies, and paying its shameful
>   debt—
> It speaks of the comforts that prisoners have, and 'holidays'
>   prisoners get.
> The visitors come with their smug, smug smiles through the gaol
>   on a working day,
> And the public hears with its large, large ears what authorities have
>   to say.
> They lay their fingers on well-hosed walls, and they tread on the
>   polished floor;
> They peep in the generous shining cans with their ration Number
>   Four.
> And the visitors go with their smug, smug smiles; the reporters'
>   work is done;
> Stand up! my men, who have done your time on ration Number
>   One!

Ration number four was the generous one available for men doing hard labour, while number one was for those in solitary confinement. Lawson refers to the 'living dead' and uses the word 'starving', 'starved' or 'starvation' eight times in his poem, highlighting how the unfair rations system affected all prisoners. Punishment also involved starvation rations, as did infringements of prison rules:

> He shall be buried alive without meat, for a day and a night unheard
> If he speak to a fellow prisoner, though he die for want of a word.
> He shall be punished, and he shall be starved, and he shall in darkness rot,
> He shall be murdered body and soul—and God said, 'Thou shalt not!'

While Lawson described deaths in Darlinghurst Gaol due to lack of food, the death rate was a concern for the prison administrators. The provision of proper clothes and shoes, bedding in separate cells to prevent cross-infection, medical care, isolation wards for infectious diseases, as well as 'medical comforts' in the form of port wine, brandy and extra food for sick prisoners, was aimed at keeping the death rate as low as possible.[21]

The inmates of Darlinghurst Gaol were also allowed daily exercise and a weekly bath with clean water. Along with a proper sewerage system, installed in 1891, these measures were designed to improve hygiene in the gaol.[22] The downside was that the gaol, built to house 420 prisoners and staff, had 732 inmates by 1900. The gaol was so plagued by lice and bed-bugs that it was nicknamed 'Lousy Bay' and 'The Booby Hatch'.

In addition to living with 'the horrible plague of boobies' which infested the gaol in the 1890s[23], Lawson's poems provide a picture of the lonely life that Sarah would have known. Each prisoner was housed in a four by eight foot cell which was 'double-lock[ed] at four o'clock' with window slits for air and '[n]o light save the lights in the yard beneath the clustering lights of the Lord'. With the 'bang' of the iron door, the 'clank' of the iron bolt, and the last contemptuous objections of some ('an ignorant oath for a last good-night—or the voice of a filthy thought'), the prisoners were locked in darkness from early afternoon until the next morning in their tiny cells to stare at the 'dead stone walls'. Rather than on mattresses, they slept in hammocks. In the morning, the prisoners would:

> rise at six, when the bell rings, and roll our blankets neat,
> Then we pace the cell unseeing—till seven, with hypnotised feet.[24]

During solitary confinement, writing and reading were not permitted, a terrible punishment for a man like Lawson, who wrote prodigiously. Lawson's poem, 'written on scraps of paper with a stump of pencil stolen from the prison printery' and smuggled out of the gaol by his friends,[25] describes prisoners left to rot from idleness:

> Warders and prisoners all alike in a dead rot dry and slow—
> The author must not write for his own, and the tailor must not sew.
> The billet-bound officers dare not speak and discharged men dare
>   not tell
> Though many and many an innocent man must brood in this
>   barren hell.

Since most of the wings housed male prisoners, there was significant overcrowding in the women's wing, so that by 1886 there were 450 female inmates in a wing that had been designed to accommodate 156. In 1896, when Sarah was one of the female inmates, one visitor to Darlinghurst Gaol described the women's dismal conditions:

> Their work is solely that of scrubbing, cleaning, washing and needlework of the most hideous and dreary description. After working at needlework from 9–12, then 2–4, they were compelled to go to bed at 5 pm. They were locked up with no lighting. They could not work in the workshops, garden or use the library as the men could do, nor could they use the schoolroom.[26]

According to Lawson, the prisoners' lives were bound by 'Rules, regulations—red-tape and rules', including enforced marching under the eyes of the warders around the exercise yard and long hours of work. But it was the inhumane conditions of solitary confinement, which included the forced wearing of a hood over a prisoner's entire face during their one hour of exercise,[27] that sent many prisoners mad:

> You get the gaol-dust in your throat, in your skin the dead gaol-white;
> You get the gaol-whine in your voice and in every letter you write.
> And in your eyes comes the bright gaol-light—not the glare of the world's distraught,
> Not the hunted look, nor the guilty look, but the awful look of the Caught.

For those who did go mad, B Wing awaited them with its medieval restraints, including a leather straitjacket and 'a conical wooden device, hollowed out in the middle, forced into prisoners' mouths to prevent them from speaking or calling out, and secured with leather straps and a buckle behind the head'.[28]

Perhaps Sarah was astute enough to avoid the torture devices of B Wing. But after 18 long years as an inmate of various gaols, Sarah's hunted and guilty look during her trial probably became 'the awful look of the Caught'.

The lonely prison years—health and other problems

After her conviction on 10 March 1893, Sarah was moved from the remand section of Darlinghurst Gaol to begin her period of solitary confinement. But Sarah only spent five more months in Darlinghurst Gaol before being sent to Bathurst Gaol on Thursay 10 August 1893, an extra punishment for her and her family because of its distance from Sydney. Bathurst Gaol was a similar vintage to Darlinghurst Gaol. Although building commenced in 1837, it was not completed until 1888 and provided similar living conditions to Darlinghurst Gaol. Sarah arrived after an overnight train journey and stayed for nearly two years.[29]

Before her journey to Bathurst, she asked to see John, since she had been told he was to be executed on the following Tuesday. On Thursday afternoon, 10 August, her wish was granted:

> she was escorted to the condemned cell, where man and wife kissed each other fervently. Neither had anything to say, and in a few moments Mrs. Makin was removed in a hysterical state just as she used to carry on during the inquest.

The journalist who reported this visit was suspicious, remarking that:

> [w]hen she reached the train she was quite composed, and chatted away as if nothing had transpired—a fact which proves that in many instances her hysterical seizures were more or less assumed.[30]

John's imminent execution and Sarah's volatile mental state may have been the reason for her transfer. Sarah's presence in the gaol at the time when John was executed would have been an extra punishment, perhaps tipping Sarah into one of her irrational and yet completely misunderstood emotional states.

By 1893, Sarah had been infected with syphilis for more than ten years. While not every infected person will develop tertiary syphilis—the final and most life-threatening phase of the disease—Sarah's fits of 'hysteria' suggest she was in the final stage of syphilis and suffering from neurosyphilis. Neurosyphilis has several forms and occurs in about 10 per cent of untreated syphilitics. About 10 per cent of neurosyphilis is caused by meningovascular syphilis, or MVS, which 'occurs as a result of damage to the blood vessels of the meninges, brain and spinal cord ... causing a wide spectrum of neurologic impairments'.[31] Sarah could also have suffered damage to the cortical regions of her brain which would have caused impairment of memory and speech, irritability, personality changes and psychotic symptoms.

With MVS, personality and behavioural changes usually manifest several years after a person is first infected with syphilis. In one case reported in the literature, a man suffering from MVS 'was easily angered and became gradually withdrawn',[32] behaviours that Sarah exhibited for some years before she and John were charged and convicted. MVS usually begins with 'weeks or months of intermittent headaches, progressive behavioural changes and movement disorders' as a consequence of meningitis—that is, inflammation of the arteries in the meninges which are the three membranes that cover the brain and spinal cord,[33] although symptoms vary from person to person depending on the extent of the damage to the brain.[34] Patients who experience MVS also tend to be younger, under the age of 50 years, as Sarah was when she was charged with murder.

One account reveals that Sarah wrote letters about how hard her life was in Bathurst Gaol and that she suffered from paranoid fantasies in which she was chased by the mothers of the dead babies,[35] a psychotic symptom that may have been the result of neurosyphilis. After two years there, for some reason Sarah was transferred back to Darlinghurst Gaol on 11 May 1895[36] where she stayed for three and a half years until 22 November 1898. She was again transferred to Bathurst Gaol where she remained for almost eleven years until 18 August 1909. By 1898, she was one of the 'long-timers' of the female inmates in Darlinghurst Gaol, with these prisoners often being assigned more important roles such as house servant to the governor.[37] During her second stint in Bathurst Gaol, Sarah had a job as a hospital attendant, perhaps using the skills she had acquired as a 'ladies' nurse'.

Not surprisingly, Sarah's health deteriorated during her imprisonment. Although infections of various types were the commonest cause of death in the gaol system, Sarah was admitted to the Bathurst Gaol hospital in 1905 with an 'intestinal haemorrhage'. The hospitals at Bathurst and Darlinghurst Gaols were similar in design with spacious wards—60 by 25 feet—and an arcaded walkway on three sides which was secured with iron grilles, where convalescing patients could exercise,[38] representing the best conditions in the gaols in terms of space, light and ventilation.

Sarah experienced several intestinal haemorrhages, suggesting she was suffering from bowel cancer or bleeding caused by diverticulosis, which is associated with chronic kidney failure. Alternatively, the haemorrhages may have been a symptom of tertiary syphilis, which can affect any organ of the body, including the production of chronic inflammation in the lining of the stomach and the intestines, also known as colitis.

Florence Makin (now a married woman by the name of Mrs Anderson) and Minnie Helbi became so concerned about their mother's worsening health that they both took the brave and bold step of writing directly to the Attorney-General. The letters written by Minnie and Florence show the different degrees of literacy of Sarah's daughters. Minnie's letter, written from 55 Mary Street, St Peters on 17 March 1907,[39] sought the mercy of the Attorney-General in relation to her mother, who was now aged 61 and had been in prison for fifteen years:

> I respectfully desire to bring under your notice for your merciful consideration the case of my mother Sarah Makin ... Her conduct in Gaol has been good throughout; thus entitling her to consideration, while at the time she was convicted the period for a life sentence was, I understand 15 years. Further, my mother has been in delicate health for several years past; and has had several attacks of Hemorrhage, another of which will prove fatal ... [M]yself and the rest of my family consider the time has now arrived for the Crown ... to exercise its prerogative of mercy, and release our mother, who ... has surely satisfied Justice by such a long expiation of her crime ... All of her children ... have always been respectable and law abideing [*sic*], and one of her sons fought in the South African war. We have all felt our mothers position very keenly; and surely, Sir, you would not have our pain and Grief added to by having her die in Gaol, for that, I am certain will take place very shortly if she is not quickly released. Trusting therefore, Sir, that you will take all the above facts into consideration, both for my unfortunate mother and her children.

Florence's letter, written from 243 Abercrombie Street, Redfern on 20 March 1907,[40] uncorrected for errors, begs the Minister of Justice's mercy:

> I beg to bring under your notice the case of my Poor Dear Mother Mrs Sarah Makin ... She as nearly complied 18 years in Prison.

And in all that time her conduct as been of the very best. And now I think it is time that the Crown dun something for her and release her from Prison. For her own Sake and that of her Children She has Shurley surffed for the Crime She has been imprisond for. And there is another reasones why she should be released and that is of her bad health. She as suffered very much of late. I have been to See her this month … And she was very bad indeed in bed in the Hospital. And I am very much afrade that if she as another attack of her Sickness. It will prove fattel … And I hope and trust with Gods help and yours Sir is the ernest Prayers of her Family that she will soon be released. And Dear Sir I will provide a Home for her and keep her for the rest of her life. I will go scurty for her good behavoure. So Trusting Dear Sir that you will give this your Consideration for my Dear Mothers Sake … Hopping this will meet with your approvual and waiting for a favourbel repley.

A report from the Visiting Surgeon to Bathurst Gaol, Dr Bassett, stated that Sarah:

> has been continuously ailing in hospital for the last two years. Latterly she has been subject to frequent attacks of Meloua (intestinal Haemorrhage). From a severe attack of this kind she is now slowly rallying—repetitions of the attack may be anticipated—one, as severe as the last, now, would probably prove, in my opinion fatal.[41]

But it was to be a few more years before Sarah breathed the air of freedom because she had only served fourteen years of her sentence and was not eligible under 'the remission scale applicable to death commuted sentence' to petition for her release until 8 March 1913. The Attorney-General, Mr C Wade, wrote in a departmental minute: 'I am unable to recommend the remission of any portion of this prisoner's sentence.' The Governor, Mr Harry Rawson, merely wrote 'Refused'.[42]

Two years later, Sarah was removed to the State Reformatory for Women at Long Bay Gaol. This was a separate prison that had been built for women in 1909, with all the female inmates of Darlinghurst Gaol being transferred in August of that year.[43] Eighteen months later, Sarah and her family began another campaign for her release on the grounds of her feeble health after a new Attorney-General, Mr Holman, visited Long Bay and gave Sarah permission to petition the government. On 28 February 1911, Sarah wrote the following:[44]

> PRISONER'S APPLICATION OR STATEMENT
> Subject:- Asking to be released so that she can spend her last days with her family.
>
> The above named prisoner respectfully makes statement ... that for years past she has been in bad health, though she suffered more during her time in Bathurst Gaol.
>
> She often feels that her life may not be long spared to her, and asks that she may be released to spend her last days with her family.
>
> She also stated that during her eighteen years imprisonment, she has nothing against her conduct and that the same may be taken into consideration.

The government also received another formal letter from Florence to the Minister of Justice.[45] This time the letter did not contain the numerous spelling and grammatical errors of Florence's first letter, suggesting that Florence had asked someone else to write on her behalf.

Although the wheels of bureaucracy creaked slowly, the Attorney-General wrote on 15 March 1911:

> In view of the great age and declining health of this prisoner I will recommend her release at the end of April (I do not wish this to be a Coronation date remission). This must be brought up in Cabinet.[46]

The Coronation was that of George V, who was crowned King on 22 June 1911. Sarah had seen the end of the reign of Queen Victoria, followed by the ascension of the 59-year-old playboy son of Queen Victoria, King Edward VII, to the throne on 22 January 1901 and then his early death in 1911.

After considering Sarah's 'advanced age and declining health', the government recommended her release on 26 April 1911.[47] More bureaucracy followed—a letter to the State Reformatory for Women at Long Bay which stated she would be released on 29 April 1911. And finally, a letter notifying Florence. After 18 years, Sarah cried at the thought that her time was up as the officer in charge of the gaol reported to the government:

> I have the honor to acknowledge receipt of order for the release of prisoner Sarah Makin ... on 29th April 1911. The prisoner was discharged at 4 PM to the Care of her daughter & Son-in-law, Mr. and Mrs. Anderson ...
>
> The prisoner when informed of her release was very much affected & asked for a Female officer to accompany her home.
>
> The prisoner had no Complaints of any kind to make & spoke of the Considerate & just manner in which she was treated during her imprisonment.[48]

Enfolded into the bosom of the family that still cared for her, Sarah left the prison quietly and anonymously, with the public none the wiser about the release of the most infamous murderer of her day. A government official, Mr Moss, observed that Sarah was:

> accompanied by a female Warder (Mrs Sparkes) and as the release party preceded me quietly along the road from the Reformatory to the Long Bay tram waiting room nobody atall [sic] could be seen either in the vicinity of the Reformatory or along the way to the tram.[49]

One can imagine the picture as Sarah and her daughter waited with quiet excitement for the tram and, once on board, Sarah taking in all the extraordinary sights of a city that had expanded and grown in the 18 years since she was arrested, as the tram trundled along what is now called Anzac Parade and then down Cleveland Street to her new home in Abercrombie Street. She had arrived back in Redfern where it had all begun. But the Sarah Makin who left prison at the age of 65 was a very different person to the one who had threatened to 'ribbon' Mrs Hill at the first Burren Street inquest 19 years earlier. Time, self-reflection, hardship and a newly found belief in God had softened Sarah Makin, murderer, into a person of gratitude in her letter to the matron of the gaol hospital:

> Just a few lines, to express my deep gratitude to you, the Governor and all the staff connected, for the many kindness I received while with you. My life being such a very sad one, you did all you possibly could, to brighten it. May God keep you and every blessing that can be sent to one, who always did her best to brighten the life of others.
>
> Dear Mrs. Braithwaite I shall never forget while it is God's wish to spare me, to be truly thankful, to the Minister of Justice, and the Controller General, and Deputy Controller for all they have done for me. I have not been very well since, I came home, being very nervous, but with the Lord's help I will have strength given me to keep a brave heart. Thanking you one and all, kindly remember me to all the officers, and may the good Lord send every blessing to you all.[50]

Sarah's final years

Constable James Joyce was still alive when Sarah was released although he was retired. He may not even have known she was free since her release was not reported in the newspapers. Although Sarah outlived him by six and a half years, her life outside prison was not a life of comfortable retirement. A few months after her release she moved in to live with her eldest daughter, Minnie, who was suffering from bowel cancer. At Eva Cottage in Belgrave Street, Petersham, Sarah cared for Minnie until her death on 7 February 1912.[51] When Minnie died, the following, strange death notice appeared in the newspaper:

> HELBY,—February 7, 1912, at Lewisham Private Hospital, Minnie Josephine, dearly-loved wife of Charles Helby, only daughter of the late Captain Charles Edwards, and granddaughter of Mr. and Mrs.

Emanuel Sutcliffe, late of Wollongong and Maitland, in her 45th
year. R.I.P.[52]

There was no mention that Minnie (who had Anglicised her name to
Helby) was the eldest daughter of (the infamous) Sarah Makin, indicating that a veil of shame still hung over Sarah's family, 19 years after her
conviction. The year before, Minnie had celebrated her silver wedding
anniversary with a proud notice in the newspaper:

SILVER WEDDINGS
HELBY EDWARDS,—March 9, 1886 at St. Luke's Church,
Sydney, by the Rev. T. W. Unwin, Carl Helby, of Germany, to
Minnie Josephine, only daughter of the late Captain Charles
Edwards, of Dundee, Scotland, and Sarah Jane Edwards, only
daughter of the late Emanuel Sutcliffe, Millowner, of West
Maitland. Perth and Dundee (Scotland) papers please reply.[53]

With a little rewriting of history, Minnie had erased the fact that her
mother had been Mrs Sarah Makin for nearly 40 years.

Six funeral notices appeared two days after Minnie's death, inviting the
friends of Minnie's sons, daughter and son-in-law, as well as the friends
of Blanche, Clarice, Florence, Daisy and their husbands, to attend Eva
Cottage for the funeral procession to Rookwood Cemetery via Petersham
train station.[54] There was no funeral notice inviting the friends of Mrs
Sarah Makin to her daughter's funeral.

Sarah remained living in Eva Cottage with Carl Helby, who sorely
missed his wife.[55] When Sarah's own health worsened, Florence and
husband moved in. Sarah lingered for another six years until, at the age
of 72, she died on 13 September 1918 at Eva Cottage from senile decay
and heart failure. It is possible her decline was due to tertiary syphilis
since heart failure and dementia are symptoms of the disease.[56] No notice
appeared in the newspapers announcing her death.

Buried in Rookwood Cemetery, in death Sarah joined some of the babies
who were placed into her not so kindly hands, including Mignonette and

Horace. Constable Joyce was also buried there, as was her husband, John. In fact, most of those who were involved in the most notorious baby-farming case of its time—Sarah, John, their children Blanche and Clarice, two of their victims and James Joyce—are all buried in Rookwood Cemetery, as if their final coming together completes a fable from which others may learn.

❧

CHAPTER TWENTY-THREE

Was Sarah Makin really an evil, deadly woman?

There was more to Sarah Makin's story than John's family's descriptions of her as 'a fiend' and the 'arch-aggressor' who would not be wound round the fingers of any man.

Rather than being a wicked woman looking for ways to indulge her 'fiendish' temper, baby farming was the desperate dead-end in which Sarah found herself with an unemployable husband and limited employment for the working-classes as the depression of the 1890s loomed. One cannot forget John's announcement to Mr Hill, the morning after the Makins moved into 25 Burren Street with six babies, that 'there is a very good thing to be made out of this business', referring to his wife's job as a ladies' nurse. Not so much a fool, as John's family had claimed, but a man who had found an easier option for earning an income. As the family's chief negotiator, John's ability to control his emotions—remaining 'immobile as marble' when his death sentence was announced[1]—along with his easy resort to lies and fantasy, ensured his indifference to the mothers and babies he dealt with.

While it is almost certain that both John and Sarah were involved in serial murder or manslaughter, they were the economic victims of the 1890s depression and the diseases that went hand in hand with Sydney's underclass. At the same time, the Makins took advantage of a moral climate which shunned unmarried mothers and illegitimate children, and a society which accepted the necessity of infanticide as a solution to illegitimate children. Just who out of the Makin family killed the 13 babies discovered by Constable Joyce and the two drain-layers we will never know. The evidence suggests that all of them—John, Sarah, Blanche, Florence and even Clarice—were involved in the underfeeding, drugging and final despatch of several dozen babies, not just the ones discovered by the police.

A working-class woman of her times, Sarah had married a man who was a bankrupt and petty criminal with an unstable work history. Early in the marriage, when she had six children aged eight days to nine years, she had been left to feed her family when John was imprisoned for theft. When she contracted syphilis, perhaps as a casual prostitute, and continued to produce more children, she added to the family's economic decline. This decline was aided and abetted by John who, either because of gambling, alcohol or opium addiction, had a reputation within his Wollongong family as a wastrel who could not be trusted with money.

The economic reality of baby farming meant that, in order to keep costs down, the Makins could not afford to feed the number of babies they adopted, while Godfrey's Cordial was guaranteed to pacify a hungry infant. So normal was underfeeding in the Makin household that John took Miss Stacey's hungry and distressed baby to see her, apparently oblivious to a young mother's reaction. So indifferent were the Makins to a baby's wellbeing, they starved Baby Mignonette despite receiving ten shillings per week for her upkeep.

Even with John's monthly inheritance, the Makins were living on the precipice of penury, a step away from debtors' prison. The economic crisis in the Makin household—through John's inability to work—increased the burden on Sarah and her daughters.

Sarah's and John's crimes were also the crimes of a society that condoned infanticide while, paradoxically, stigmatising unmarried mothers. The legal status of an illegitimate child was described as 'filius nullius', child of no-one,[2] which sums up the legal and social reality of those times. Since these children had no legal status, it is hardly surprising they had little or no social value. Life was cheap for illegitimate babies. Baby farmers provided an unsavoury but necessary service that filled the vacuum left wide open by government policies, the market economy and the limited assistance available through charitable organisations.

For those who believed that John's death would serve as an example, their satisfaction was short-lived, since baby farming continued long after the Makins were sentenced. Economic conditions for unmarried mothers, working-class families and deserted women did not improve. It would be another 70 years before reliable contraception became available and then another 10–20 years before a child born outside of marriage became a socially acceptable event.

❧

CHAPTER TWENTY-FOUR

The lives that were left

The Makin daughters all suffered as a result of their parents' baby-farming activities, since every one of them was conscripted into the business. Their education, in particular, suffered—Florence's literacy was poor compared to her mother's and father's, while Clarice could only read a little and Daisy could neither read nor write.

During the inquest into Baby Horace's death, Blanche had been distressed by being unable to see her gentleman friend who had come to Darlinghurst Court to see her. This may have been the man she married on 8 May 1894 at the age of 19, nine months after the death of her father and a few months after she gave birth to her own illegitimate daughter, Ruby May Makin, on 7 January 1894. Blanche's half-sister, Minnie Helby had given consent to the marriage as Blanche's guardian. When Blanche visited her father in Darlinghurst Gaol the day before his execution, she was four months pregnant. Blanche was one of the lucky unmarried mothers whose child did not end up with a baby farmer since the father of her child, Charles William Deacon, had been willing to make an 'honest' woman of her. Perhaps the hurried nature of the marriage accounts for the fact that no marriage notice appeared in the local newspapers.

Blanche and Charles had another seven children after Ruby, who was registered as Ruby Makin when she was born then as Ruby Deacon in 1910. Three more daughters and four sons were born between 1895 and

1909, although Blanche's first son, Charles, died in the year of his birth in 1895. Blanche died on 9 February 1953, aged 78.

Clarice was the next Makin daughter to marry when she promised to love and obey Charles Henry Ellis, a 22-year-old bootmaker, on 25 March 1896 at the age of 20. Like her sister Blanche, she was pregnant before she married. Charles saved her from being the mother of another illegitimate child in the family by marrying her six weeks before she gave birth to Ruby Pearl on 7 July at 80 Botany Road, Alexandria, close to where her other sisters were living. Curiously, the permission of Sarah Makin, who was in Darlinghurst Gaol at the time, had been obtained in writing for Clarice to marry. Blanche and her husband were witnesses at the wedding, suggesting a reconciliation between the sisters.

Clarice had one more child, Reginald, born ten years later in 1916. She died on 26 June 1951 at Bondi Junction aged 73 years after being a widow for 20 years.[1] Her husband died on 6 September 1930 after an accident in which he was struck by a car on the corner of Oxford Street and Green Road in Paddington. Clarice sued the driver of the car, seeking £1000 compensation for her husband's death, although she eventually settled her claim for £250.[2] It appears she was eventually reconciled with her whole family, since she attended the funeral of her half-sister, Minnie Helby, with her other sisters and her mother in February 1912.

More mysterious is the life of Florence, who married Edward Anderson on 27 February 1900. The marriage notice, which was not published in the newspaper until April, stated they were both of Wollongong, suggesting that Florence lived with John's family after her parents were convicted.[3] They appear to have had no children. Florence died quite young at the age of 47 in 1922, although there is no record of a death certificate for Florence Eileen Elise Anderson in Australia for that or any other year. An online family history states that she lived in the Northern Cape of South Africa—a long way from the Makin family shame—where she may have died.[4] Her husband outlived her, dying in Sydney in 1930. The names of Mrs (Daisy) Maloney, Mrs (Blanche) Deacon, and a daughter of Minnie Helby in Edward Anderson's death notice indicate the Makin siblings maintained contact over the decades.[5]

A few days after Daisy gave evidence at the inquest into the death of Baby D, she was sent to the Benevolent Asylum after 'being turned out' by Minnie Helby, who denied this, saying Daisy had run away. The Journal of the Benevolent Asylum recorded that Daisy was 'sent to the Asylum ... as she stayed away from home'.[6] Daisy's admittance to the Asylum was recorded as an 'emergency' and ordered by the Colonial Secretary after the Redfern police had sought an order from the courts.

With both parents in gaol and disagreements with her eldest sister, Daisy was treated as an orphan. Her new home was run by the Benevolent Society of New South Wales, a Christian organisation established in 1818. An imposing two-storey building built on the corner of Pitt and Devonshire Streets, Sydney, it originally provided basic shelter and relief for abandoned women and children, the aged, the homeless and the sick. By the time Daisy was admitted, the Benevolent Asylum only cared for single and destitute married women giving birth and children over the age of eight years. Although the Asylum had been designed to house 60 people, on the day that Daisy was admitted there were 108 women and 145 children.[7]

When Daisy was discharged on 29 April 1893, she was given into the care of a Boarding-Out Officer. Such officers oversaw the boarding-out system that had been introduced to replace institutional care by placing abandoned children into the care of families who were willing to become foster parents,[8] although this was sometimes a euphemism for free domestic labour. Perhaps Daisy returned to live with Minnie after a four month cooling off period, although at the age 12, she was old enough to go into domestic service.

Twelve years later, Daisy married John Patrick Molony (or Maloney), a 22-year-old tanner, on 21 March 1905, with Blanche and Florence as witnesses. Like her sister Clarice, Daisy was employed in 'home duties' at the time. She and John had two children, Edward, born in 1905, and Eveline, born in 1907. And like Blanche and Clarice, Daisy was pregnant before she married. She gave birth to Edward five months later on 6 August 1905 at 243 Abercrombie Street, the home of her sister, Florence. Daisy died in 1930 at the young age of 49.

Cecil, also known as Tommy, was two years old when his parents were arrested in 1892. Although he was looked after by Minnie Helby in the short term, it appears he ended up living with the Makin family in Wollongong. He changed his name to Meakin after his marriage in 1916, the same name as his brother William. Cecil died in 1950 aged 60 years. William remained in Wollongong after he spent most of his teenage years with one of his father's brothers 'learning the trade of wool classer' and died in 1953. The Makins' second son, Percy, also spent his teenage years in Wollongong with an uncle learning the blacksmith's trade; he died in 1922.[9]

Sarah's eldest daughter, Minnie Helby, had five children (Alma, Vincent, Gerald, Lorenzo and Minnie) with her husband Carl, who was still giving gymnastic performances in 1893.[10] Their youngest daughter, nicknamed Queenie, died when she was two on 28 June 1898. Minnie and Carl remembered their daughter with a notice in the newspaper a year after her death. As with other family notices, Minnie emphasised her paternal parentage, noting that her 'little Queenie' was the granddaughter of the late Captain Charles Edwards and grandniece of Captain John Garthley, with no mention that she was also the granddaughter of Mrs Sarah Makin.[11] As we know, Minnie died at the age of 45 on 7 February 1912 from bowel cancer. Her husband died in 1941, aged 88.

The unmarried mothers

Although they were the victims of baby farming, and, unwittingly, the lead players in the drama of Sarah and John Makins' lives, Minnie Davies and Horace Bothamley found a happy ending of sorts when they married in 1894.

Minnie had been born Mignonelle (or Mignonette) Lavinia Davies on 23 October 1876 at Woodburn in northern New South Wales, the daughter of William and Elizabeth Davies.[12] Her beau, Horace William Henry Bothamley, was an Englishman who was born in the cathedral city of Salisbury in Wiltshire. He had arrived in Australia at the age of nine on 2 May 1884 with his father, Henry, aged 38, mother, Mary, aged 48, and brother Oliver, aged seven, on the *Belgravia*. His father was a painter, glazier and agricultural labourer who could read and write, as could his mother. Mr and Mrs Bothamley were one of the 'general assisted married couples' who emigrated to Australia that year, the men on the ship being trades-people or labourers for a growing colony.

The Bothamley family had paid £21 for their passage to Australia, more than double the amount paid by other couples. The £15 ticket for Mary Bothamley was almost four times that of her husband (who paid £4) and seven times that of other, younger spouses listed on the ship's passenger list (who paid £2). In fact, all passengers over the age of 40 paid £15, possibly to deter them from applying.[13]

Minnie Davies was only 17 when she gave birth to Baby Mignonette, while Horace was 19. Perhaps they had intended to marry when Minnie reached her majority and reclaim their child from the Makins. A year after the execution of John Makin, Minnie was pregnant a second time but this time she and Horace married on 9 August 1894 at the Newtown Registry Office with the consent of Minnie's father, William Davies, a miner. By this time, Horace was 21 and a reader with the *Daily Telegraph* while Minnie's occupation was listed as 'private life'.

Minnie and Horace only had one more child, a son, Harold Lawrence, who was born three months after their marriage on 6 November 1894 in Balmain. Minnie died young at the age of 53 on 11 December 1929 while Horace lived to 92, dying in 1967.

The fate of Miss Amber Murray, whose gentleman friend had encouraged her to give up her baby son to baby farmers, has been impossible to track down. She was the only mother to find some comfort from the Makins' conviction, since they were tried for the murder of her child. There is no record of an Amber Murray born in Australia who would have been 18 years old in 1892. Although there was an Amber Constance Murray born in 1880, she was too young to be the 18-year-old who gave birth to Horace Amber Murray in 1892. While Amber Murray could have been illegitimate, it is more likely she was born in Britain given the comment made by Mrs Patrick who, when identifying the baby clothing made by Amber, said 'colonials do not sew like that'. It has not been possible to find out what happened to Miss Murray—no records of her marriage or death were found.

Miss Agnes Jane Todd was 25 years old when she gave birth to her baby, Elsie May, on 1 January 1892. After Agnes paid £3 for the adoption of her daughter by the Makins, she never saw her child again. It is likely that Elsie was one of the babies buried by the Makins in the backyard of 25 Burren Street. Agnes had been born on 22 November 1866 to William and Agnes Todd in Sussex Street, Sydney. She married William Hart, a blacksmith, on 2 January 1895, almost three years to the day after Elsie May had been born in 1892, a happy ending in St Barnabas Anglican Church, George Street, Sydney. She and William spent a busy life rearing seven children, Gladys (b.1895), Alice (b.1897), Henry (b.1900), Isabella (b.1904), Elsie (b.1907), Alma (b.1909), and Kathleen (b.1910).

Miss Clara Florence Risby was another of the unmarried mothers who encountered the Makins. She was admitted to Sydney's Benevolent Asylum on 7 March 1892 where she gave birth to her daughter, Elizabeth May, on 16 April 1892. The admission records state that Clara was pregnant by 'Henry Holmes, shipping clerk, now supposed to be in New Zealand'. On her discharge, it was recorded that '[t]he putative father of [her] child is supposed to be in Brisbane', suggesting she kept in touch with Henry, who was possibly not of the marrying kind.[14] Clara's real name was Florence Rigby and she was born on 22 May 1873 to Thomas and Barbara Rigby in Glebe, Sydney. Although Clara had two older half-sisters from her father's first marriage, it is curious she was not able to give birth at the home of one of them. She was discharged from the Asylum on 16 May into the care of her sister, Mrs Sargent, the same day she relinquished her baby to the Makins, who were living in East Street, Redfern. No babies were found in the backyard of East Street and it does not appear her daughter was one of the babies dug up at 109 George Street. She married William Alfred Davis several years later on 8 April 1909. They had one child, Cecil, who died the year he was born, 1909.

Miss Agnes Ward, the unmarried domestic servant who handed over her 'delicate' baby boy to the Makins in April 1892, was born in Goulburn in 1873, the third youngest of 16 children born to John and Sarah Ward. In 1910, Agnes Ward married Walter Edward Dolan but had no children. She died in 1957 aged 84.[15]

The final player in this drama, who has been assigned a rather small role, was the man responsible for a dozen inquests, a sensational trial, two appeals, several petitions and one execution. That man is Patrick Mulvey, who one day in October 1892 innocently employed two drain-layers to solve what he thought was a drainage problem in his backyard. The day after John Makin's execution, Mr Mulvey, the owner of 25 Burren Street, passed away and was buried in Waverley Cemetery:

> MULVEY, — August 16, at his late residence, Eileen, Burren-street, Macdonaldtown, Patrick Mulvey, age 39. Deeply regretted.[16]

There is no record of Patrick's birth in Australia, suggesting he was an immigrant. The passenger lists for ships arriving in New South Wales reveal that Patrick Mulvey, a groom aged 22 years, arrived in Sydney on 20 February 1878 aboard the *Tyburnia* from Leitrim in Ireland, the son of a farmer.[17] He married Mary Grogan in Sydney on 2 September 1880. At the time of his death, Mr Mulvey was the manager of the wine and spirits stores of Messrs J T and J Toohey, brewers.[18] Dead at a young age, he had been suffering from a lung condition, possibly tuberculosis. It was Mr Mulvey's illness that forced him to move out of his house in Burren Street and enabled its later occupation by the Makins. If Mr Mulvey had not done so, most likely the Makins would have remained living in the Sydney underworld of buying and killing babies, rather than becoming the most infamous baby farmers of their time and providing us with a sobering insight into the social and economic reality of times past.

Notes

Abbreviations in notes:

BC	*The Brisbane Courier*
BFPMJ	*Bathurst Free Press and Mining Journal*
CLJ	*Colonial Literary Journal*
CRE	*Clarence and Richmond Examiner*
DT	*The Daily Telegraph*
EN	*The Evening News*
MMHRGA	*The Maitland Mercury & Hunter River General Advertiser*
SAR	*South Australian Register*
SGNSWA	*The Sydney Gazette and New South Wales Advertiser*
SMH	*The Sydney Morning Herald*
SRO	State Records Office of New South Wales, Kingswood
TA	*The Argus*
TG	*The Guardian*

Author's note

1 Buttercup in *HMS Pinafore* by Gilbert & Sullivan.
2 *South Australian Register* (henceforth *SAR*), 10/3/1893, p.5.
3 *The Sydney Morning Herald* (henceforth *SMH*) was the lawyers' preferred source of law reporting because it employed legally trained reporters, unlike some of its competitors (see http://www.law.mq.edu.au/scnsw/html/introduction.html; accessed 25 October 2010).

Prologue

1 Rima Dombrow Apple (1987) *Mothers and Medicine: A Social History of Infant Feeding 1890–1950*, University of Wisconsin Press, Madison, Wisconsin, p.9.

Chapter 1

1 John's last days and hours and his hanging are taken from *The Brisbane Courier* (henceforth *BC*), 19/8/1893, p.6; the *Bathurst Free Press and Mining Journal* (henceforth *BFPMJ*), 16/8/1893, p.2; Inquest No. 849/93.
2 T Flannery (ed) (1999) *Watkin Tench 1788*, Text, Melbourne, pp.49–50.

3 P Norrie (2007) An Analysis of the Causes of Death in Darlinghurst Gaol 1867–1914 and the Fate of the Homeless in Nineteenth Century Sydney, Master of Arts (Research) Thesis, School of History, University of Sydney, p.104; <http://ses.library.usyd.edu.au/bitstream/2123/1862/5/01whole.pdf> [27 March 2011].

4 ibid., p.103.

5 Deborah Beck (2005) *Hope in Hell: A History of Darlinghurst Gaol and the National Art School*, Allen & Unwin, Sydney, p.137.

6 The first cervical vertebra transected the spinal cord, stopping John's breathing instantly: Norrie, p.102.

7 Carol Herben (1997) *From Burren Street to the Gallows: The John and Sarah Makin Story*, J & C Herben, Fairy Meadow, NSW, p.170.

Chapter 2

1 Emanuel Sutcliffe's convict record was obtained from the Archives Office of Tasmania, digitised record Item: CON31–1–40, <http://search.archives.tas.gov.au/ImageViewer/image_viewer.htm?CON31–1–40,262,57,F,36> [25 October 2010].

2 <http://www.rootsweb.ancestry.com/~austashs/convicts/conships_s.htm> [25 October 2010].

3 Archives Office of Tasmania, digitised record Item: CON18–1–20, <http://search.archives.tas.gov.au/ImageViewer/image_viewer.htm?CON18–1–20,247,122,L,27> [25 October 2010].

4 Terry Newman, extract from 'Becoming a Penal Colony', p.1, <parliament.tas.gov.au/php/BecomingTasmania/convictresistance.pdf> [26 October 2010]. The word 'dust' is thought to have referred to something more basic. Approximately 160,000 convicts were transported to Australia, with over 65,000 being sent to Tasmania.

5 L L Robson (1985) *A Short History of Tasmania*, Oxford University Press, Melbourne, p.118.

6 Newman, p.2.

7 E Barnard (2010) *Exiled: The Port Arthur Convict Photographs*, National Library of Australia, Canberra, p.74.

8 ibid.

9 Newman, pp.4–5; A Atkinson (1979) 'Four Patterns of Convict Protest', *Labour History*, 37: pp.28–51.

10 Barnard, p.63.

11 Newman, p.6.

12 ibid.

13 <www.tocal.com/homestead/vandv/vv26.htm>, [25 October 2010].

14 H de Bougainville (translated by M Serge Riviere) (1999) *The Governor's Noble Guest: Hyacinthe De Bougainville's Account of Port Jackson, 1825*, Melbourne University Press, Carlton, Victoria.

15 *The Teetotal Advocate*, 10/4/1843, p.2.

16   A Summers (1975) *Damned Whores and God's Police: The Colonisation of Women in Australia*, Penguin Books, Ringwood, Victoria, p.277.

17   *The Colonial Times*, 19/8/1834, cited in ibid.

18   Herben, p.3.

19   J C R Camm and J McQuilton (1987) *Australians: A Historical Atlas*, Fairfax, Syme & Weldon Associates, Sydney, p.204.

20   *The Colonial Observer*, 31/10/1844, p.4.

21   Camm and McQuilton, p.90.

22   Barnard, p.48.

23   ibid., p.49, citing a patron called Alexander Harris.

24   *Colonial Literary Journal* (henceforth *CLJ*), 27/6/1844, p.1.

25   ibid., p.298.

26   *CLJ*, 31/10/1844, p.289.

27   ibid., p.303.

28   S C McCulloch (1966) 'Gipps, Sir George (1791–1847)', *Australian Dictionary of Biography*, Volume 1, Melbourne University Press, Carlton, Victoria, pp.446–53.

29   *The Guardian* (henceforth *TG*), 5/10/1844, pp.233–5.

30   ibid., p.236.

31   ibid., emphasis in original.

32   ibid., p.235.

33   ibid.

34   M Steven (1967) 'Macarthur, John (1767–1834)', *Australian Dictionary of Biography*, Volume 2, Melbourne University Press, Carlton, Victoria, pp.153–9, <http://adb.anu.edu.au/biography/macarthur-john–2390> [31 August 2012].

35   *TG*, 5/10/1844, p.235.

36   *The Maitland Mercury & Hunter River General Advertiser* (henceforth *MMHRGA*), 24/7/1852, p.3.

37   *MMHRGA*, 17/3/1855, p.2.

38   *MMHRGA*, 8/8/1855, p.2.

39   *MMHRGA*, 27/11/1856, p.2.

40   *MMHRGA*, 6/1/1857, p.3.

41   *MMHRGA*, 29/1/1857, p.3.

42   *MMHRGA*, 24/2/1857, p.1. New South Wales was an English colony. This calculation was based on the price index of 1750–2005 set out in Table 1 of D Webb (2006) Inflation: The Value of the Pound 1750–2005, Research Paper 06/09, House of Commons Library, London, pp.12–15. The Australian dollar value was calculated according to its value on 23 July 2012 at 0.6618 GBP.

43   *MMHRGA*, 26/12/1857, p.2.

44   *SMH*, 12/2/1858, p.5.

45   *SMH*, 9/5/1865, p.1. Emanuel Sutcliffe was described as her father, late of Maitland. The marriage certificate is in the author's possession (1865/000355).

46   According to her death notice on 7 February 1912, Minnie was in her 45th year, making her year of birth either 1866 or 1867.

47   *The Australasian Sketcher with Pen and Pencil*, 12/6/1875, p.38.

48   <http://investigator.records.nsw.gov.au/entity.aspx?path=\agency\1726> [25 October 2010].

49   Email communication from Faye Stevenson, 4/6/2010.

50   Herben, p.4. The admission card for Ellen Sutcliffe's admission to Newington Asylum is not held by the State Records Office of New South Wales, Kingswood (henceforth SRO).

51   *SMH*, 12/8/1893, p.7.

Chapter 3

1   Herben, p.1; marriage certificate of William Makin and Ellen Bolton, number 1336/ volume 21; death certificate of William Samuel Makin, number 1887/009536; copies held by author.

2   1837 Convict Muster, <http://search.ancestry.com.au/iexec?htx=View&r=5544& dbid=1185&iid=IMAUS1787_114233–00770&fn=William&ln=Makins&st=d&ss- rc=&pid=272170> [18 December 2010].

3   See ancestry.com.au, public family trees for John Makin, which contain contra- dictory and conflicting information. I have relied on the information in these trees and the family history by Herben only when they concur in relation to dates and personages.

4   Mary and William Bolton's children were William (b.1803), Anne (b.1806), Mary (b.1807), Eliza (b.1812), Ellen (b.1816) and Sarah (b.1818).

5   The Convict Muster of 1823 states that William Bolton was convicted in Warwick, although his convict record states his conviction was in Stafford. Since he was convicted of more than one crime this accounts for the discrepancy. It appears he received a life sentence for coining and seven years for sacrilege, <http://search. ancestry.com.au/Browse/view.aspx?dbid=1185&path=Tasmania.List+of+convicts+ (incomplete).1823.71> [19 December 2010].

6   Tasmanian   Archives,   <http://search.archives.tas.gov.au/ImageViewer/image_ viewer.htm?CON31–1–1,433> [15 December 2010].

7   <http://www.turnbullclan.com/tca_genealogy/tca_all2-o/exhibits/turnbull_adam_ md.pdf>, [19 December 2010].

8   P Robinson (1993) *The Women of Botany Bay*, Penguin Books, Ringwood, Victoria, pp.160–1.

9   Quoted in ibid., pp.102, 161–3.

10 England & Wales, Criminal Registers, 1791–1892, Record for Mary Boulton, pp.240–4.

11 Robinson, p.185.

12 Ellen was born on 28/6/1816 or 1817 in Birmingham.

13 Robinson, p.26.

14 ibid., pp.63, 102.

15 J Ramsland (1986) *Children of the Back Lanes: Destitute and Neglected Children in Colonial New South Wales*, New South Wales University Press, Sydney, p.1.

16   ibid., pp.3, 5.

17   The population in 1800 was 5217 (3780 men and 1437 women): Australian Bureau of Statistics, *Australia's Population Since 1788 and Gender Composition Since 1796*, Australian Bureau of Statistics, Canberra, 2007.

18   Ramsland, p.5, quoting Governor King.

19   ibid., p.11; quoting Governor Macquarie.

20   S and K Brown (1995) *Parramatta: A Town Caught in Time, 1870*, Hale & Iremonger, Sydney, p.103.

21   B M Bubacz (2008) The Female and Male Orphan Schools in New South Wales, 1801–1850, Ph.D Thesis, Department Education and Social Work, University of Sydney, p.105, citing Governor Macquarie.

22   ibid., pp.105, 107, citing Rule 15 of Rules and Regulations of the Female Orphan School.

23   ibid., p.108.

24   ibid., p.118.

25   Ramsland, pp.11–12.

26   *Sydney Gazette*, 11/2/1810, p.1, cited in Bubacz, pp.93–4.

27   Ramsland, pp.18–19.

28   ibid., p.14.

29   Bubacz, pp.106, 226.

30   ibid., p.225.

31   Ramsland, p.16.

32   ibid.

33   Marriage certificate of Ellen Bolton, Volume 21/1336; copy held by author.

34   Ramsland, p.26, citing Reverend Walker.

35   ibid., pp.29, 30.

36   ibid., pp.30–1, emphases in original.

37   ibid., p.31.

38   ibid., pp.20, 40.

39   Bubacz, p.223.

40   All letters about Ellen Bolton's discharge from the Female Orphan School were obtained from SRO, citation NRS 783[1]; [4/333]; pp.243–8, Reel 2776; copies held by author.

41   All documents concerning Sarah Bolton's discharge from the Female Orphan School were obtained from SRO, citation NRS 783[2]; [4/334]; p.051–3, Reel 2777; NRS 798 [4/390]; p.161, Reel 1484; copies held by author.

42   O'Meara was one of 11 conductors working under the wardsmen who were in control of the five police districts in Sydney Town, <http://www.policensw.com/info/history/h2a.html> [19 December 2010].

43   <http://www.claimaconvict.net/index_files/Page452.htm> [17 December 2010].

44   <http://home.vicnet.net.au/cgi-bin/betsie/parser.cgi/0001/cd2.slv.vic.gov.au/Volumes/PJAnthology/9.+Marriage+Licences.pdf> [17 December 2010].

45   <http://search.ancestry.com.au/iexec?htx=View&r=5544&dbid=1783&iid=32245_223265–00451&fn=Mary&ln=Boulton&st=d&ssrc=&pid=48488> [18 December 2010].

46   R Hughes (1987) *The Fatal Shore*, The Harvill Press, London, p.256.

47   Barnard, p.91; Summers, p.280.

48   Hughes, p.256.

49   ibid., citing Dr Reid, emphasis in original, footnote omitted.

50   References to the riot at the Female Factory include: *The Sydney Gazette and New South Wales Advertiser* (henceforth *SGNSWA*), 31/10/1827, p.2; *The Australian*, 31/10/1827, p.3.

51   *SGNSWA*, 17/8/1830, p.3.

52   Barnard, pp.40–1. Mary Bolton's ticket-of-leave and certificate of freedom obtained from SRO, citation [4/4307; Reel 987]; [4/4071; Reel 912]; copies held by author.

53   *SMH*, 2/2/1853, p.3.

54   *SMH*, 8/4/1882, p.6. On 9/9/1856, 21/4/1857 and 20/4/1858, William Samuel Makin was granted a publican's licence for a recognisance of £50: Certificates for Publicans' Licences, 1830–1849, 1853–1860, Record for William Samuel Makin.

55   *The Empire*, 26/2/1864, p.5.

56   *SMH*, 4/1/1871, p.2; see also *The Empire*, 2/11/1870, p.2.

57   A W Martin (1974), 'Parkes, Sir Henry (1815–1896)', *Australian Dictionary of Biography*, Volume 5, Melbourne University Press, Carlton Press, Victoria, pp.399–406.

58   *SMH*, 2/11/1870, p.2; 9/12/1870, p.2.

59   Marriage certificate 1871/000870; copy held by author.

60   *SMH*, 24/6/1872, p.2; 3/7/1872, p.2.

Chapter 4

1   Herben, p.4.

2   *Sands Directories: Sydney and New South Wales, Australia, 1858–1933* <www.ancestry.com> [21 May 2011].

3   References to the sheep-stealing charge and trial are from *SMH*, 20/10/1881, p.7; 2/11/1881, p.7.

4   *SMH*, 6/4/1883, p.7.

5   *SMH*, 23/8/1889, p.3.

6   Although the horse owner paid Makin £20, he then announced he had stopped payment on the cheque.

7   *SMH*, 29/11/1889, p.4.

8   Death certificate 1886/005417; copy held by author.

9   Death certificate 1888/001900; copy held by author.

10   *SMH*, 16/11/1892, p.3.

11   M Lewis (1998) *Thorns on the Rose: The History of Sexually Transmitted Diseases in Australia in International Perspective*, AGPS, Canberra, pp.16–17, 21.

12   D Hill (2008) *1788: The Brutal Truth of the First Fleet*, William Heinemann, Sydney, p.154, quoting Surgeon Bowes Smyth of the *Lady Penrhyn* who witnessed 'a scene of

debauchery and riot which ensued during the night' of 5 February 1788. Although this orgy is disputed by historian Grace Karskens, Lieutenant Watkin Tench also noted in his diary the 'licentiousness' and 'habits of depravity' which occurred when the male and female convicts disembarked: T Flannery (ed) *Watkin Tench 1788* (1996), Text, Melbourne, p.45.

13   Lewis, pp.22–4.

14   ibid., pp.22–4, 36.

15   J Allen (1990) *Sex and Secrets: Crimes Involving Australian Women Since 1880*, Oxford University Press, Melbourne, pp.20, 25.

16   World Health Organization (2001) *Global Prevalence and Incidence of Selected Curable Sexually Transmitted Infections: Overview and Estimates*, World Health Organization: Geneva, p.22, <http://www.who.int/hiv/pub/sti/pub7/en/> [25/8/2011]; E Tridapalli, M G Capretti, V Sambri, A Marangoni, A Moroni, A D'Antuono, M L Bacchi and G Faldella (2007) 'Prenatal Syphilis Infection is a Possible Cause of Preterm Delivery Among Immigrant Women from Eastern Europe', *Sexually Transmitted Infections*, 83, pp.102–5; R Behrouz, A R Malek and R I Chichkova (2011) 'Meningo-Vascular Syphilis: Revisiting an Old Adversary', *Practical Neurology* (July/August), p.32.

17   M Genç and W J Ledger (2000) 'Syphilis in Pregnancy', *Sexually Transmitted Infections*, 76, pp.73, 74.

18   ibid., p.73.

19   For the contraction, symptoms and stages of syphilis see Genç and Ledger, p.74; K Nessa, A Alam, F A H Chawdhury, M Huq, S Nahar, G Salauddin, S Khursheed, S Rahman, E Gurley, R F Breiman, M and Rahman (2008) 'Field Evaluation of Simple Rapid Tests in the Diagnosis of Syphilis', *International Journal of STD & AIDS*, 19, p.316.

20   Lewis, pp.53–4.

21   Elisabeth Kehoe (2005) *Fortune's Daughters: The Extravagant Lives of the Jerome Sisters*, Atlantic Books, London, pp.xvii, 177.

22   For the symptoms and contraction of congenital syphilis see: Genç and Ledger, pp.74–75; Nessa et al., 'Field Evaluation of Simple Rapid Tests', p.316; A E Singh, K Sutherland, B Lee, J L Robinson and T Wong (2007) 'Resurgance of Early Congenital Syphilis in Alberta', *Canadian Medical Association Journal*, 177, p.34; C C Wu, C N Tsai, W R Wong, H S Hong, Y H Chuang (2006) 'Early Congenital Syphilis and Erythema Multiforme-like Bullous Targetoid Lesions in a 1-Day-old Newborn: Detection of Treponema Pallidum Genomic DNA from the Targetoid Plaque using nested Polymerase Chain Reaction', *Journal of the American Academcy of Dermatology*, 55, pp.S11–5, <http://www.dermatologyinfo.net/english/chapters/chapter09.htm> [3 September 2009].

Chapter 5

1   *The Argus* (henceforth *TA*), 10/3/1893, p.4.

2   *SMH*, 22/12/1892, p.5. One pound equalled 20 shillings and one shilling equalled 12 pence.

3   The following is a list of their addresses after 1880 when the Makins were living at 190 Goulburn Street: Darling Street, Ultimo (October 1881); 149 Goulburn Street, Darlinghurst (February 1882); on or near Bourke Street, Surry Hills (November 1883); 47 Oxford Street, Darlinghurst (1884); 58 George Street, Redfern (November 1885); 207 Wells Street, Redfern (July 1886); 113 Bullanaming Street, Redfern (in August 1888); 26 Dale Street, Chippendale (October 1888); Glebe (part of 1889); Richard Street, Newtown (1890); Cook's River Road, St Peters (June 1891); 56 Howard Street, St Peters (1891); Bay Street, Glebe (1891); Harbour Street, Darling Harbour (date unknown) and Queen Street, opposite the mortuary (date unknown). Sources: *Sands Directories: Sydney and New South Wales, Australia, 1858–1933*, <www.ancestry.com> [21 May 2011]; death certificates of Leslie, Linda and Harold; various newspaper reports.

4   Ruth Ellen Homrighaus (2001) 'Wolves in Women's Clothing: Baby-Farming and the British Medical Journal 1860–1872', *Journal of Family History*, 26, pp.350–72; S Swain (2005) 'Toward a Social Geography of Baby Farming', *History of the Family*, 10, pp.151–9; B Waugh (May 1890) ' "Baby-Farming"', *Contemporary Review*, pp.700–2.

5   In 1875, a report found that illegitimate babies in England and Wales had 'double the mortality risk of those born in marriage': A Levene, 'The Mortality Penalty of Illegitimate Children: Foundlings and Poor Children in Eighteenth Century England' in A Levene, T Nutt and S Williams (2005) *Illegitimacy in Britain, 1700–1920*, Palgrave Macmillan, Hampshire, p.34.

6   Allen, p.26.

7   ibid., p.27.

8   ibid., p.26, 30.

9   Judith Allen 'Octavius Beale Reconsidered: Infanticide, Babyfarming and Abortion in NSW 1880–1939' in Australian Labour History Group (ed.) (1982) *What Rough Beast? The State and Social Order in Australian History*, Allen & Unwin, Sydney, p.115; Barbara Burton (1986) Bad Mothers? Infant Killing in Victoria 1885–1914, Honours Thesis, University of Melbourne, cited in G A Carmichael (1996) 'From Floating Brothels to Suburban Semirespectability: Two Centuries of Nonmarital Pregnancy in Australia' *Journal of Family History*, 21, p.293; Kathy Laster (1989) 'Infanticide: A Litmus Test for Feminist Criminological Theory' *Australian and New Zealand Journal of Criminology*, 22, pp.151, 153.

10   *SMH*, 16/1/1892, p.7; 29/2/1892, p.7; 24/3/1892, p.2.

11   *Criminal Law Amendment Act* 1883.

12   Allen, *Sex and Secrets*, p.28.

13   ibid., pp.29–30.

14   According to the Australian Institute of Criminology, between 1989–90 and 2006–07, the offending rate of men for the crime of homicide fluctuated from 2.5 to 4 times the offending rate of women for the crime of homicide, <http://www.aic.gov.au/statistics/homicide/offenders.aspx> [24 August 2011].

15   Allen, *Sex and Secrets*, p.31.

16   Carmichael, p.293.
17   Allen, *Sex and Secrets*, p.33.

Chapter 6

1   A-M Whitaker (2002) *Pictorial History of South Sydney*, Kingsclear Books, Alexandria, New South Wales, p.114.
2   J Beard (1983) Newtown 1892–1922: A Social Sketch, Honours Thesis, Department of History, University of Sydney, p.5.
3   The description of suburban life in Newtown is taken from ibid., pp.7–8.
4   *BC*, 11/11/1892, p.6.
5   *SMH*, 5/11/1892, p.10.
6   ibid.
7   *TA*, 4/11/1892, p.6; *BC*, 8/11/1892, p.6.
8   Joyce's visit to 6 Wells Street is taken from *SMH*, 16/11/1892, p.3; *BC*, 16/11/1892, p.3.

Chapter 7

1   Allen, *Sex and Secrets*, p.35.
2   Mr Neild (1892) Second Reading Speech, Infants Protection Bill, Legislative Assembly, *NSW Parliamentary Debates (First Series) Fifteenth Parliament Session*, 1891–92, 55° Victoire, Volume 52, Charles Potter, Government Printer, Sydney, p.758.
3   Mr Haynes and Mr Garvan (1892) Second Reading Speech, Infants Protection Bill, Legislative Assembly, *NSW Parliamentary Debates (First Series) Fifteenth Parliament Session*, 1891–92, 55° Victoire, Volume 52, Charles Potter, Government Printer, Sydney, pp.763–5.
4   Mr Wall (1892) Second Reading Speech, Infants Protection Bill, Legislative Assembly, *NSW Parliamentary Debates (First Series) Fifteenth Parliament Session*, 1891–92, 55° Victoire, Volume 52, Charles Potter, Government Printer, Sydney, p.768.
5   The legislation was originally named the Infants Protection Bill. Enacted as the *Children's Protection Act* on 31 March 1892, it was renamed after the upper age of baby-farmed children was increased to three years.
6   *The Daily Telegraph* (henceforth *DT*), 28/10/1892, p.4; 13/10/1892, p.5.
7   Allen, *Sex and Secrets*, p.35.
8   S Swain (2009) 'Birth and Death in a New Land: Attitudes to Infant Death in Colonial Australia', *History of the Family*, 15, p.25.
9   As described in Allen, *Sex and Secrets*, pp.36–7.
10   *DT*, 9/11/1892, p.5.
11   Allen, *Sex and Secrets*, p.36.

Chapter 8

1   All references to these inquests are to Inquest Numbers 1196/92 and 1177/92, Register of Coroner's Deaths, 1892. The evidence from these inquests was published in *SMH*,

27/10/1892, p.8; 29/10/1892, p.8; 8/11/1892, p.6; 15/11/1892, p.3; *BC,* 8/11/1892, p.6; *The Evening News* (henceforth *EN*), 27/10/1892, p.6; 29/10/1892, p.6.

2 L Mellor (2008) 'Milford, Frederick', Faculty of Medicine Online Museum and Archive, University of Sydney, <http://sydney.edu.au/medicine/museum/mwmuseum/index.php/Milford,_Frederick> [25 April 2012].

3 See *SMH,* 27/10/1892, p.8; 11/11/1892, p.3; 15/11/1892, p.4; *EN,* 28/10/1892, p.6; 11/11/1892, p.6.

4 R W Mann, W M Bass and L Meadows (1990) 'Time Since Death and Decomposition of the Human Body: Variables and Observations in Case and Experimental Field Studies', *Journal of Forensic Sciences,* 35, pp.103–11.

5 <http://en.wikipedia.org/wiki/Decomposition> [10 June 2010].

6 Flies will burrow through cracks and crevices in the soil after burial, especially following heavy rain. They also lay their eggs on the surface of the soil after a burial: W C Rodriguez and W M Bass (1985) 'Decomposition of Buried Bodies and Methods That May Aid in Their Location', *Journal of Forensic Sciences,* 30, pp.836–52, 848–9.

7 <http://www.deathonline.net/decomposition/body_changes/grave_wax.htm> [26 July 2009].

8 D H R Spennemann and B Franke (1995) 'Decomposition of Buried Human Bodies and Associated Death Scene Materials on Coral Atolls in the Tropical Pacific', *Journal of Forensic Science,* 40, pp.356–67.

9 *SMH,* 5/11/1892, p.5.

10 *EN,* 27/10/1892, p.6.

11 A A Vass (2001) 'Beyond the Grave—Understanding Human Decomposition', *Microbiology Today,* 28, p.190.

12 A Morovic-Budak (1965) 'Experiences in the Process of Putrefaction in Corpses Buried in Earth', *Medicine, Science and the Law,* 5, pp.42–3.

13 Rodriguez and Bass, p.839.

14 ibid., pp.839–43.

Chapter 9

1 SRO, Australian Birth Index, Volume number V1849380 66 and Register of Police Appointments (1862–1913) 8/3253.

2 Constable Joyce's employment history is taken from SRO, Register of Police Appointments (1857–1883) 8/3251; Register of Police Appointments (1862–1913) 8/3253.

3 <http://www.sydneyarchives.info/jubilee-souvenir-1912/book/2?firstPage Number=50> [10 August 2011].

4 SMH, 27/9/1901, p.7.

5 <http://search.ancestry.com.au/cgi-bin/sse.dll?rank=1&db=pubmembertrees& gsfn=James&gsln=Joyce&_8000C002=John&_80008002=Jane&_81004010= 1849&msbpn__ftp=Sydney%2c+New+South+Wales> [9 and 10 July 2011].

6   SMH, 15/10/1881, p.7.

7   These directories are known as the *Sands Directories*, <www.sydneyarchives. info/sands-directories> [16 August 2011]. In 1882, a James Joyce lived in O'Connell Street, south side, Newtown; in 1883, a James Joyce lived in O'Connell Street, west side, Newtown; in 1884 and 1885 there is no James Joyce listed although in 1886–1887, James Joyce, constable, is listed at Camden Street, south side 86. There is no *Sands Directory* for 1888 but in 1889 James Joyce had moved to Camden Avenue, Newtown where he lived from 1889 to 1891. In 1892, the year of his marriage to Agnes, he was listed as living at 29 Australia, east side, Newtown where he lived from 1892 to 1907.

8   *SMH*, 16/5/1912, p.8.

9   *SMH*, 14/5/1914, p.8.

10 *SMH*, 14/5/1915, p.8.

11 *SMH*, 14/5/1917, p.6.

Chapter 10

1   *SMH*, 4/11/1892, p.4.

2   *SMH*, 4/11/1892, p.5; 5/11/1892, p.10.

3   *BC*, 8/11/1892, p.6.

4   All information about this police dig is taken from *SMH*, 4/11/1892, p.5; 5/11/1892, p.10; *BC*, 8/11/1892, p.6.

5   *BC*, 4/11/1892, p.5; *TA*, 4/11/1892, p.6; *The* [Hobart] *Mercury*, 5/11/1892, p.3.

6   Evidence of the arrests is taken from *BC*, 8/11/1892, p.6; *SMH*, 14/11/1892, p.5; *EN*, 7/11/1892, p.6. At this time, the Makins had three other children who were not living with them. William, aged 20, lived in Wollongong, as did Percy, who was 13 years old. Clarice, aged 14, was a domestic servant in Sydney.

7   See <www.sydneyarchives.info/sands-directories> [16 August 2011]. I am grateful to Ms Naomi Crago, Archivist at the City of Sydney, for this information (email communication, 27 July 2011).

8   Sources for the police interview include *SMH*, 8/11/1892, p.3; 15/11/1892, p.3; *BC*, 11/11/1892, p.6.

9   Stories about the Makins were reported in *SMH*, 12/11/1892, p.7; 14/11/1892, p.5; 16/11/1892, p.3; *MMHRGA*, 17/11/1892, p.7; *Clarence and Richmond Examiner* (henceforth *CRE*), 19/11/1892, p.2; *BC*, 17/11/1892, p.3; *DT*, 16/11/1892, p.6.

10 See footnote 42, Chapter 2 for method of calculation.

11 SRO, Will number 19812, Eleanor Makin; 17/2339, probate packet of Eleanor Makin. Part of her very long will stated, 'And I declare that the shares of my said son John Makin and of my said daughter Emily Roberts shall be paid to them respectively by monthly instalments of Four pounds each'.

12 The symptoms of opium addiction include greater and greater tolerance to the drug with a need for increasing concentrations to satisfy the addiction; mood swings, anxiety, paranoia and hallucinations, <http://www.wrongdiagnosis.com/o/opium_ addiction/symptoms.htm> [24 August 2011].

Chapter 11

1   References to these inquests are to Inquest Numbers 1204/92, 1205/92, 1252/92, 1253/92 and 1254/92, Register of Coroner's Deaths, 1892.

2   All evidence from the inquest into the death of Baby 1 of Burren Street is taken from *SMH*, 5/11/1892, p.10; 7/11/1892, p.5; 9/11/1892, p.4; *DT*, 8/11/1892, p.3; 9/11/1892, p.5; *BC*, 11/11/1892, p.6; *EN*, 8/11/1892, p.6.

3   *SMH*, 9/11/1892, p.4.

4   *The Moreton Bay Courier*, 7/5/1859, p.4.

5   *SMH*, 28/10/1850, p.3.

6   D Manderson (1993) *From Mr Sin to Mr Big: A History of Australian Drug Laws*, Oxford University Press, Melbourne, p.53.

7   *Colonial Times*, 2/12/1851, p.2.

8   Manderson, p.82.

9   A S Wohl (1983) *Endangered Lives: Public Health in Victorian Britain*, Harvard University Press, Cambridge, p.34.

10 T E C Jr, (1970) 'What Were Godfrey's Cordial and Dalby's Carminative?', *Pediatrics*, 45, p.1011.

11 E Cobham Brewer (1898) *Dictionary of Phrase and Fable*, Henry Altemus, Philadelphia.

12 T E C Jr, p.1011.

13 Wohl, p.34.

14 Brewer, *Dictionary of Phrase and Fable*.

15 The Australian Academy of the History of Pharmacy, A Scandalously Short Introduction to the History of Pharmacy, <http://www.psa.org.au/site.php?id=771> [20 December 2009].

16 Wohl, p.35.

17 *Colonial Times*, 27/8/1855, p.3.

18 *SMH*, 10/5/1856, p.6.

19 Wohl, p.35.

20 *SMH*, 21/6/1845, p.2.

21 Evidence concerning the inquests into the deaths of Babies 2, 3 and 5 is taken from *SMH*, 9/11/1892, p.4; 12/11/1892, p.7; *DT*, 9/11/1892, p.5; *R v Makin and Wife* (1893) 14 NSWLR 1 at 10, per Windeyer J.

22 *SMH*, 14/11/1892, p.5.

Chapter 12

1   *DT*, 11/11/1892, p.5.

2   *BC*, 16/11/1892, p.3; *The Advertiser*, 17/11/1892, p.5.

3   Registration Number 26156/1892; copy held by author.

4   All references to this inquest are to Inquest Number 1252/92, Register of Coroner's Deaths, 1892. Evidence from the inquest is taken from *SMH*, 9, 15 & 16/11/1892, p.3; 14/11/1892, p.5; *TA*, 14 & 18/11/1892, p.6; *EN*, 14, 15, 17, 18, 22, 24 & 25/11/1892,

p.6; *DT*, 14/11/1892, p.5; 15 & 16/11/1892, p.6; *BFPMJ*, 17, 18, 23 & 25/11/1892, p.2; 19/11/1892, p.3; *The Advertiser*, 17/11/1892, p.5; *BC*, 17/11/1892, p.3; *The West Australian*, 18/11/1892, p.3; *MMHRGA*, 18/11/1892, p.2.

5 *DT*, 17/11/1892, p.5.

6 *SMH*, 9/3/1886, p.1.

7 According to the Register of Coroner's Deaths, 1892, the inquest was heard on 7, 8, 11, 14, 15, 16, 17, 18, 21, 22, 23, 24, 25 and 28 November.

Chapter 13

1 Birth certificate number 26156/1892; copy held by author.

2 Although the date stamps on the telegrams sent by John Makin to Horace Bothamley are out by a month and a few days, nothing turned on this odd discrepancy. The first was dated 4/7/1892 and the second 9/7/1892, both signed by John Burt, whom a post-office clerk recognised as John Makin: *SMH*, 22/11/1892, p.3.

3 P Saukko and B Knight (2004) *Knight's Forensic Pathology*, Arnold, London, p.414.

4 *EN*, 1/10/1892, p.4.

5 The evidence of this part of the inquest is taken from *SMH*, 18 & 23/11/1892, p.6; *BFPMJ*, 23/11/1892, p.2; *TA*, 29/11/1892, p.5; *EN*, 23/11/1892, p.6.

6 Allen, *Sex and Secrets*, p.26.

7 The evidence of Agnes Todd is taken from *TA*, 18/11/1892, p.6; *The Queenslander*, 26/11/1892, p.1024; *DT*, 18/11/1892, p.6; *R v Makin and Wife* (1893) 14 NSWLR 1 at 11, per Windeyer J.

8 References for this part of the inquest are taken from *TA*, 29/11/1892, p.5; *SMH*, 12/12/1892, p.7.

9 Nonetheless, the cause of death entered in the Register of Coroners' Inquests, 1892, for Inquest Number 1252/92 was 'Marasmus the result of negligence and carelessness on the part of John and Sarah Makin'.

10 *SMH*, 1/12/1892, p.4.

Chapter 14

1 Descriptions of the George, Botany, East and Kettle streets digs are taken from *SMH*, 10 & 11/11/1892, p.5; *DT*, 10/11/1892, p.5; *BFPMJ*, 10/11/1892, p.2; *EN*, 14/11/1892, p.6.

2 Description of the Alderson Street dig is taken from *SMH*, 12/11/1892, p.7; 14/11/1892, p.5; 12/12/1892, pp.4, 7–8.

3 Inquest No.1259/92 (the Register of Coroners' Inquests, 1892). The jury returned an open verdict in relation to the death of Baby E on 14/12/1892.

4 Description of the Levey Street dig is taken from *EN*, 14 & 16/11/1892, p.6; 15/11/1892, pp.4, 6; *BFPMJ*, 15/11/1892, p.2; *CRE*, 19/11/1892, p.2; *SMH*, 14/11/1892, p.5; *BC*, 17/11/1892, p.3.

5 William Redfern was a naval surgeon in the Royal Navy who was sentenced to death for his part in a mutiny in 1797, although his death sentence was commuted

to transportation. He was granted 100 acres in 1817 in the Redfern area. William Chippendale, a free settler, was granted 95 acres in 1819: B Diggs and C Bickerton, 'Pre and Post Colonial History of Redfern', <http://people.arch.usyd.edu.au/web/current/topic1/Digges+Bickerton(T1)/Pre_and_post_colonial_histo.doc> [21 July 2010]; S Fitzgerald (2008) 'Chippendale', <www.dictionaryofsydney.org/entry/chippendale> [21 July 2010].

6   B Diggs and C Bickerton.

7   W S Jevon, 'Sydney in 1858', *SMH*, 7/12/1929, p.13.

8   G F J Bergman (1967) 'Levey, Solomon (1794–1833)', *Australian Dictionary of Biography*, Volume 2, Melbourne University Press, Carlton, Victoria, pp.110–11, <http://adbonline.anu.edu.au/biogs/A020096b.htm> [17 September 2010].

9   *BC*, 17/11/1892, p.3.

10   Inquest No.1259/92 (the Register of Coroners' Inquests, 1892) on 15 November into the deaths of Babies G and H returned an open verdict because there was no cause of death.

11   *MMHRGA*, 17/11/1892, p.7.

12   *DT*, 14/11/1892, p.5.

13   *SMH*, 14/11/1892, p.5; *EN*, 15/10/1892, p.6.

14   *MMHRGA*, 17/11/1892, p.7; *BC*, 16/11/1892, p.3.

15   *BC*, 16/11/1892, p.3.

16   *BFPMJ*, 12/11/1892, p.2; *SMH*, 14/11/1892, p.5.

17   *SMH*, 11/11/1892, p.5.

18   *DT*, 15/11/1892, p.6.

Chapter 15

1   *EN*, 29/11/1892, p.6.

2   Herben, p.36.

3   *SMH*, 14/11/1892, p.5; 15/12/1892, p.4; 21/12/1892, p.7; *EN*, 29/11/1892, p.6.

4   Inquest No. 1371/92, Register of Coroners' Inquests, 1892.

5   Evidence from the second George Street inquest is taken from *EN*, 17/11/1892, p.6; 15/12/1892, p.6; *BFPMJ*, 15/12/1892, p.3; *SMH*, 15/12/1892, p.4; 17/12/1892, p.2; *The Advertiser*, 17/12/1892 p.4; *MMHRGA*, 22/12/1892, p.5.

6   One report said that Clarice revealed there were four babies in the house in George Street (*SMH*, 15/12/1892, p.6). Six babies accords with evidence given by other witnesses, as well as the Notes of Evidence of *R v Sarah Makin and John Makin*, Justice Stephen, 3 April 1893, SRO, Register 10/11136.

7   Clara's evidence is taken from *EN*, 15/12/1892, p.6; *SMH*, 15/12/1892, p.4; 16/12/1892, p.3; 17/12/1892, p.10.

8   The evidence for day two of the second George Street inquest is taken from *EN*, 15/12/1892, p.4; 16/12/1892, pp.4, 6; *SMH*, 16/12/1892, p.3; *DT*, 22/11/1892, p.6; 16/12/1892, p.2.

9   *EN*, 18, 20, 21, 22, 23 & 24/6/1892, p.1.

10 This evidence and account of proceedings is taken from *EN*, 17/12/1892, p.6.

11 The account of the incident between Makin and Joyce and the juryman is taken from *EN*, 17/12/1892, p.6; *Barrier Miner*, 16/12/1892, p.4.

12 The evidence from post-lunch on day two is taken from *SMH*, 17/12/1892, p.10; *BFPMJ*, 17/12/1892, p.2; *EN*, 17/12/1892, p.6; *DT*, 10/11/1892, p.5.

Chapter 16

1 Inquest number 1369/92, Register of Coroners' Inquests, 1892. Evidence at the inquest into Baby D is taken from *SMH*, 7/12/1892, p.3; 21/12/1892, pp.4, 7; 22/12/1892, p.4; 7/3/1893, p.3; *EN*, 20/12/1892, p.4; 21 & 22/12/1892, pp.4, 6; *TA*, 21/12/1892, p.5; 22/12/1892, p.6; *DT*, 21/12/1892, p.5; *The Advertiser*, 22/12/1892, p.5; *MMHRGA*, 22/12/1892, p.5; *BC*, 17/11/1892, p.3; *R v Makin and Wife* (1893) 14 NSWLR 1 at 7–8, per Windeyer J; depositions of Amber Murray, Mrs Patrick, Clarice Makin, 21 December 1892, filed in Register 9/6839 Clerk of the Peace, Central Criminal Court, Sydney, February 1893; *R v John Makin and Sarah Makin* (murder) held by the SRO.

2 *BC*, 17/11/1892, p.3.

3 ibid.

4 The accounts of the Makins' reactions are taken from *SMH*, 22/12/1892, p.4; 26/12/1892, p.3; *The Advertiser*, 22/12/1892, p.5; *TA*, 22/12/1892, p.8.

5 G Robbins, 'Age Estimation', quoting Fazekas and Kosa (1978), <http://www.appalachianbioanth.org/week7.pdf> [29 January 2012].

6 J Kiesler and R Ricer (2003) 'The Abnormal Fontanel', *American Family Physician*, 67, pp.2547–52; G Duc and R H Largo (1986) 'Anterior Fontanel: Size and Closure in Term and Preterm Infants', *Pediatrics*, 78, pp.904–8; see also W Derkowski, A Kedzia and M Glonek (2003) 'Clinical Anatomy of the Human Anterior Cranial Fossa during the Prenatal Period', *Folia Morphologica*, 62, pp.271–3.

7 M Nyström, L Peck, E Kleemola-Kujala, M Evälahti and M Kataja (2000) 'Age Estimation in Small Children: Reference Values Based on Counts of Deciduous Teeth in Finns', *Forensic Science International*, 10, pp.179–88.

Chapter 17

1 Letter 93/1251 and statement 93/449, filed in Register 9/6839 Clerk of the Peace, Central Criminal Court, Sydney, February 1893; *R v John Makin and Sarah Makin* (murder), held by the SRO. The statement, signed by John Makin, was not written in his own hand.

2 Letters 93/1051, filed in ibid.

3 ibid., emphases in original.

4 See *HML v The Queen*; *SB v The Queen*; *OAE v The Queen* [2008] HCA 16 at [443]-[444], per Crennan J.

5 Descriptions of the courtroom scene before the trial commenced, including opening addresses, are taken from *SMH*, 7/3/1893, p.3.

6 *R v Makin and Wife* (1893) 14 NSWR 1 at 6, per Windeyer J.

7 *SMH*, 14/11/1892, p.5.

8 *R v Makin and Wife* (1893) 14 NSWR 1 at 30, per Windeyer J.

9 *R v Makin and Wife* (1893) 14 NSWR 1 at 5; argument for the Crown on appeal.

10 The evidence from this trial is taken from *SMH*, 7/3/1893, p.3; 8/3/1893, p.4; 9/3/1893, p.8; 20/3/1893, p.3; *BFPMJ*, 10/3/1893, p.2.

11 *Pfennig v R* (1995) 182 CLR 461; *Uniform Evidence Acts*, s101(2).

12 <http://www.babycenter.com.au/baby/health/thrush>; <http://newbornbaby.com.au/newborn/baby-health/oral-thrush> [17 January 2011].

13 See Chapter 20.

14 This tunnel was built to prevent prisoners from escaping when being transferred from the gaol to the court and back again.

15 *SAR*, 10/3/1893, p.5.

16 See section 20, Uniform Evidence Acts; *Azzopardi v R* (2001) 205 CLR 50 at [51], per Gaudron, Gummow, Kirby and Hayne JJ.

17 *Dyers v R* (2002) 210 CLR 285.

18 This is confirmed in the Notes of Evidence of *R v Sarah Makin and John Makin* written by Justice Stephen on 3 April 1893 in which he stated: 'I left the case to the Jury upon the latter', that is, the second count charging John and Sarah Makin with the murder of an infant whose name was unknown. SRO, 5/7913, Register 10/11136.

19 Several newspapers reported that the Makins had been found guilty of the murder of Horace Amber Murray: *Gippsland Times*, 10/3/1893, p.3; *BFPMJ*, 10/3/1893, p.2; *Northern Star*, 1/4/1893, p.3; *The Advertiser*, 10/3/1893, p.5; *SAR*, 1/4/1893, p.4; *SMH*, 10/3/1893, p.3; *BC*, 11/3/1893, p.4.

Chapter 18

1 *SAR*, 10/3/1893, p.5; *TA*, 10/3/1893, p.4.

2 *SMH*, 31/3/1893, pp.4–5.

3 *SAR*, 10/3/1893, p.5.

4 *SMH*, 31/3/1893, p.5; *R v Makin and Wife* (1893) 14 NSWLR 1 at 18, per Windeyer J.

5 S Edgar and B Nairn (1976) 'Salomons, Sir Julian Emanuel (1835–1909)', *Australian Dictionary of Biography*, Volume 6, Melbourne University Press, Carlton, Victoria, pp.81–3, <www.adbonline.anu.edu.au/biogs/A060093b.htm> [1 August 2010].

6 ibid.

7 ibid.

8 ibid.

9 P Serle, 'Salomons, Sir Julian Emanuel (1836–1909)', *Dictionary of Australian Biography*, <http://gutenberg.net.au/dictbiog/0-dict-biogSa-Sp.html#salomons1> [2 August 2010].

10 He made what was at the time the longest speech in the history of the Council, an eight hour recitation on the Federation Bill on two consecutive days, 28 and

29 July 1897 (Parliament of New South Wales, 'Miscellaneous NSW Parliamentary Facts'), <http://www.parliament.nsw.gov.au/prod/web/common.nsf/key/Resources-Factsmiscfact> [2 August 2010].

11   (1976) 'Windeyer, Sir William Charles (1834–1897)', *Australian Dictionary of Biography*, Volume 6, Melbourne University Press, Carlton, Victoria, pp.420–2, <http://adb.anu.edu.au/biography/windeyer-sir-william-charles–1062/text8145> [24 February 2011].

12   G D Woods (2002) *A History of Criminal Law in New South Wales: The Colonial Period 1788–1900*, The Federation Press, Sydney, p.389.

13   ibid., p.390. See his famous judgment in *Ex parte Collins* (1888) 9 NSWLR 497 at 515–17.

14   Woods, p.389.

15   This chapter is based on the court report in *SMH*, 24/3/1893, pp.2–3 and *R v Makin and Wife* (1893) 14 NSWLR 1.

16   Justice Innes' argument was based on s9 of the *Criminal Law Amendment Act* which he said altered the rule that a defendant had to rebut the presumption of murder when an unlawful killing is established.

17   The law in relation to unreasonable or unsafe and unsatisfactory verdicts is summarised in *Castagna v R* [2012] NSWCCA 181 at [91], per Latham J.

18   Today, there is no presumption of murder. The prosecution bears the onus to prove, beyond reasonable doubt, that an accused (i) committed the act that caused the victim's death and (ii) intended to kill the victim.

19   See Chapter 20.

20   *SMH*, 31/3/1893, p.4.

21   *SAR*, 1/4/1893, p.4.

Chapter 19

1   The sentencing hearing was reported in *SMH*, 31/3/1893, p.3.

2   ibid., p.4.

Chapter 20

1   Minutes and Papers Respecting the Respite of John Makin, pending hearing of appeal to the Privy Council, SRO, filed in Register 4/909.1.

2   *SMH*, 5/5/1893, p.5.

3   *SMH*, 20/4/1893, p.6.

4   Woods, p.400.

5   *SMH*, 5/5/1893, p.5.

6   *SMH*, 4/8/1893, p.3.

7   This discussion of the appeal is based on *Makin v Attorney-General for New South Wales* [1894] AC 57. The appeal proceeded on the incorrect basis that there had been sufficient evidence at trial to identify Baby D as Horace Amber Murray.

8   Woods, p.393.

9 *Pfennig v R* (1995) 182 CLR 461; the *Pfennig* test applies in Australian common law jurisdictions.

10 Infant mortality rates represent the number of infant deaths in the first year of life for each 1000 live births. Reliable figures are only available for Australia from 1870 onwards. In NSW in 1871–75, the rate was 101–110, rising to 121–130 during 1881–85 and falling to 111–120 during 1896–1900: Camm and McQuilton, p.165.

11 See <www.indexmundi.com/australia/infant_mortality_rate.html>; <www.index mundi.com/g/r.aspx?c=as&v=29> [27 August 2011].

12 *R v Betts* (1889), unreported.

13 Swain, 'Toward a Social Geography', p.158.

Chapter 21

1 *BFPMJ*, 25/7/1893, p.2; Beck, p.130.

2 *SMH*, 11/8/1893, p.4.

3 B E Mansfield, 'Dibbs, Sir George Richard (1834–1904)', *Australian Dictionary of Biography*, National Centre of Biography, Australian National University, Canberra, <http://adb.anu.edu.au/biography/dibbs-sir-george-richard–3408/text5179> [1 September 2011].

4 *SMH*, 12/8/1893, p.7. The following account is taken from this edition of the newspaper.

5 *SMH*, 16/8/1893, p.7.

6 *SMH*, 15/8/1893, p.4.

7 *SMH*, 11/8/1893, p.6.

8 *SMH*, 12/8/1893, p.7.

9 *SMH*, 15/8/1893, p.4.

10 *SAR*, 1/4/1893, p.4.

11 *CRE*, 18/3/1893, p.3; Mrs Collins was the last woman hanged in NSW after being convicted of murdering her husband and five-month-old baby.

12 *SAR*, 10/3/1893, p.5.

13 *SMH*, 15/8/1893, p.4.

14 *BFPMJ*, 17/8/1893, p.3; see also *SMH*, 16/8/1893, p.2.

Chapter 22

1 Norrie, p.19. The walls were based on a design by Francis Greenway, Government Architect from 1816 to 1822.

2 Beck, p.1.

3 The gaol is now the National Art School.

4 John Moroney (1988) *The More Things Change—A History of Corrections in NSW*, New South Wales Department of Corrections, Sydney, p.76, quoting Thomas Macquoid, the High Sheriff, in 1835.

5 For a summary of the Royal Commission of Inquiry, see J M Bennett, 'Bigge, John Thomas (1780–1843)', *Australian Dictionary of Biography*, National Centre of

Biography, Australian National University, Canberra, <http://adb.anu.edu.au/biography/bigge-john-thomas–1779/text1999> [September 2011].

6   Norrie, p.20.

7   Beck, p.44.

8   ibid., p.6.

9   ibid., pp.27, 95.

10 ibid., p.93.

11 ibid., p.46.

12 Norrie, pp.52, 90.

13 ibid., pp.93, 144. Norrie discusses how life for the working classes in late Victorian NSW was possibly worse than in England.

14 Beck, p.110, quoting Governor of Darlinghurst Gaol, Arthur Collis.

15 One ounce is equal to 28.4 grams, which means that 16 ounces of meat is about 454 grams (nearly half a kilogram) and 24 ounces of bread is 680 grams.

16 The title of Henry Lawson's poem *One Hundred and Three* refers to his prison number.

17 Brian Matthews, 'Lawson, Henry (1867–1922)', *Australian Dictionary of Biography*, National Centre of Biography, Australian National University, Canberra, <http://adb.anu.edu.au/biography/lawson-henry–7118/text12279> [17 August 2011].

18 Norrie, p.123.

19 ibid., pp.124–5.

20 Beck, p.20.

21 Norrie, p.100.

22 ibid.

23 Beck, p.130.

24 *Song of a Prison* by Henry Lawson, published in 1908.

25 Beck, p.20.

26 ibid., p.48, quoting Rose Scott.

27 ibid., p.62.

28 ibid.

29 Archives Office of NSW, Prisons: Bathurst Gaol Entrance Books No.87/411 to No.94/340 (1887–1894), Year 1893, August; held at the SRO.

30 *BFPMJ*, 16/8/1893, p.2.

31 Behrouz et al., p.33.

32 M D Holmes, M M Brant-Zawadzki and R P Simon (1984) 'Clinical Features of Meningovascular Syphilis', *Neurology* 34, pp.553–6.

33 Behrouz et al., p.33.

34 Holmes et al., pp.553–6.

35 Herben, p.175.

36 Archives Office, 'Prisons'. The gaol card and description for Sarah Makin is missing from the Bathurst Gaol records for prisoners who were first incarcerated in 1893.

37 Beck, p.46.

38   ibid., p.124.
39   Letter 07/4496, SRO, Register 10/11136.
40   Letter 07/4527, SRO, Register 10/11136.
41   Letter 07/3250, SRO, Register 10/11136.
42   Letter 07/4527, SRO, Register 10/11136.
43   Norrie, p.21.
44   Letter 11/347, SRO, Register 10/11136. Sarah was given permission to make this application in letter 11/3403, SRO, Register 10/11136.
45   Letter 11/6593, SRO, Register 10/11136.
46   Letter 11/8289, SRO, Register 10/11136. Section 462 of the *Crimes Act* 1900 (NSW) allowed for the remission of the whole or part of a prisoner's sentence at the discretion of the Executive Council.
47   Letter 11/4535, SRO, Register 10/11136.
48   Letter 11/8289 by George Steele, SRO, Register 10/11136.
49   J J Moss to the Comptroller General of Prisons, 1 May 1911, Memorandum 11/8289, SRO, Register 10/11136.
50   Letter 11/8853, SRO, Register 10/11136.
51   Herben, p.192.
52   *SMH*, 9/2/1912, p.8.
53   *SMH*, 9/3/1911, p.8.
54   *SMH*, 9/2/1912, p.7.
55   *SMH*, 7/2/1914, p.20s.
56   Holmes et al., pp.553–6.

Chapter 23

1   *SAR*, 1/4/1893, p.4.
2   William Blackstone (1770) *Commentaries on the Laws of England, Book I: The Rights of Persons*, Oxford, Clarendon Press, p.455, cited in T Nutt, 'The Paradox and Problems of Illegitimate Paternity in Old Poor Laws Essex', in Levene et al., *Illegitimacy in Britain*, p.102.

Chapter 24

1   *SMH*, 27/6/1951, p.26.
2   *SMH*, 2/10/1931, p.6.
3   *SMH*, 7/4/1900, p.1.
4   <http://trees.ancestry.com.au/tree/5067081/person/112622961> [6 December 2011].
5   *SMH*, 11/8/1930, p.7.
6   *The Advertiser*, 3/12/1892, p.5. She was the only person admitted on that Friday (Register 1 – CY Reel 1817; the Admissions Register of the Benevolent Asylum); see also the Journal of Benevolent Asylum, Journal 1 – CY Reel 1977, p.20.
7   Benevolent Asylum, Register 2 – CY Reel 1817.
8   Woods, p.388.

9   Herben, pp.172–3.

10 *SMH*, 25/8/1893, p.6.

11 *SMH*, 28/6/1899, p.1.

12 See family history at <http://trees.ancestry.com.au/tree/21814898/person/1137866422/fact/12588637306> [6 December 2011].

13 SRO, Kingswood, New South Wales, Australia, Assisted Immigrant Passenger Lists, 1828–1896, Record for Henry Bothamley, p.32.

14 Admission and discharge records of the Benevolent Asylum for March, April and May 1892; copies held by author.

15 See family histories at <http://trees.ancestry.com.au/tree/12247957/person/–304505174?ssrc=>; <http://trees.ancestry.com.au/tree/6569337/person/–932778210?ssrc=>; <http://trees.ancestry.com.au/tree/31526956/person/18074478434?ssrc=> [7 December 2011].

16 *SMH*, 18/8/1893, p.1.

17 Assisted Immigrant Passenger Lists, 1828–1896, Record for Patrick Mulvey, p.47.

18 According to the funeral notice in *SMH*, 17/8/1893, p.8.

❧

Acknowledgements

Thanks and appreciation to Rachel Fraher, Angela Kintominas and Mabel Koo who provided highly skilled research assistance at various times during the writing of this book and to Raymond Roca for his excellent work in compiling and accessing photographs and preparing the index.

I am grateful to Helen O'Sullivan for her patient reading of the legal chapters and her insightful comments. Also my appreciation to Elaine Elliott and Jacqui Kerr who read some of the chapters in Part I of the book.

Many thanks to the patient staff at the State Records Office of New South Wales, Kingswood for helping me track down historical material about the Makins, in particular Angela and Emily Hannah.

Index

adipocere 85-7, 150

Agassiz, Alfred 4, 133, 135–6, 141–2

age estimation of infants 187–8

baby farming
  advertisements 64–5
  causes 62–4
  legal response *See Children's Protection Act*

Barton, Edmund 226

Bathurst Gaol 247
  hospital 249

Benevolent Asylum 262

Bolton, Ellen
  family life 44–5
  father 30–1
  marriage 29, 40
  mother 32, 35–6, 41–4
  time in Orphan School 33, 35–40, 44

Bothamley, Horace 1–5, 116–17, 131–2, 238, 263–4

Branken Moor 17–18

Camden 21–2

capital punishment 11

Children's Protection Act 75–9
  compulsory registration of babies 76–7

Chippendale 151

congenital syphilis *See* syphilis

convicts 13–17
  women 32–3, 41–3

coronial inquest
  Burren Street deaths 79–87, 106–15, 116–46
  George Street deaths 157–88

Darlinghurst Gaol 210, 225, 241–2
  conditions 230, 243–7
  death rate 243, 245

hangings 11
hospital 249
women's wing 246
Davies, Mignonette
adoption by Makins 2–3
birth 1, 116
coronial inquest into death
of 116–46
death 4, 221, 238
Davies, Minnie
dealings with Makins 1–5,
116–17
marriage and children 263–4
testimony at coronial
inquest 131–3
decomposition of bodies 84–7
Dibbs, George 230, 233
domestic servants 63–4

Female Factory 41–3
forensic science
age estimation of infants 187–8
decomposition 84–7
proof of murder 195

Godfrey's Cordial 69, 110–13, 115,
133, 156, 195, 229
grave wax See adipocere

Helbi (Helby), Minnie 126–7,
135–6, 138, 250, 254–5, 263

infant mortality 66–7, 228
inquest See coronial inquest

J Wheel See treadmill
Joyce, James
altercation with John
Makin 167–70
birth 88
criminal investigations 9,
71–2, 95–9, 147–56, 158,
183, 191
family life 89–94
motivations 95
physical description 88
testimony at coronial inquests
80, 117, 119
testimony at Makins' trial
196–7

Launceston 17–18
Long Bay Gaol 251–2

Macdonaldtown 1, 68–9
Makin, Blanche
arrest 98
birth 48
children 260–1
conduct at coronial inquests 108,
118, 120–5, 134, 145, 160, 181,
185
coronial inquest testimony
81
marriage 260
police interview 99–100
Makin, Clarice
birth 48
children 261

coronial inquest testimony
    120–5, 159–60, 168, 171, 176,
    180–3
marriage 261
role in baby farming 138, 167–8,
    176, 182–3, 205
trial testimony 198
Makin, Daisy
    admission to Benevolent
        Asylum 262
    birth 48
    marriage 262
    testimony at coronial
        inquest 125–6, 128–30
Makin, Ellen *See* Bolton, Ellen
Makin, Florence
    arrest 98
    birth 48
    conduct at coronial inquests 108,
        118, 120–3, 125, 145, 160, 181,
        185
    coronial inquest testimony 81
    marriage 261
    petitions for Sarah Makin's
        release 250–2
Makin, John
    appeal to Privy Council
        225–9
    appeal to Supreme Court
        210–20
    arrest 98
    biological children 48, 51–2
    birth 29
    childhood 44–5

conduct at coronial inquests 108,
    126, 135, 146, 160, 169–70,
    185, 187
confession 113–15
coronial inquest testimony 83
early criminal history 45–6,
    48–51
employment situation 101–2, 108
execution 9–12
father 29–30
final letter 236–7
grandfather 30–1
grandmother 32, 35–6, 41–4
marriage to Sarah Makin 46–7
media opinions 209–10, 219–20,
    224, 233–6
mother *See* Bolton, Ellen
petition to Executive
    Council 230–3
police interview 99–100
sentencing 221–4
syphilis infection 57
trial 191–208
Makin, Sarah
    appeal to Privy Council 225–9
    appeal to Supreme Court 210–20
    arrest 98
    biological children 48, 51–2
    birth 13
    childhood 25
    conduct at coronial inquests 108,
        117–18, 120–1, 123–6, 128,
        134, 145, 160, 164, 181, 185–6
    coronial inquest testimony 82–3

father *See* Sutcliffe, Emanuel
final years 254–6
gaol life 243–53
marriage to Charles Edwards
    26–7
marriage to John Makin
    46–7
media opinions 209–10, 219–20,
    224, 234–6
mother *See* Murphy, Ellen
petitions for mercy 250–2
prostitution 53–4
release from gaol 253
sentencing 221–4, 225
syphilis infection 52–7, 248–9
trial 191–208
Macquarie, Lachlan 33–5
Mignonette *See* Davies,
    Mignonette
Milford, Frederick 80, 83, 84, 86,
    107, 109–10, 113–14, 118, 141–2,
    150, 153, 158–9, 168, 171, 183,
    187–8
Murphy, Ellen
  birth 17
  death 27
  employment as midwife 27
  life in New South Wales
      18–26
  marriage to Emanuel
      Sutcliffe 18
  migration to Australia 17–18
  relations with Sarah
      Makin 27–8

Murray, Amber 146, 158–9,
    173–80, 182–6, 197, 207, 212,
    264
Murray, Horace Amber 9, 158–9,
    177–80, 182, 186, 229
  syphilis 178–9, 198
  trial for murder of 191–208

Newtown 69
  police station 99

opium
  opium-based baby sedatives
      See Godfrey's Cordial
  use by Makins 105, 258
Orphan School
  admission of Ellen Bolton
      36–7
  foundation 34
  living conditions 34–8
  religious instruction 37

Palmyra 18–20
Privy Council
  appeal by John and Sarah
      Makin 225–9
  verdict 226
prostitution 53

Raper, Edward 39–40
Redfern Park 150
reproductive crimes 66–7
right to silence in criminal
    trials 202, 206, 216

Risby, Clara 162–5, 171, 200, 265
Rocks, the 19

Salomons, Julian 210–17
sexually transmitted
    diseases 52–53; *See also* syphilis
Stacey, Mary 165–8, 171
street children 33
Sutcliffe, Ellen *See* Murphy, Ellen
Sutcliffe, Emanuel
    death 27
    life as convict 13–19
    life in Camden 21–2
    life in Maitland 22–6
Sutcliffe, George 22, 25
    death 25
Sydney
    in 1840s 19–22
    street children 33
Sydney Gaol 241–2

syphilis 51–3, 54–7, 105, 178–9,
    198, 228, 248–9

treadmill 16
trial of John and Sarah
    Makin 191–210
    appeal to Privy Council 225–9
    appeal to Supreme Court 210–20
    media reaction 209–10, 219–20,
        224, 233–6
    petition to Executive
        Council 230–3
    sentencing 221–4
    verdict 204–5
Todd, Agnes 108–9, 137–40, 182,
    200, 265

Ward, Agnes 199, 265
Windeyer, William 211–19, 226,
    228–9